Kitchen and Bath Design

Kitchen and Bath Design
A Guide to Planning Basics

Mary Fisher Knott, CID
allied member ASID, CAPS

With CAD Illustrations by
J. Webster Knott

John Wiley & Sons, Inc.

WILEY

This book is printed on acid-free paper. ♾

Copyright © 2011 by John Wiley & Sons, Inc. All rights reserved.

Published by John Wiley & Sons, Inc., Hoboken, New Jersey.

Published simultaneously in Canada.

For general information on our other products and services, or technical support, please contact our Customer Care Department within the United States at 800-762-2974, outside the United States at 317-572-3993 or fax 317-572-4002.

Wiley also publishes its books in a variety of electronic formats. Some content that appears in print may not be available in electronic books.

For more information about Wiley products, visit our Web site at http://www.wiley.com.

Library of Congress Cataloging-in-Publication Data:

Knott, Mary Fisher.

  Kitchen and bath design : a guide to planning basics / Mary Fisher Knott ; with CAD illustrations by J. Webster Knott.

       p. cm.

  Includes bibliographical references and index.

  ISBN 978-0-470-39200-3 (pbk. : alk. paper); ISBN 978-0-470-89005-9 (ebk);
ISBN 978-0-470-89007-3 (ebk); ISBN 978-0-470-89008-0 (ebk);
ISBN 978-0-470-95098-2 (ebk); ISBN 978-0-470-95115-6

  1. Kitchens. 2. Bathrooms. I. Knott, J. Webster. II. Title. III. Title: Guide to planning basics.

  NA8330.K595 2011

  747.7'97–dc22

                                             2010016470

Printed in the United States of America

SKY10025976_033021

Contents

Acknowledgments

Over the past four decades, I have learned so much from the artisans, subcontractors, and clients for whom I've worked. It is that knowledge that I am sharing with you in this book, so I want to thank all of these master craftspersons for their practical solutions over the years.

Many thanks go to my clients, who have so willingly allowed us to photograph their homes and use their projects to illustrate design principles. In addition, I'd like to thank BSH Home Appliance Corp., Franke, Asko Appliances, Fisher-Paykel, and Sub-Zero/Wolf Appliances for their photographic support.

The support and collaboration of other design professionals helped me present a variety of design solutions. My thanks to David Dalton, David Dalton, LLC; Judy Svendsen, Raven Interiors; Brooke D'Allyrand, Sub-Zero/Wolf Southwest; Amber Carlson, BSH Home Appliance Corp.; Pam Perfect and Kristi Leudenia, Sunwest Distributors; Barbara Houston, Vancouver, BC; NY Loft Cabinetry; and Steve Johnson Poggenpohl Cabinetry.

Dr. Dylan Foster and the occupational and physical therapists I've interviewed have provided valuable information regarding body mechanics and the influence they have on our home work spaces.

Writing a book while you are working on projects under construction and in the various design stages requires a great deal of understanding and support from your family. I appreciate the support and understanding my family has shown me, especially my husband and partner, Webb, who not only did all the CAD work on our projects (thereby freeing up my time to write), but also provided the CAD drawings and illustrations for this book.

Introduction

Kitchens and baths are two rooms of the home that involve every trade of the construction industry. To effectively design these spaces, you must fully understand space planning techniques, basic construction methods and terminology, and building code constraints.

This book provides the reader with practical information gleaned from practicing design professionals, as well as craftsmen and craftswomen of the construction industry. It features practical guidelines from those who must take a design on paper and make it a reality. The prudent designer will seek out the specialty trades involved in the project and ask about installation procedures; the answers will often influence the designer's vision for the space during the design concept phase. Design details often require specific clearances and construction constraints affecting various other components of the room.

As one can see from Figure i-1, the coordination of several construction trades is involved in achieving one specific detail. By first researching installation requirements of the finish materials selected for use, the designer can accurately

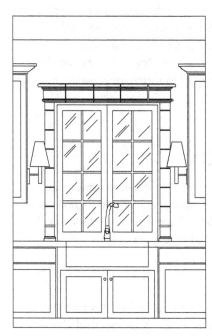

Figure i-1 A special stone-tile surround at a window affects the window size and placement, wall space on all sides, crown moldings and cabinetry adjacent to the window, window coverings, and lighting fixtures.

create design details that are ready for execution in the field. This requires close collaboration with the architect, general contractor, and subcontractors.

The checklists, case studies, and problem-solving techniques in this book will help the reader isolate and correct some potential problems prior to construction. This book also serves as a reference guide for designers of kitchens and bathrooms, and can significantly aid in the understanding and teaching of kitchen and bath design in real applications.

Written from a residential space planner's point of view and underlain by four and a half decades of experience, this book provides insight into proven techniques for designing kitchens and baths.

Who Are Residential Space Planners?

Residential space planners are experienced design professionals who approach kitchen and bath design as problem solvers. By isolating a set of design criteria from the client, the space planner begins by tackling the space planning process first; then makes product selections to meet those criteria functionally and aesthetically; and then creates solutions unique to that client and space.

Winston Churchill once stated, "We shape our dwellings and afterwards, our dwellings shape us." It is the space planner's goal to shape the dwelling to fit the client.

Overview of the Book

Initial chapters focus on **design criteria** common to kitchens and baths. These criteria include construction methods, basic plumbing and electrical applications, national codes, and anthropometric information. Anthropometric information is thoroughly covered in Chapter 3, Universal and Ergonomic Design.

Basic Construction Methods

It is the responsibility of the architect, engineer, and general contractor to ensure the integrity of the building envelope. Decisions affecting the structural elements must be engineered by those qualified and licensed professionals. However, it is critical that kitchen and bath designers understand general construction methods and terminology, so that they can work effectively with the allotted space and communicate with the construction tradespersons.

This book examines types of building foundations that directly influence locations of the mechanical systems in the kitchen and the plumbing layout in the bath. The difference between load-bearing and nonload-bearing walls is explained to illustrate how optional alterations of walls can be executed. Unless the designer is also a licensed general contractor, decisions on whether a wall can be removed must be made by those who are licensed and qualified to do so. However, by understanding how a house is framed, the designer can recognize design possibilities should structural alterations be planned. Mechanical systems, air returns, ductwork and special plumbing applications must be housed within the framework of the structure; all these are covered in Chapter 10.

Chapter 2 discusses window and door types and how they affect kitchen and bath space planning and ergonomic considerations. Because windows are a major focal point within a space, how they look and function affects the entire space.

Architectural features such as niches, arches, columns, ceiling treatments, exposed beams, and soffits are examined as they relate to design of the kitchens or baths in the case studies.

Codes: ANSI Regulations and ADA Guidelines

The International Building Code (IBC) is a compilation of the Uniform Building Code (UBC), the Building Code Officials and Code Administration National Building Code (BOCA), and the Standard Code. Some states and municipalities have not adopted these codes, so it is necessary for designers to be aware of the code constraints governing their practice and project locations. This is particularly important for designers working in multiple states. Chapter 2 defines and discusses various codes relating to fire, health, and safety issues. Codes and ANSI standards specific to kitchens and baths are covered in Chapters 4 and 7, on kitchens and baths, respectively.

Plumbing Basics

The plumbing system provides a means of bringing water to the house and distributing it to water appliances and fixtures, as well as a means of taking used water (graywater or wastewater) away from the house. In addition, it involves the proper venting of fixtures and appliances. When natural gas is being used to power appliances, a qualified plumber is required for installation. Chapter 8 illustrates a typical plumbing system, showing gas and water supply and drainage in a single-story and a two-story house. Island vents, sewer vents, and gas appliance vents are defined and illustrated, showing their influence within the design. Certain shower systems require a higher-capacity water supply than normal. Case studies are presented that show these installations. The selection of plumbing fixtures for kitchens and baths is covered in each of the respective chapters (4 and 7).

Energy-efficient water heaters are important to both kitchen and bath design and we examine the several options available in Chapter 10.

Electrical Basics

Just as a plumbing system is concerned with conveying gas and water to and from the house, so the electrical system is concerned with acquiring power from the supplier, bringing it to the house, and distributing it throughout the house. Chapter 9 covers how electrical energy comes to the house and how the distribution occurs from the main panel throughout the home. Reading the main electrical panel capacity and understanding how circuits work is necessary for planning adequate power supply to appliances. Electrical plans from actual projects illustrate electrical layouts, as well as means of calling out convenience outlets, ground fault circuit interrupters, switches, and controls. Motion sensors and other automatic controls are defined based on code constraints.

Lighting systems, both structural and decorative, are studied in detail to illustrate basic applications and their relationship to the construction package. Specific lighting layouts are featured in Chapter 4 for kitchens and Chapter 7 for bathrooms.

Mechanical Systems

The importance of mechanical systems, including sound control, air and water quality, ventilation, and moisture control cannot be overemphasized. Because the layout of such mechanical systems as the heating/cooling and ventilation systems is done by other licensed professionals during the framing stage (new construction) or rough-in stage (remodeling), it is very important that the designer be involved in providing space planning information related to the location of controls, registers or diffusers, and air returns to the architect before the architect submits final plans to the client and all pertinent agencies. Poor location of these items dramatically affects the space planning of the kitchen and bath.

When the project is a remodel rather than new construction, certain constraints already exist that will influence the design of the space. Available options are studied to give the designer basic knowledge, so that communication among the designer, architect, and contractor can be achieved. Although aesthetic considerations are very important, it is the heating, ventilation, and air conditioning (HVAC) contractor and architect that must set the mechanical plan.

Moisture control is critical in both kitchens and bathrooms. We discuss how this is effectively done to maximize comfort within the space, using case studies to illustrate these applications. An examination of moisture barriers and how they protect the structure and surfaces is provided.

Sound control is often ignored in the design process. With open-plan kitchens and the exposure of appliances and kitchen task areas to the social spaces of the home, sound control is a critical element of design. Designers must understand sound emission levels so that they can select products and materials conducive to sound suppression. Refer to Chapter 10. Construction methods for reducing sound with sound board, insulation wraps, and other sound-deadening materials are investigated.

Steam appliances and fixtures are frequently being used in kitchens and bathrooms. A water supply of the proper size coming to the house and the extraction of ambient steam in the room are primary concerns of an adequate ventilation system. Mold and mildew can result if ventilation is not planned effectively. Building code requirements and manufacturers' guidelines are examined.

Sustainability, Conservation, and Energy Resources

Sometimes deciding what is really a sustainable and environmentally responsible material can be extremely confusing. How and where a product is manufactured, how it should be correctly used for maximum benefit, and budget constraints should all be considered. An examination of the benefits of sustainability, opportunities for reuse of material, energy conservation programs, and understanding alternative energy sources applicable to kitchens and baths appears in Chapter 12.

Solar systems, natural gas applications, efficient electrical uses such as induction cooking and laser-monitored cooktops, and wireless technology are all explored as they apply to kitchen and bath design.

Basic Design Principles

Chapter 1 presents a review of the basic principles and elements of design. Kitchens and baths lacking these basic design disciplines turn out to be mediocre at best. Aesthetic principles—scale, proportion, rhythm, balance, harmony, and emphasis—must be employed.

Design elements consist of pattern, texture, line, form or mass, color, space, and light. Checklists have been developed to assist designers in the development of their plan. Though this is second nature for most seasoned designers, these checklists of basics can be particularly helpful to designers who are just beginning their career. No two projects are exactly the same.

Universal and Ergonomic Design

Accessibility of a completed space should be a prime consideration. There is a difference between universal design and ergonomic design. Ron Mace, founder and program director of the Center for Universal Design, is credited with coining the term *universal design*, which he defined as "[t]he design of products and environments to be usable by all people, to the greatest extent possible, without the need for adaptation or specialized design."

Karl H. E. Kroemer in his book, *Extra-Ordinary Ergonomics* (2006), states, "Design to match the characteristics of the user is the guiding principle of ergonomics or human factors, also called human factors engineering." He goes on to say, "For most designs, the common user population is not a unitary, homogeneous assemblage but rather a group of individuals with diverse characteristics and varying capabilities."

It has been my experience that when the capabilities of the individual are accounted for and incorporated into the kitchen or bath design, the designer can integrate the individual traits of the client into the space place(s) in a way that meets the client's particular ergonomic profile.

Everyone has some physical challenge when dealing with movement and stress in their lives. Each person accesses a space differently based on physical stature alone. In this book, we recognize that *universal design* is the umbrella for human-factors design common to all; *ergonomic design* is the act of defining specific design applications for the individual user. Ergonomic design considerations are featured in every aspect of this book. Many resources, and hours of research by respected ergonomists and physical and occupational therapists, have been pared down to provide the basic, practical information needed for good design of kitchens and baths. Chapter 3 expands on these principles and includes a practical format for retrieving ergonomic information and measurement techniques. One section deals with weights and measurements of items used in the kitchen and how they affect movement and body mechanics.

How the body works physically is considered to help the designer fully understand the importance of designing space that works in concert with the body rather than against it. Good body posture and alignment can be encouraged when the design of the kitchen or bath minimizes the fatigue and stress of tasks performed.

Throughout the book, the symbol (E) can be found next to products and applications with ergonomic relevance.

Kitchen Design Principles

Industry standards for kitchen and bath design are presented along with codes affecting the kitchen specifically. Ergonomic design principles are introduced here for the first time. Techniques for developing a client/project inventory, space planning methods used in creating a bubble plan and plan variations, and ergonomic considerations regarding the space lead off Chapter 1.

Allowances for stagnant and active space, minimum to maximum clearances for movement and work zones (Figure i-2), and space planning principles are given.

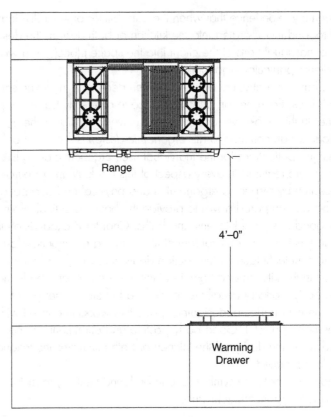

Range

4'–0"

Warming
Drawer

Figure i-2 The residential space planner measures traffic-lane clearances as the distance between the two most protruding parts on opposite sides of the lane.

Reference charts of industry standards have been developed to make this valuable information readily available.

A new kitchen design concept, the CoreKitchen™, is introduced. This concept plays an important role in today's kitchen design philosophy. The unique features of each are given and the designer is shown how to implement them in a design. The design flexibility created by the CoreKitchen™ is phenomenal. All this is discussed in Chapter 4.

Introduction

Furniture, storage systems, color, texture, lighting, and sound are issues arising in open kitchen concept plans, and each is addressed as it relates to the kitchen and adjoining spaces. Implementation of the elements and principles of design are particularly evident, as we understand that the kitchen should not be designed in isolation from adjoining areas.

Matching appliance and plumbing selections to the client and space is explored in detail. A surface cooking unit, for example, should match the food-preparation skills of the cook. Unfortunately, many kitchens are built with professional-style appliances for their look alone. Ergonomic considerations are a prime factor in selecting the right appliances for the project. We investigate ways to use standard appliances creatively in solving ergonomic design criteria; see Chapter 5. Case studies of various kitchen sizes are utilized to illustrate these planning techniques.

Structural and decorative lighting systems are explained as they relate to the kitchen. The extensive section on fixtures equips the designer with the product knowledge necessary to create lighting plans that feature task lights, ambient or general lighting, and decorative or accent lights.

A reference guide to lamps and definitions of each type (including incandescent, fluorescent, CFL, halogen, xenon, and LED), along with new technology being introduced, is provided. In addition, the benefits of each type of fixture as it relates to light output, color, temperature, and energy efficiency are studied. Knowledge of the Kelvin scale, lumen output, and heat index is necessary for an understanding of lighting systems and their influence on the safety and ambience of the space. Wired, wireless, motion-sensor, and remote-control systems are also featured in the kitchen lighting section. The important role of controls in energy conservation, ergonomic applications, and creation of a soothing atmosphere is examined. Case studies illustrate the options available to designers.

Appliances

For years, appliance manufacturers have been bringing restaurant cooking techniques into the residential kitchen. By calibrating appliances to meet code constraints, manufacturers have given the home cook many options. This is both a blessing and a curse. How the designer selects the right appliance for the client depends on how well the designer listens to the client. With the popularity of television chefs and cooking shows, a whole new breed of cook has appeared. Many men now are the primary cooks in the family. Direct questions must be asked of cooks as to what they prepare, how they entertain, and what appliances they want. An appliance questionnaire is provided to help guide the designer. An additional section of this chapter features food preparation techniques and terminology. It is difficult to ask the right questions and understand the answers if the designer has never held a whisk or zester in her or his hand!

Appliances are defined by type, size, and use. Cooking, cold storage, and specialty appliances such as water quality units are all covered. Explanations are given as to why one model may be a better choice than another. Alternates for standard appliances, such as modular cooktop units, give the designer insight into installation options that are often overlooked.

Appliance finishes are covered in Chapter 11 on surfaces.

Cabinetry

It is important to have a thorough understanding of cabinet construction and current industry standards, as well as cabinet terms and options. Terms such as *custom, semi-custom, custom modular, modular, inset, overlay, framed*, and *frameless* must be understood before the design process begins. When dealing with independent cabinet shops or dealerships, the designer needs to have the style of construction clearly in mind. We also study design trends and classic looks as they relate to cabinets. Cabinetry makes a major statement about the aesthetic and functional aspects of the kitchen and bath design. Scale and proportion are emphasized in relation to the size of the space, as well as adjacent cabinets. Techniques in using moldings and architectural elements to add character and unique storage to the space are illustrated, as are the ergonomic influences on storage systems, access to interior cabinet space, and custom options in standard and custom cabinetry.

Bath Design Principles

Bathrooms range in size from small powder rooms to large, spa-inspired master baths. Selecting the right fixtures and designing them into a functional, aesthetic space requires a full understanding of plumbing basics and mechanical systems.

Bathrooms must include moisture barriers, sound controls, appropriate ventilation and lighting, and fixture and finish materials that work in wet areas. Water supply lines, water heating requirements, extraction of moist air, and sound control are dictated by code; the plumbing contractor implements those codes and the manufacturer's suggested installation procedures. Industry standards for heights, clearances, and code constraints are fully detailed. Methods of creating full-access bathrooms that are visually pleasing and meet universal-design and ADA standards are illustrated in case studies. A bathroom checklist provides guidelines for the phase of the design process prior to submission of the plans; it features structural, decorative, and ergonomic checks and notes.

Methods of choosing fixtures that fit the ergonomic profile of the client are discussed in detail; by reviewing client characteristics and specifying a toilet, tub, or other fixtures meeting those criteria, the designer achieves many goals. Barrier-free showers, shower seats, shower sound and audiovisual systems, steam showers, soft bathtubs, walk-in tubs, and wall-mounted toilets are just a few of the fixtures and applications studied. Each application presents its own set of issues that the designer must confront and solve. Case studies of actual bath projects show the developmental process used to achieve the final design.

Installed heights of counters, toilets, and tubs have changed over the years, as homeowners may have been exposed to unique design features in resort hotels, spas, and even television and movies. Exposure to the resort/spa environment is a driving force in bath design today. An extensive section examines why and how bathroom design should reflect this feeling, no matter what the size of the space. Creating an atmosphere of tranquility that is easy to maintain is a common request from clients seeking their dream bathroom design.

Surfaces and Materials

The elements making up a space—color, texture, form or mass, and pattern— create the visual impact of the room. Balance between these elements must be achieved for harmony in the room. Surfaces include floor covering, wall and ceiling finishes, countertops and backsplashes, tile and stone surfaces, recycled products, metals, fabric, wood, and paint. Because of the many options for materials in each category, methods of selecting the correct surface for each area within the kitchen or bath are illustrated in photographs of completed projects.

Each potential material must be considered regarding its appropriate use in the kitchen and bath.

Installation procedures for selected materials are presented from the subcontractor's point of view. The guidelines drawn from on-the-job experience give the designer more freedom in considering how materials will be used. This practical information on the proper use of material can help alleviate costly installation errors. Communication among all parties is paramount.

Kitchen and Bath Design

Design Basics

Design must embrace how people live and work in a space. Creation of spaces that enhance the client's lifestyle is achieved through careful design and design implementation.

Combining principles and elements of basic design, specific kitchen and bath design guidelines, and product technology in a creative approach will produce appropriate solutions in kitchen and bath space planning.

Following are basic guidelines of theory and application as they relate to kitchen and bath design.

Basic Design

Basic design falls into two categories, *structural* and *decorative*. Both categories can be easily recognized as they apply to kitchens and bathrooms.

Structural Design

Structural design relates to the size and shape of an object that is an integral part of the structure. Architectural elements (such as stone walls, wood beams, columns, arches, doors, and windows, among many others) will affect the space through shape, form, and mass. However, these elements work in concert with the structural design found in cabinetry, appliances, fixtures, and surfaces within the kitchen or bath.

Four characteristics essential to successful structural design are simplicity, good proportion, and appropriate and suitable materials.

- *Simplicity:* A kitchen or bathroom will be the structural framework within which decorative and structural components are installed. Such components include cabinetry, fixtures, and accessories. It is important to keep these elements simple to create a sense of balance and serenity within the space.

- *Good proportion:* Any object that is well proportioned structurally will be visually pleasant, whether decorated or plain. It is difficult to plan the spaces in a badly proportioned room without making changes to the structure. The rule of good proportion also includes elements within the room (Figure 1-1).

Figure 1-1 Lack of variety in shapes and sizes can lead to elements that are out of proportion.

- *Appropriate materials:* Environmental concerns will influence your selection of finish materials and surfaces. The ability of a material to be cleaned; to stand up to water, heat, and steam; and to fit the client's lifestyle must be carefully considered.

- *Suitability:* When selecting materials, the end use of each material and its structure must be considered. For example, a counter surface that will deteriorate when exposed to moisture is an unsuitable material.

Decorative Design

The ornamentation of the basic structure constitutes decorative design. Hand-carved doors, moldings, and on-lays are specific examples.

Color, texture, and line play important roles in creating kitchen and bath spaces that meet the decorative scheme of the space. Four basic classifications make up the decorative scheme:

- *Geometric,* in which geometric shapes and patterns are the basis of the plan.

- *Conventional*, where traditional uses of patterns and shapes create balance within the space.
- *Abstract*, where traditional forms and shapes are transposed into nonrepresentational design.
- *Naturalistic*, where realism of shape and pattern makes a design statement in its natural form.

Elements of Design

- *Texture:* Refers to the surface quality of objects and materials. It adds interest to the design.
- *Pattern:* Line, shape/form, space, light, and color all create pattern within a space.
- *Line:* The direction and movement of the eye through a space create serenity. This is especially obvious in kitchens and baths. Line can alter the perceived proportion of an object or room (Figure 1-2).
- *Diagonal* lines introduce action to a room; *curved* lines lend a feeling of softness and grace. Careful balance of line is essential to the feeling of comfort and harmony in a space.

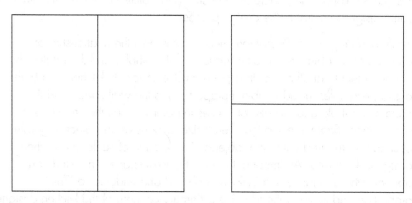

Figure 1-2   Vertical lines give height and strength to a space; horizontal lines create a feeling of repose and make the space appear wider.

- *Form or Mass:* Three-dimensional shapes are the form or mass in a room. In kitchen and bath design, cabinetry, appliances, and such shapes as islands and peninsulas all create mass and form within the space. Careful attention must be paid to scale and proportion. Too much variety of shape and form will lead to perceptual confusion. In contrast, little or no variety of shape and form creates a feeling of monotony. An easy transition of the eye from form to form as it views the space should be achieved.
- *Space:* One of the most important elements of kitchen and bath design is a feeling of space. When carefully crafted, well-organized spaces help create an atmosphere and perception of ample space.
- *Color:* The most economical tool of the designer, color is a key element of design. The appearance of color is directly affected by natural and artificial light, so it should be viewed in the atmosphere in which it will be seen at different times of the day.
- *Light:* All design elements are based on perception and any space lacking in light cannot properly incorporate the elements of design. Refer to Chapter 9 for an in-depth study.

Principles of Design

A designer's grasp of the principles of design and ability to implement them in a specific design is central to the design process.

- *Scale and Proportion: Proportion* encompasses both the relationship of one part of an object to the other parts or to the whole, and the relationship of one object to another—both aspects involve shape. In kitchen and bath design, examples include cabinet proportions to the wall space and the room as a whole and the size of fixtures in bathrooms as they relate to room space. *Scale* refers to the overall size or parts of an object, regardless of shape, compared with other objects. An example of scale in a kitchen design is the island. An important form in the total space, an island can appear either too large and bulky or too small and undersized. The proportion and scale of the island is a primary concern of the kitchen designer (Figure 1-3).

Figure 1-3 The lighting fixture, island size and shape, and overall size of the hood fit the volume of space of the kitchen. The volume of space in this kitchen required a large island and lighting fixture. In addition, the range-top hood had to be designed to reflect the proportions of the room and its relationship to the cabinetry and other elements within the space. (Courtesy of Northlight Architectural Photography.com; Mary Fisher Designs.com)

- *Balance: Balance* is the quality of a room that engenders a sense of equilibrium and serenity. There are three types of balance to consider: bisymmetrical, asymmetrical, and radial.

  - *Bisymmetry* is also referred to as *formal balance* or *symmetry,* in which identical things are arranged equally on each side of an imaginary line (Figure 1-4).

  - *Asymmetry* is more informal and typically is found in contemporary designs. For example, rather than placing a cabinet centered on an opening, the cabinetry is offset, creating an asymmetrical balance.

  - With *radial* balance, all the elements of the design radiate from a central point (Figure 1-5).

3'-0"	3'-0"	3'-0"

BISYMMETRY

pot filler

sink

1'-0"	3'-0"	1'-0"	1'-8"	1'-8"	1'-8"

ASYMMETRY

FIGURE 1-4 Bisymmetry is created with cabinets of equal size flanking the range and hood that are centered on the wall. Asymmetry is achieved by off-setting the cooktop and hood from center.

- *Rhythm:* Rhythm is an intangible component of a complete design composition. To most people, rhythm suggests a flowing quality. In interiors, it is the visual guide that assists the eye to move comfortably about a room from one area to another. This principle can be embodied through repetition, progression, opposition, transition, and radiation.
  - *Repetition* is rhythm established by repeating color, pattern, texture, line, or form.
  - *Progression* is rhythm produced by a succession of the sizes of objects. It can also be produced with color, going from dark to light.
  - *Opposition* is found in a composition wherever lines come together at right angles. Casework in kitchens and baths is a good example.
  - *Transition* is rhythm created by a curved line that carries the eye easily over an architectural element, such as an arch, or around an item of furnishing.
  - *Radiation* is a method of creating rhythm by having lines extend outward from a central axis.

Figure 1-5 An example of radial balance. (Courtesy of Schreiber & Associates Architects)

- *Focal Point:* The central point of interest or emphasis in a room is the *focal point.* Emphasizing a feature within a kitchen or bath will bring unity and order to the space. In the kitchen, this may be a wall of windows or a large hood over the range (Figure 1-6). In bathrooms, it is most often a beautiful vanity area with lights or a spa tub. The focal point is important but should not be overpowering.

- *Harmony/Unity:* Harmony or unity is an essential ingredient in any well-designed kitchen or bath. A common denominator should run throughout the space. This consistency is best achieved by carrying out a basic theme or style, although the juxtaposition of a seemingly unrelated object can add relief and interest. In the bathroom, it may be a piece of furniture converted to function as a vanity; in the contemporary kitchen, it might be an antique piece of furniture used for storage.

Figure 1-6 Natural light always commands attention in a space. By emphasizing natural light with a large window, you create a focal point. (Photo courtesy of Mary Fisher Designs.com, Northlight Architectural Photography.com)

- *Contrast:* Contrast within a space adds vitality and vigor to that space. A monochromatic scheme can be boring if not deliberately planned and executed. For example, an all-white kitchen can be stunning, and yet a kitchen with light-stained cabinetry and beige counters, backsplash, and floors can look uninteresting and mediocre.
- *Variety:* Variety adds interest to a space but can lead to disorder if not carefully monitored. A little bit goes a long way (as noted in the discussion of harmony/unity).

Kitchen and Bath Design Guides

- *Work Flow:* The food preparation process from storage to preparation to serving to cleanup.

- *Traffic Flow:* The circulation of people through the space.
- *Storage Systems:* The organized storage of utensils, cookware, dishes, and food, with convenient access to appliances and cookware.
- *Clearances:* Space dimensions needed for safe movement and access to appliances, fixtures, and cabinetry.
- *Ergonomics/Universal Design:* Fit of the kitchen and bath and their components to the physical characteristics of the users.
- *Appliance Selection:* Appliances matched to the client's cooking skill, menus prepared, and the interior style of the space.
- *Plumbing Fixtures:* Selection based on use, ergonomics, and environmental concerns.
- *Lighting and Controls:* Lighting systems designed with multiple controls for balanced lighting in the space and easy access to controls.
- *Ventilation:* Properly sized to provide healthful and comfortable interior air quality.
- *Sound Control:* Appliances and materials designed to minimize the emission of sound.
- *Surfaces:* Materials and finishes that balance the space.
- *Architectural Elements:* Selected to lend interest to and create structure in the room.

The location of the kitchen or bath in the home as a whole is critically important in planning spaces that unite the interior design of the home. No room should be designed in isolation. Each part of the home must be in balance with the structure and design as a whole.

Planning Procedures in Kitchen and Bath Design

An organized plan for approaching kitchen and bath design will enable designers to use their creative skills in shaping and outfitting the space.

- Analyze how the space relates to the house as a whole.

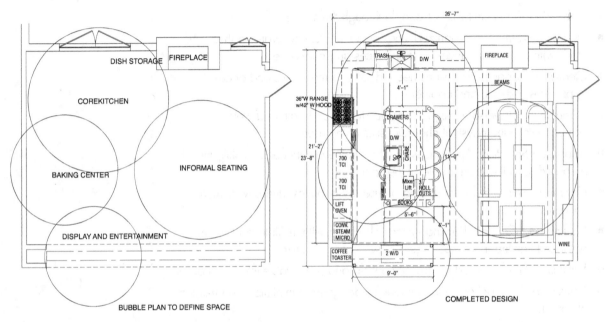

Figure 1-7 The bubble plan will help the designer distribute space for the various activities in the room.

Where is the kitchen or bath located in the home? How does it relate to point of entry from the front and back doors, garage, and adjacent interior rooms? Do the location and orientation of the room take advantage of the site, views, and natural light? Note the compass points of the exterior walls of the space.

- Create a bubble plan based on how the family uses the space.

Determine the primary uses of the space by designating specific areas to be planned. Locating the CoreKitchen™ and support layers for storage and cooking activities can be done in a general format at this time.

Procedures

1. *Review inventory list and set priorities.* List cooking equipment, utensils, dishes, glasses, serving items, and furniture to be included in the kitchen. Food storage must be planned within the CoreKitchen™ and pantry. Note dimensions and door hinge locations on furniture so proper access is allowed. In addition to the kitchen inventory, note the methods used in cooking, along with any specialty cooking that might be done (see "Project Inventory List" in the Appendix).

2. *Lay out the space plan and elevation views.* Variations of the space can be helpful in determining the optimal design. Often, a good way to begin is to decide on the plumbing locations. Reviewing space plan options with the clients will involve them in the decisions and help the designer refine the plan to meet specific client needs.

3. *Select appliances and plumbing fixtures.* Select appliances that meet food preparation needs and match the intended users' cooking skills. Ergonomic considerations should be incorporated at this time. Bath plumbing fixtures should be selected to fit functional and ergonomic criteria. Counter and cabinet depths will be affected by the selections.

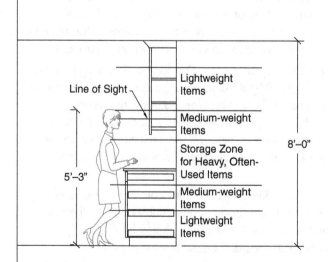

ERGONOMIC STORAGE SYSTEM
Storage by Weight and Frequency of Use

Figure 1-8 Plan storage systems based on size, weight, and frequency of use.

4. *Plan storage systems.* Access to stored items must meet ergonomic considerations.

5. *Design cabinet types and locations.* Cabinets must be structurally sound to support appliances, plumbing fixtures, stored items and counter surfaces, as well as to be stylish in appearance. Furniture can often be altered to house appliances. This is a way to add interest to a kitchen or bath.

6. *Analyze ergonomic considerations.* Check every aspect of the plan to make sure it meets ergonomic criteria established by the client. These considerations influence the selection of equipment, fixtures, cabinets, counter heights, and appliances and appliance installation.

7. *Check space clearances.* Verify clearances between counter edges, appliance door openings, right-angle corners, drawer operation with hardware at right angles, passage with appliance doors open, furniture placement, and entrances into the space. Refer to the ADA Design Guidelines when a mobility device is being used (see Chapters 2, 3, 4, and 7).

8. *Adjust the plan to fit planned surfaces.* Prior to construction, countertop thickness and edge shape, projection of surfaces, hardware, handles, crown moldings and trims, and thickness of flooring must be planned. Plan adjustments may be needed to allow use of a chosen product, for example, adequate clear space when using faucets and controls on appliances.

9. *Create a lighting plan.* Develop a general plan for location of light fixtures and controls. Size and style of light fixtures must be considered. Placement of fixtures and varied light levels must be planned early, not as an afterthought. Effective lighting systems are carefully planned using the space plan with all furniture and fixtures in place. Do a furniture plan when the kitchen includes a breakfast nook, family room, dining room, or other adjacent space.

10. *Plan sound control measures.* Kitchens and baths can be the source of high levels of sound. Kitchens are often open to adjacent spaces, so the control of emitted sounds must be planned. Bathrooms should be effectively designed to mute sound emissions and create a serene space.

11. *Verify ventilation location and sizing.* As homes are built more airtight, the proper design and use of ventilation are critical. Make sure the hood is

sized for the selected range or cooktop. If an in-line blower, remote motor, or downdraft system is planned, location and duct runs must also be planned.

12. *Assemble finish materials.* Gather samples of finishes and textures being used in the design. Check to see if design principles and elements have been properly employed, especially with regard to color, pattern, texture, contrast, and balance.

13. *Create color boards.* Use a color board for each room to bring all elements into focus and harmony.

14. *Make up specification books.* Specification books are a critical part of project documentation. Three-hole binders are usually used for ease of reference and updating. A master specification book should be prepared for the job site and updated as required. Specification books should also be prepared for the contractor and various subcontractors. Monitor and update specification sheets and product information. Remove and discard old material and date the current materials.

Basic Construction Methods for Kitchens and Baths

2

Introduction

Architects, engineers, and licensed building contractors bear the responsibility for the construction and integrity of the building. However, it is critical that the designer understand the building envelope, especially as it relates to residential kitchens and baths. Knowledge of construction terms and building methods will help the designer better understand the design constraints in an existing dwelling and more effectively communicate with architects, builders, and subcontractors during the construction process. The term *system* is used often in this book. It designates a given construction method. For example, a floor system would include the sole plate, floor joists, subflooring, and finished floor material.

Design variations and construction costs are calculated on the building envelope and its parts. The methods by which the foundations and walls are framed allow for adequate plumbing and electrical installation and play a major role in the efficiency of a design. Consider the raised foundation. Having a basement or crawl space to distribute water, gas, electricity, and ductwork allows more flexibility than the slab-on-grade foundation, which requires exact placement of distribution runs before the concrete slab is poured. You can also understand why remodeling an existing space with a slab foundation presents additional challenges to the designer and builder. When moving utilities within a space, the slab must be cut, new utility runs installed, and then concrete poured in the cut channels. If the foundation is raised above grade with a basement or crawl space, new utility runs can be made more easily. This saves time and money. In this section we discuss construction methods and their influence on kitchen and bath design.

Codes and Standards

Code councils, industry associations, and government regulatory agencies initiate rules and guidelines concerning building safety and structural integrity, thus forming building codes. These entities periodically modify codes to meet current building and energy efficiency mandates. The Internet may be used to contact almost all of these various agencies. Following are groups common to the construction industry:

IRC: International Residential Code®. Establishes minimum regulations for one- and two-family dwellings and townhouses using rigid standards governing material uses, installation processes, and structural considerations. This residential building code establishes minimum regulations required for the public health and safety of the community.

ICC: International Code Council®. An ongoing council dedicated to the current use of new building materials and designs. The regulations presented by the current code council are compatible with the International Building Code®, International Energy Conservation Code®, International Existing Building Code®, International Fuel Gas Code®, International Mechanical Code®, International Plumbing Code®, International Private Sewage Disposal Code®, and International Zoning Code®.

The International Residential Code (IRC) is widely accepted throughout North America. However, some jurisdictions may not recognize the IRC and may have adopted their own regional building codes. In some remote areas, no building codes exist at all. In these cases, the wise designer employs IRC guidelines to assure project integrity.

An example of regional differences can be found in Title 24 of the California Energy Code, which employs additional standards for energy use and lighting standards. A copy of the *California Title 24 Residential Lighting Design Guide* can be downloaded free online at: www.energy.ca.gov/title24.

Because of such variations, it is imperative that the designer become familiar with state and local codes governing the project location. Licensed builders, plumbers, electricians, architects, and engineers carry the liability for knowing and meeting the applicable codes. The designer should develop a close relationship with the builder and subcontractors for correct application of code criteria to the design. The designer must always apply code restrictions throughout the design prior to presentation of plans to the client.

Electrical, plumbing, and accessibility codes and standards are covered in their respective chapters.

In addition to building code councils, government agencies set standards for energy, air and water quality.

ADA: American with Disabilities Act; a federal law. Accessibility guidelines are administered by the Architectural and Transportation Barriers Compliance

Board (ATBCB), and regulations are administered by the U.S. Justice Department. Many state housing codes incorporate the ADA requirements.

ANSI: American National Standard Institute; does not itself develop standards. The ANSI mission statement is "to enhance both the global competitiveness of U.S. business and the quality of life by promoting and facilitating voluntary consensus standards and conformity assessment systems, and safeguarding their integrity."

DOE: Department of Energy.

Energy Guide Label: Defines energy consumption by appliance.

Energy Star®: A joint program of the U.S. Environmental Protection Agency and the U.S. Department of Energy, intended to help us all save money and protect the environment through energy-efficient products and practices.

EPA: Environmental Protection Agency; sets parameters governing energy and water use.

NEC: National Electrical Code; sponsored by the National Fire Protection Association. The NEC is approved as an American standard for the safe installation of electrical wiring and equipment by the ANSI.

NEMA: National Electrical Manufacturers Association; comprised of more than 430 manufacturers of electrical products. Technical standards are developed within the organization's core departments.

USGBC: U.S. Green Building Council; a partnership with the American Society of Interior Designers (ASID) to develop guidelines for environmental stewardship through sustainable design and building practices. REGREEN Guidelines are ever-evolving sets of principles dedicated to green design materials and practices and quality design and construction projects.

Water Sense®: A partnership program sponsored by the U.S. Environmental Protection Agency; makes it easy for Americans to save water and protect the environment.

State Building Codes: Each state has a separate and distinct code adoption process. Many states allow local adoption of codes, so adjacent jurisdictions in the same state may have different building codes based on different model codes. Be certain of the code with which you are working!

Local Building Codes: Most local jurisdictions adopt state code documents with little or no change. However, city and county jurisdictions may differ within the same state. Be aware of local modifications and be prepared for varying interpretations of the same code sections among various jurisdictions. Do not proceed into the design process based on review of similar designs in another jurisdiction without first verifying the code and code interpretation applicable to the project location.

Foundations

The design of foundation elements is based on calculations of the kinds of loads the foundation must bear. These loads are divided into two categories:

Dead loads: constant weight of the superstructure and foundation.

Live loads: weight that is not constant, such as furniture, people, and snow/ice. Dynamic forces, such as wind and earthquakes, can shift live loads, which is why regional building codes specify the parameters that the architect and builder must follow. When adding space to a kitchen or bath requires alteration of, or addition to, the foundation, the architect, engineer, and builder must be involved. Codes must be met and the space must be properly engineered to meet all applicable local (and other) codes.

The three basic typical foundation types are as follows:

Slab on grade
Crawl space
Basement

Slab on Grade

Slab construction depends on the slab type, site preparation, ground or surface moisture, and any required thermal control. The architect must plan for removal of water from the site to prevent transfer of moisture through the slab. It is suggested that a vapor barrier of 4-mil Visqueen plastic be used prior to pouring of the slab. Heat loss on the perimeter of the slab must also be calculated by the architect and HVAC contractor (Figure 2-1).

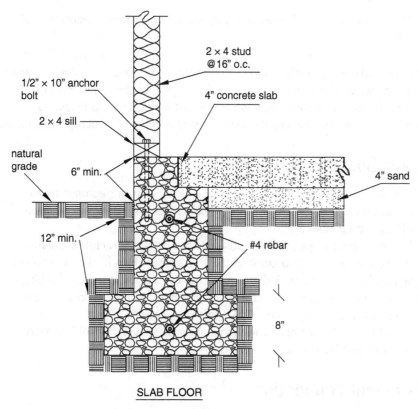

1/2" × 10" anchor bolt

2 × 4 stud @16" o.c.

2 × 4 sill

4" concrete slab

natural grade

6" min.

4" sand

12" min.

#4 rebar

8"

SLAB FLOOR

Figure 2-1 Slabs reinforced with steel can be installed on most soil content. Most slabs are poured in conjunction with a perimeter concrete footing.

As with all phases of construction, the performance of the slab depends on quality control over the concrete and workmanship.

Plumbing pipes, drains, electrical wire conduits, wireless and fiber-optic wiring conduits, ductwork, and any interior footings needed within the slab must be installed before the concrete is poured. When a gas line is required for an island location, local codes will dictate how deep the gas pipe must be placed and the type of pipe to be used. It is important to remember that when a designer wants to open up a load-bearing wall or change its location, foundation and footings must be engineered for the new location. Therefore, it is critical that the liability of this process be passed on to qualified, licensed architects, engineers, and builders.

It is the job of the designer to explore the design options available through altering load-bearing walls, enlarging windows and doors, or moving plumbing fixture locations. Cutting into a concrete slab is possible but adds cost to the project. Acquiring structural information from the builder prior to proposed changes in a design will help the designer stay within project budget constraints.

Crawl Space Foundation

The International Building Code calls out 18-inch minimum clearance for the crawl space in residential construction. Local codes will dictate the minimum height allowed (Figure 2-2).

Currently, there is quite a discussion as to the benefit of a closed crawl space versus the traditional vented crawl space. The primary benefit of a crawl space is the distribution of utilities. When it is necessary to gain access to plumbing pipes, electrical conduits, or ventilation ducts located under the floor, a crawl space (though restricted) will accommodate such access.

An additional benefit of a crawl space is installation of thermal insulation to cut the heat loss from heated interior space.

Basement Foundation

A typical basement is created by digging out the ground 8 feet deep, then forming and pouring footings and a concrete slab floor (Figure 2-3). Walls of reinforced concrete, foam block, and concrete or concrete block, as well as exposed support posts and beams, are found throughout the space as required by the architect's design and the engineer's calculation.

In some situations, the basement may be only one foundation section of the house footprint. A slab or crawl space may make up the balance of the foundation of the home. It is very important that the designer determine the type of foundation upon which the kitchen and/or baths rest, especially when the project is a remodel rather than a new construction.

Knowing how the utilities are distributed to the space is critical when changes to the space plan are contemplated. Needless to say, altering the location of the

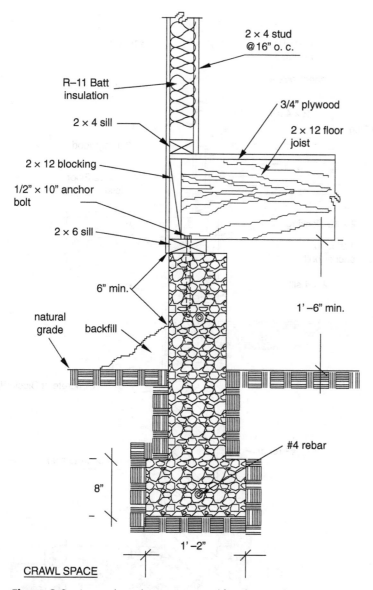

2 × 4 stud
@ 16" o. c.

R–11 Batt
insulation

3/4" plywood

2 × 4 sill

2 × 12 floor
joist

2 × 12 blocking

1/2" × 10" anchor
bolt

2 × 6 sill

6" min.

1' –6" min.

natural
grade

backfill

#4 rebar

8"

1' –2"

CRAWL SPACE

Figure 2-2 A typical crawl space is a raised foundation with 18 to 24 inches of clear space.

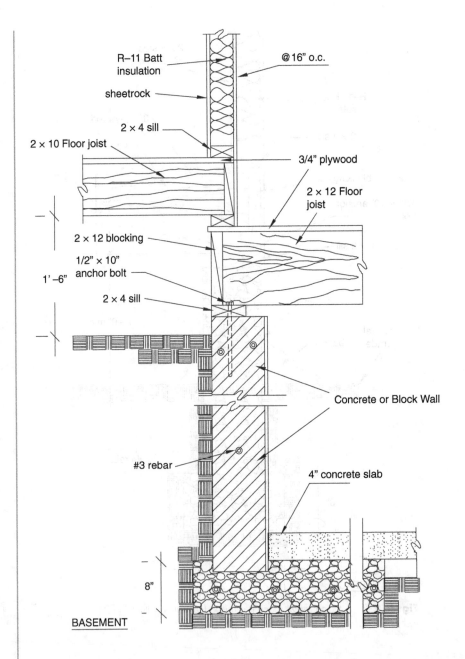

R–11 Batt insulation

sheetrock

2 × 4 sill

2 × 10 Floor joist

@ 16" o.c.

3/4" plywood

2 × 12 Floor joist

2 × 12 blocking

1/2" × 10" anchor bolt

1' –6"

2 × 4 sill

Concrete or Block Wall

4" concrete slab

#3 rebar

8"

BASEMENT

Figure 2-3 A basement is the excavated space of a house; it is either completely or partially below ground level.

utilities is much simpler and less costly when a basement or crawl space exists. When a house is built on a slope, the basement is often referred to as a "walk-out" or "daylight" basement. This configuration may allow access to the basement space from outside without the use of stairs.

A basement built with windows located above the ground level is referred to as a "look-out" basement.

Cellars (walk-up or storm) or basements typically have exterior stairs that are covered by doors to protect the space from the elements.

Foundation Walls

Poured, reinforced concrete and concrete block have been the standard foundation wall construction for decades. Currently, a combination of foam sheathing or foam block with poured concrete; concrete block; and poured, reinforced concrete make a sturdy, energy-efficient foundation wall system. Basements, crawl spaces, and slabs must all have foundation footings and perimeter walls. The exterior and interior wall finishes must be calculated into the equation and therefore selected early in the design process. If the designer and architect plan on using stone in the kitchen or bath design, the weight of the material must be calculated and an appropriate footing and foundation designed into the structural plans.

Footings

A footing is required to spread the loads on the supporting soil. Footings are sized for soil conditions and the magnitude of dead and live loads. Footings are located far enough below ground level to protect them from frost damage caused by the freezing of wet soil. Reinforced footings contain steel "rebar" to strengthen the footing in poor soil and where it must span a pipe trench. Stepped footings are found on lots having sloping grades. These are the responsibility of the architect and engineer.

Foundation Anchorage

The building structure must be anchored to the foundation to provide resistance to lateral forces from wind pressures, earthquake movement, shearing, and racking.

Typically, this is achieved through a bolt system that is secured in the concrete foundation and bolted through the bottom plate of the framed walls. Along with this anchorage, shear wall panels are used to stabilize the structure.

Why is this important to the designer? It may be desirable to open up an exterior corner wall to enlarge a window or add a glass door. Architectural engineering may be required for this because of the shearing aspects of the wall.

Water and Moisture

Water, in its liquid, vapor, and solid forms, must be planned for when engineering the foundation plans. If water penetrates the walls of a basement or crawl space, or seeps below a slab on grade, unlivable conditions can result. Basements cannot be occupied, and crawl spaces can become conducive to decay, musty odors, mold growth, and corrosion. Moisture can migrate through the slab on grade, causing delamination and warping of floors, as well as condensation on interior walls.

The two external sources of water affecting foundation design and construction are surface water and ground water. Both water sources are addressed by local building codes. The architect and builder are responsible for engineering the correct solution for the structure and location.

Framing

Every structure's walls are made up of specific components. Wall systems include the sole plates, top plates, studs, headers, blocking, and bracing. Today's typical wall heights in new construction range from 8 feet to 10 feet. Vaulted and beam ceilings represent two systems affecting ceiling height, which is typically 8 to 10 feet.

Standard Structural Dimensions

Residential construction prior to 1990 was typically built to the following standards for interior spaces:

- Ceiling height: 8'-0"
- Interior wall thickness: 4"-5"

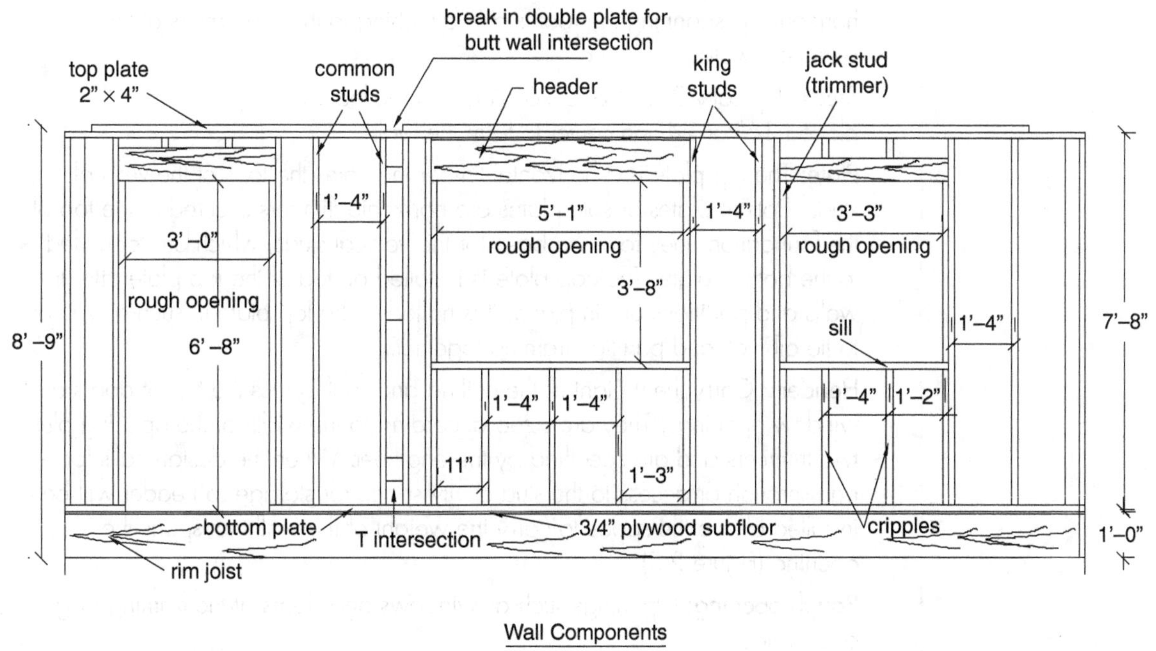

break in double plate for
butt wall intersection
top plate
2" × 4"
common
studs
header
king
studs
jack stud
(trimmer)
1'–4"
5'–1"
1'–4"
3'–3"
3'–0"
rough opening
rough opening
rough opening
3'–8"
8'–9"
6'–8"
sill
1'–4"
7'–8"
1'–4"
1'–4"
1'–4"
1'–2"
11"
1'–3"
bottom plate
T intersection
3/4" plywood subfloor
cripples
1'–0"
rim joist
Wall Components

Figure 2-4 Wall components.

- Exterior walls: 6″
- Doors 6′-8″ minimum height, 2′-8″ minimum width
- Windows headers finished at 6′-8″

The designer should know the basic components (Figure 2-4).

Framing Terms

Effective communication with trade professionals is enhanced by an understanding of construction terms.

Joists, studs, plates, headers, posts, and rafters are common structural members of the wood-framed home.

Joists: There are two types of joists: floor joists, which run horizontally and support the floor system and furnishings; and ceiling joists, which also run horizontally, spanning the rooms and attaching to the roof rafters at the perimeter walls.

Studs: Typically 2"x 4" or 2"x6" timbers installed vertically and typically placed 16" or 24" on center to form the walls.

Plate: The top plate is a horizontal timber that joins the tops of the vertical studs. Bottom plates or sole plates are horizontal timbers secured to the top of the foundation; they form the base for the vertical studs, which are toenailed to the bottom plate. The cap plate is installed on top of the top plate after the walls and partitions are in place. It is nailed to the top plate in such a way as to tie all wall and partition framing together.

Headers: Carry the weight of the ceiling and roof across the top of doors and window openings. They are sized according to the width of the opening plus two trimmers and are specified by the engineer. When the design calls for a pass-through or access to the stud cavity space for storage, a header will be installed above the space to carry the weight of the wall that spans the opening (Figure 2-5).

Rough opening: Openings such as windows and doors at the framing stage of a project.

Trimmer stud: Supports the header in an opening.

Post: An engineered vertical support member usually larger than a single stud.

Rafters: A series of structural members that form the skeleton support of the roof. They can influence the location of a skylight.

Cripple stud: A 2"x4" framing member that has been cut off to fit below or above a framed opening in an exterior or interior wall. This is also found in the pony (partial) wall.

Bracing: Exterior walls typically need some type of bracing to add rigidity. Local codes will dictate the type and amount. Bathrooms should always have bracing or blocking installed during the rough framing stage to support grab bars that may be installed later.

Pony wall: A partial wall forming a separation within a space; often used to support plumbing and electrical systems (Figure 2-6).

On center (o.c.): The distance from the center of an object to the center of another object; usually used in framing when referring to the measurement

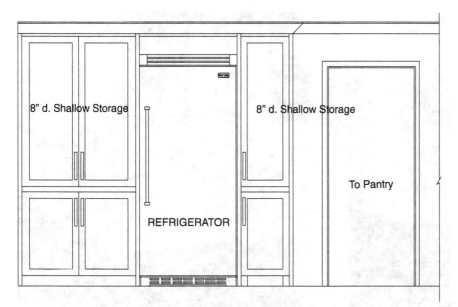

8" d. Shallow Storage   8" d. Shallow Storage

To Pantry

REFRIGERATOR

Elevation View – Recessed Refrigerator in Wall

Note: Air space must be provided for refrigerator.

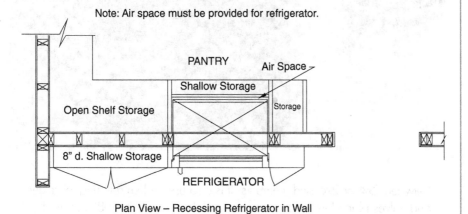

PANTRY   Air Space

Shallow Storage

Open Shelf Storage   Storage

8" d. Shallow Storage

REFRIGERATOR

Plan View – Recessing Refrigerator in Wall

Figure 2-5 When recessing a refrigerator into a wall, a header will be necessary to support the opening.

Figure 2-6 The pony wall is used to secure island cabinets and provide structure to run plumbing and electrical in the island. (Photo courtesy of Downsview Kitchens, www.downsviewkitchens.com)

between 2x4 or 2x6 stud members. It is also used when referring to faucet and valves placed in the countertop or sink (e.g., 4" o.c. or 8" o.c. wide spread).

Subfloor: The floor underlayment; usually plywood or wafer board that is nailed on top of the floor joists to form a rigid base for the finish flooring material. Typically, it is 1/2" to 3/4" thick.

Tongue-and-groove: A method of constructing materials that are specifically designed to fit together; a "tongue" on one edge fits into a corresponding "groove" on the adjoining sheet or plank. This method may be used with plywood, bead board, or wood planks for ceilings, walls, and floors.

Windows and Doors

Windows and glass doors often create the focal point of the kitchen or bath. Careful attention must be paid to window size and exposure, as well as to door size and shape. During the selection process, careful consideration must be directed to their visual impact on the interior and exterior elevations of the structure. In new construction, the architect will call out a particular style, size, and location for windows and doors. Because any change to the design may affect the balance of the exterior elevations, the designer should work with the architect in modifying window or door sizes and placement to make sure the integrity of the design is maintained.

When designing for an existing space, the designer should carefully select windows and doors that repeat the existing style, unless all windows and doors are being replaced. In that case, a new style can be achieved, but must also be consistent. Careful thought must also be given to size of and access to space.

In today's kitchen and bath designs, consumers are asking for more expansive glass areas and integration of indoor and outdoor living spaces. This affects heating and air conditioning loads, artificial lighting systems, and the general feeling within the space. Double and triple thermopane glass will help diminish heat loss and gain. Heat loss calculations will be done by the HVAC contractor to determine selection of an appropriate air-conditioning unit.

Understanding the window and door choices available, and how each type operates, leads to better decision making in the planning stages. Manufacturers offer a volume of technical and visual information that should be accessed when selections are being made.

Important considerations when selecting windows:

1. What are the local code requirements regarding window size and egress?
2. Can the window be opened easily when reaching over a countertop?

3. Does the window type fit the architectural style of the home?

4. What direction does the window face? The quality of direct and indirect sunlight will be influenced by its orientation (north, south, east, or west). This will also affect the amount of heat loss or gain during winter and summer months.

5. Will a window treatment be required for light control and/or privacy?

6. Has space been planned to install the window treatment selected? Shade pockets, shutters, and many other window treatments must be planned for in advance.

7. Is the window energy-efficient? Low-emission (low-E), dual- and triple-pane glass will add to the efficiency of the window.

8. Are structural changes necessary for installation of the new windows? Any time a window is added or moved, appropriate framing and support must be done as well.

9. Are you specifying the size correctly?

HOW TO READ AND SPECIFY WINDOW AND DOOR SIZES

Reading window and door sizes can be confusing at first. For example, a window that is 48 inches wide by 42 inches high may be specified as 4036 (4 feet 0 inches wide by 3 feet 6 inches high). Most manufacturers now clearly list window and door sizes in feet and inches.

A door that is 36 inches wide by 6 feet 8 inches high is specified as 3068 (3 feet 0 inches wide by 6 feet 8 inches high).

It is the responsibility of the builder to order the windows and doors. You will want to verify the ordering information with the builder before the order for doors and windows is placed.

WINDOW TERMS

Glazing: The actual glass installed in a window or door.

Single glazed: One sheet of glass is installed.

Double glazed or **insulated glass:** Two sheets of glass are installed and the space between the panes hermetically sealed. Argon or krypton gas may fill the space for added insulation properties.

Triple glazed: Three sheets of glass are installed and the space between the panes hermetically sealed. Argon or krypton gas may fill the space for added insulation properties.

Heat loss/gain: Refers to heat transfer through the glass, either *lost* from the inside to the outside or *gained* from the outside through the glass into the interior.

Egress: Means of exiting a space through a window or door; especially important regarding an emergency exit.

Casing: Molding (door casing) installed on each side and on top of the door frame to cover the space between the jambs and the wall.

Pane: The glass section(s) of a window or door.

Argon: A colorless, odorless, nonreactive gas used to fill the air space between panes of insulating glass. The gas increases the thermal performance of the window.

Divided lites:

Mullion (muntin) bars: Divide the glass areas of doors and windows and thereby create a pattern.

True or authentic divided lites: Individually glazed between the muntin bars; come in single- and dual-glazed products.

Simulated divided lites: Muntins permanently adhered to the interior and exterior of the glass.

Grilles: Wood muntins fastened to the interior of the sash to create the effect of divided lites; removable for cleaning.

Spacer bars: Small aluminum bars inserted between simulated divided lite muntins to emulate authentic divided lites.

Jamb: Member that runs parallel to the frame of the door.

Low-E-II glass: Low-emissivity material designed to improve thermal performance. Low-E-II glass is coated twice with microscopic metal or metallic oxide layers to reflect or absorb the sun's heat and to reduce damaging UV rays.

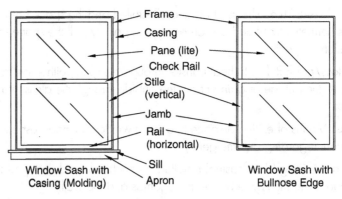

Frame
Casing
Pane (lite)
Check Rail
Stile (vertical)
Jamb
Rail (horizontal)
Sill
Apron

Window Sash with Casing (Molding)

Window Sash with Bullnose Edge

Figure 2-7 Window components.

Mulling: Attaching two or more windows or a door and transom unit together.

R-value: The resistance a material has to heat flow. Higher numbers indicate greater insulating capabilities.

Rough opening: The framed space in a wall where a niche, window, or door unit is to be installed. Openings are larger than the window or door to allow room for insulation and squaring of the units.

Sash: The glass-and-wood (or other material) moveable or stationary portion of a window, separate from the frame. The sash consists of the *stiles* (the vertical sides of the window sash), the *rails* (horizontal sides of the sash), and the *check rails* (the horizontal rails of the sash that meet at the center of a double-hung window or the vertical stiles that meet in a sliding window or door).

Skylight: An operating or stationary window installed between the ceiling and the roof to allow natural light to illuminate a room.

Tempered glass: Glass having an additional degree of hardness, which causes it to shatter into small pieces, rather than into large shards, when broken. Tempered glass is required by code for exterior glass doors, shower doors, and windows within 12 inches from a finished floor. Because of the heat process used to create it, tempered glass cannot be trimmed or recut.

DOORS

Important considerations when selecting doors:

1. Does the swing of the door interfere with traffic patterns?
2. What type of door allows the best access to the space? Hinged doors, pocket doors, and barn doors all have applications conducive to kitchens and baths.
3. How thick is the door? It will be necessary to know the thickness of the door to do correct framing.
4. Does the swing of the door interfere with the operation of appliances, fixtures, or cabinetry?
5. How does the bathroom door open in relation to the shower door or toilet?
6. Are the door width and selected hardware conducive to the user's ability to access the space?
7. Where will the door stand when in the open position? A door fully opened must not interfere with traffic or access to fixtures, appliances, or storage.
8. On what side should the hinges be installed? The contractor will ask where the door will hinge, so that it opens in the direction planned (Figure 2-8).

Sliding doors travel on an overhead and/or bottom track. Sliding doors will have either one active door and one stationary panel, or two or more doors that pass by each other. The width of the track varies according to the number of active doors and screens (Figure 2-9).

A *pocket door* is a sliding door on a track that recesses into the wall space when opened.

Sliding glass doors open completely out of sight by telescoping into an end wall and thus allowing interior space to open unimpeded to the outside. Most often found in warmer climates, this application is generally planned in new construction projects or room additions where wall pockets can be constructed to store doors. Multiple bifold doors can be designed to create a feature that is similar in terms of access, but you must allow for the door stack on the inside or exterior of the space.

A *Dutch door*, sometimes referred to as a *stable door*, is divided horizontally to allow the bottom half to remain closed while the top half is open. This is an excellent choice for keeping pets in a separate but adjacent space.

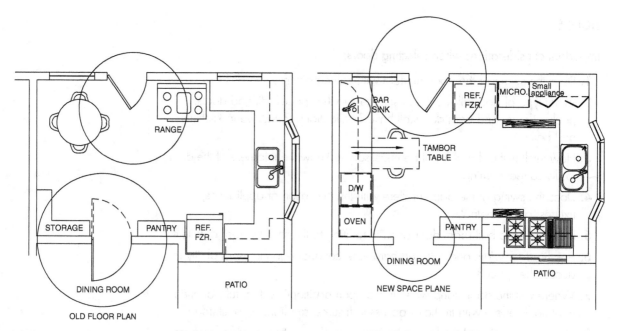

Figure 2-8 Change the hinge side of the door, or eliminate the door when appropriate, to improve access to the space.

Bifold doors are doors connected into pairs with special hinges and move along a track installed at the top and bottom of an opening. They are often used in storage areas within the kitchen or bath where the use of a larger swinging door would interfere with traffic flow. Smaller bifold doors can provide access without intruding into the room.

A *barn door* is a sliding door that slides laterally on an exposed track fixed to the wall (Figure 2-10). When the door is open, it becomes a decorative part of the wall. If barn doors are to be installed in front of stone walls with irregular material depths or adobe walls (which are typically uneven) or any other type of wall, any irregularities must taken into account during the design process. The hardware for these installations will be calibrated to handle the weight of an active door as well as the protrusion of the surface and should be confirmed by the manufacturer.

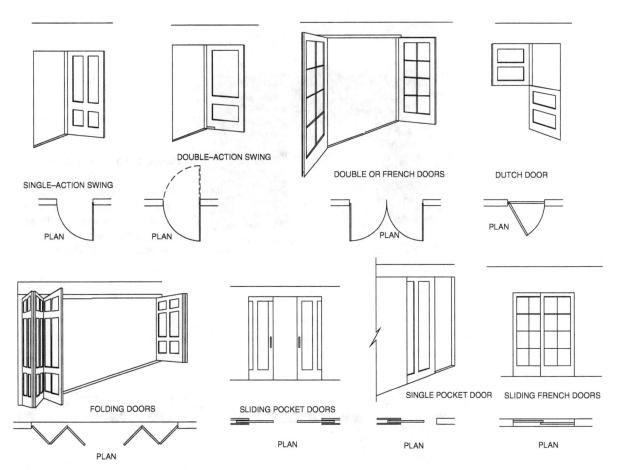

Figure 2-9 The selection of a door type should be based on the access requirements, intrusion into the space, where the door stands when open, and the type of doors used throughout the rest of the house.

ADA-ANSI Standards

Entry Doors

ANSI 404.2.3: Measure swinging doors between the face of the door and stop, with the door open at 90°.

Figure 2-10 Sliding doors on an exposed track are also used on cabinetry. Consider where the door hangs when opened, whether as an entry door or a cabinet door. (Photo courtesy of Downsview Kitchens, www.downsviewkitchens.com)

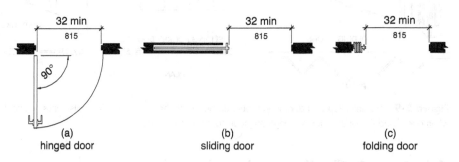

| (a) | (b) | (c) |
| hinged door | sliding door | folding door |

Figure 2-11 Measurements for doors.

ANSI A117.1 404: When an entrance into a room exceeds 24″ in depth, the minimum clear opening increases to 36″.

Access Standard

ANSI A117.404.2.3.1: For a standard hinged door, the clearance space on the pull side of the door should be the door width plus 18″ by 60″.

ANSI A117.1 404.2.3.1: On the push side of the door, the clearance should be the width of the door by 48″ long.

IRC R 303.1, IRC R 303.2: A window or skylight area, equal to at least 8% of the total square footage of the kitchen, or a total living space which includes a kitchen, is required.

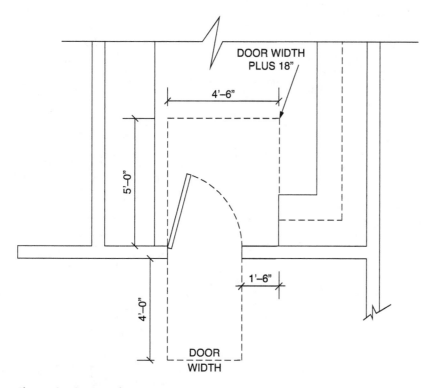

Figure 2-12 Door clearances.

Universal and Ergonomic Design

3

Definition of Terms

Ron Mace, who founded the Center for Universal Design at the School of Design at North Carolina State University in Raleigh and acted as its program director until his death in 1998, is credited with coining the term *universal design*. He defined the term as "[t]he design of products and environments to be usable by all people, to the greatest extent possible, without the need for adaptation or specialized design" (www.adaptiveenvironments.org).

The term *ergonomics* is defined in Britannica's Micropedia Reference as: "human engineering, science of dealing with the application of information on physical and psychological characteristics to the design of devices and systems for human use. Its data and principles apply to activities of the home, the workplace, and recreation" (*The New Encyclopedia Britannica*, Vol. 6, Micropedia, Ready Reference, Human Factors, Encyclopedia Britannica, 1990).

Although these definitions are similar, there is a major difference between the two design principles that use these terms. The first principle, universal design, deals with implications applicable to the general population. The second principle, ergonomic design, deals specifically with individual human factors. Both principles, when properly employed, will encourage spatial design that minimizes physical stress on the body.

Anthropometric (Human Factors) Data

Successful ergonomic design depends on specific human factors information, also known as *anthropometric data*. Data specific to your client is essential when designing the ergonomic kitchen and bath.

There are two basic types of body dimensions: structural or static dimensions that provide basic information in general terms and functional or dynamic dimensions of the body in working positions.

Body Mechanics

To better understand body mechanics, it is important to know some basic anatomical information.

POSTURE AND MOVEMENT

Posture and movement play a critical role in design of kitchens and bathrooms that are ergonomically sound. Design that accounts for the body's ability to move and perform tasks within the space involves knowledge of the working system of the skeleton, muscles, ligaments, and joints. Poor posture and movement often lead to stress of the neck, back, shoulders, and wrists.

When combined with other physical activities poorly done at work or in the home, it's not hard to understand why less stressful kitchen and bath designs should be our goal.

Following is elementary information on how the musculoskeletal system works.

FUNCTION OF BONES

The skeletal system provides shape and support for the body. When you are standing erect with good posture, internal organs can function properly and efficiently. As poor posture distorts the body, organs must compensate for the added stress placed on them.

Try this little experiment. Stop what you are doing and, whether seated or standing, assume a proper posture. Feel the difference in your breathing and the distribution of weight on your bones and muscles.

Standing and sitting tall allows the weight of your body to travel down from the head through the spinal column, to then be distributed throughout the skeletal system. The term *neutral position* refers to the natural, relaxed, or resting position of joints and limbs (Figure 3-1).

Think of it as the weight of the roof on a house being transferred via the load-bearing walls, down to the foundation, then to the ground. Steidl and Bratton write in their book, *Work in the Home* (1968), "It is useful to consider the body as made up of three major weights which must be supported: the head, the chest and the pelvis. As long as the balance of the head over chest and chest over pelvis is maintained at work, sitting, standing, walking, and climbing stairs, a minimum of muscular effort and ligament strain is required to hold the body upright."

JOINTS AS LEVERS

Design to keep joints in the neutral position whenever possible (Figure 3-2). An example of this design application is the height of the cooktop. By placing the

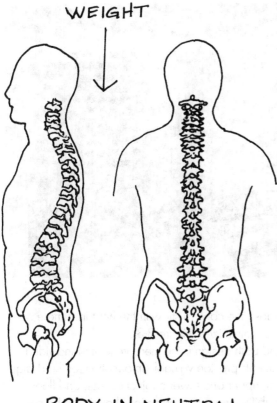

WEIGHT

BODY IN NEUTRAL
POSITION
WEIGHT DISTRIBUTED
DOWN SPINE

Figure 3-1 Body in neutral position.

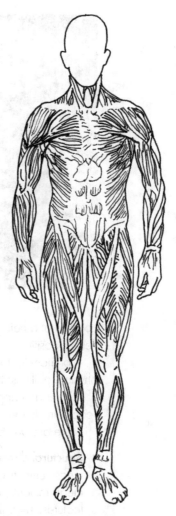

Figure 3-2 With ergonomic
design, the muscles and ligaments
that span the joints are stretched to
the least possible extent, and are
thus subject to less stress.

Figure 3-3 An ergonomic cooktop application. (Photo courtesy of Sub-Zero/Wolf Photograph)

cooktop at a height that encourages the cook to stir with the wrist in a more neutral position, joint stress can be minimized (Figure 3-3).

A primary factor in kitchen and bath design is the measurement of individual physical abilities; these measurements provide valuable information for the design of counter and appliance heights, upper and lower cabinet access, and floor-space circulation. A person's flexibility and range of motion should also be noted.

There are two basic types of body dimensions: structural and functional.

- **Structural dimensions**, often referred to as *static dimensions*, include such measurements as the size of the head, size of the pupil of the eye, torso measurements, and limb sizes; these relate to very specific anatomical features. Though important when designing apparel, eyewear, and clothing, they have minimal impact on the design of the kitchen or bath.

- **Functional dimensions**, also referred to as *dynamic dimensions*, involve body movement associated with certain tasks. Cabinet layout, appliance selection and placement, lighting, and clearances are all affected by the person's ability to reach and move. Assessment of these human factors gives the designer the necessary information to design a space that fits the client,

Kitchen and Bath Design

whether tall, short, young, old, wheelchair-assisted, or mobility-device-using (walkers, crutches, canes, scooters).

Physical and occupational therapists confirm that proper body alignment through good posture and body mechanics will enable you to live a more healthful and more productive life for a longer period of time. The weight of items you lift, turn with, bend to reach, and pull down from above is a controlling factor in minimizing body stress, strain, and injury (Figure 3-5). Factors causing

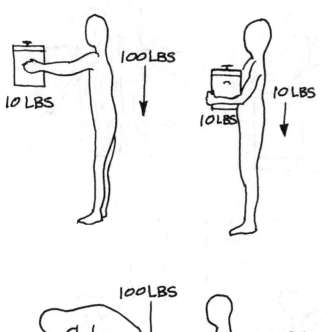

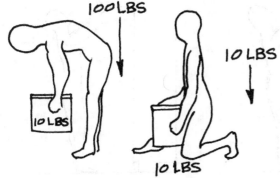

Figure 3-4 How the body moves within a space and how the body performs tasks in that space will dictate how the design should be approached.

fatigue and stress on the body can be positively dealt with through design. For example, a person who uses a wheelchair, when sitting erect, may have limited capacity to bend or turn, resulting in a restricted reach. By measuring the physical ability of the individual, the designer can create a space that fits his or her physical characteristics.

Heavy items should be held close to the body when moving them. Lift with the legs, not with the back (Figure 3-4).

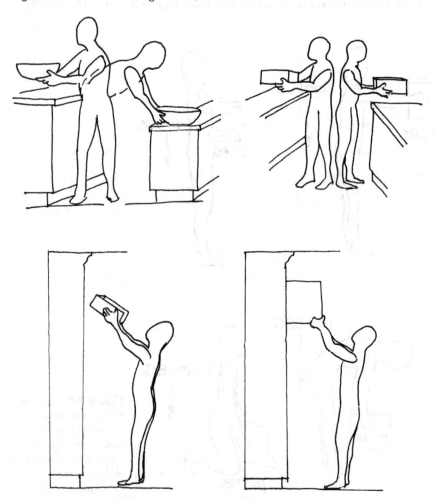

Figure 3-5 When transferring items, turn the body rather than twist it. Only lightweight items should be stored over head height.

Kitchen and Bath Design

Figure 3-6 The installation height of the oven(s) enables the cook to access the oven utilizing the triceps and biceps muscles of the upper arm to carry the weight. (Photo courtesy of NY Loft, Phoenix, AZ)

Body mechanics can be enhanced through design solutions that favor advantageous working positions. By creating environments conducive to good posture and body mechanics, the designer enables the client to maintain better body health during daily activities and prevent strain to the body, thus helping to avoid injuries. Homes and home interiors that are designed ergonomically can enable the body to interact within ideal conditions, definitely promoting total body health regardless of age.

In kitchen and bath design, the underlying supposition that most users are "normal adults" is a fundamentally flawed assumption. Humans are not homogeneous; rather, they are diverse individuals with varying capabilities and characteristics. You have only to consider the differences between short and tall people to recognize how differently they use and move within a space.

Assessment Methods and Techniques

To gather the necessary anthropometric data, begin by analyzing the movement associated with certain tasks. Because individual physical characteristics and ability levels vary, gathering specific data eliminates some of the assumptions made by using general population statistics. An individual's ability to access space, and to work and move within that space, greatly influences the design.

Explain to your client the purpose of the measurements and how the information will be integrated into the plan. This gives you an opportunity to explain the benefits of ergonomic design, as well as to set yourself apart from other designers.

The information gathered in your assessment will enable you to be a problem solver regarding access to space and the use of equipment. Under some circumstances, additional accommodations must be made. An occupational or physical therapist should be engaged as a consultant in these instances. They can be your greatest ally.

Line of Sight

Clear vision of control panels, appliance interiors, food being prepared and cooked, stored items, traffic patterns, and furniture will require a line-of-sight (LOS) measurement. Explain that this measurement will provide the ideal height for locating the control panel of built-in ovens, as well as upper cabinet storage. To make the measurement, you need not touch the person; just hold a measuring tape about 8 to 12 inches from the side of the face (Figure 3-7). Use the "Ergonomic Profile" and "Ergonomic Profile Measurements" forms in the Appendix as an aid.

You will need to discuss light levels during the day and at night and ask whether the client experiences any problems with existing lighting. You will also want to ask about the direction of natural and artificial light in the existing space and whether the client experiences unusual areas of glare or notices areas that lack light.

Note whether the person wears glasses. When oven doors are opened or lids on pots removed, steam is released which can quickly fog eyeglasses. Good ventilation and proper access to the oven must be planned.

Ability to Reach

Measure the distance from the floor to the elbow bent at 90°. This figure indicates the height best suited to the use of large muscle sets.

Safe access into space in appliances, cabinetry, and counter surfaces is achieved with good balance and flexibility. Knowing the client's ability to stand;

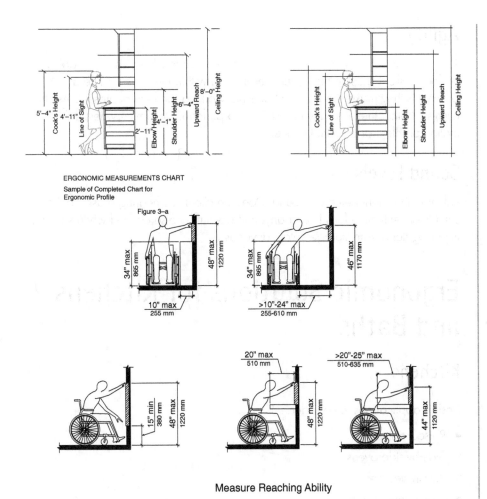

ERGONOMIC MEASUREMENTS CHART

Sample of Completed Chart for
Ergonomic Profile

Figure 3–a

Measure Reaching Ability

Figure 3-7 With a sturdy measuring tape, measure the distance from the floor to the client's eye level, elbow height and upper reach.

to reach up, down, and out; or to reach in all directions enables the designer to plan space that works with the body. For example, islands are sometimes designed so wide that it is difficult for a person who uses a wheelchair to clean the surface in the middle of the island.

Record this information by measuring the client's ability to reach up and out.

Agility

The physical agility and posture of a person relate directly to his or her ability to perform tasks. Observe how your clients move within the space. Note any comments they make regarding what is not working for them at present. Ask the clients whether they find any task difficult to perform. Determine whether this is a motion problem or a spatial concern.

Sound Levels

Ask how the client perceives sound. Does the client use hearing aids? Do the sounds of ventilation fans bother anyone? Does the noise created when someone is getting items from storage irritate anyone?

Ergonomic Solutions for Kitchens and Baths

Kitchens

Design applications to consider:

- Raised dishwasher
- Side-by-side ovens
- Built-in steamer
- Matte counter surfaces
- Sink with mid-level rack position
- Varied counter heights
- Lower cooktop
- Screening of light sources
- Resilient floor covering
- Soundproof materials

Bathrooms

Design applications to consider:

- Shower seat
- Grab bars
- Hand shower
- Thermostatic pressure balance valve
- Shampoo niches
- Valves and tub faucet on front side
- Dressing table
- Different vanity heights
- Barrier-free shower entrance
- Walk-in tubs
- Radiant heat in floor or ceiling
- Nonslip floor covering
- Light fixtures that illuminate either side of face

Grasp and Motion

ANSI A117.1 309.4 states that "[m]oving parts should operate with one hand and not require tight grasping, pitching, or twisting of the wrist. The force required to activate operable parts should not exceed 5 pounds."

Ergonomic Storage System

An ergonomic storage system encourages good body mechanics when retrieving cookware, food, and appliances. It improves safety by encouraging the use of good posture and the larger muscle sets (Figure 3-8).

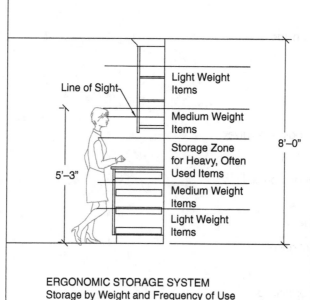

Line of Sight

Light Weight Items

Medium Weight Items

Storage Zone for Heavy, Often Used Items

Medium Weight Items

Light Weight Items

8'–0"

5'–3"

ERGONOMIC STORAGE SYSTEM
Storage by Weight and Frequency of Use

Figure 3-8 The ergonomic storage system locates items based on the weight of the item, how often the item is used, and where the item is used first.

The guidelines established by the Americans with Disabilities Act are helpful in planning clearances and access. CAD drawings and resource information can be accessed online at www.ada.gov.

Additional ADA and ANSI standards are found in Chapter 4, "Kitchen Design Basics," and in Chapter 7, "Bathroom Design Basics."

Kitchen Design Basics

4

"Cooking is a series of related tasks, with specific demands in terms of space, equipment and storage. Planning these separate functions into a cohesive plan is the job of the kitchen planner who works to integrate the technical infrastructure with the practical needs of food preparation to a given layout of space."

Author unknown

Space is a fundamental consideration in kitchen design. A space that is too small or that is awkwardly shaped, with little natural light, can be as challenging as an enormous space with inefficient work patterns. Setting design priorities based on the needs of the chef and the type of food he or she cooks is the first step in the kitchen design process. Refer to the "Planning Procedure Checklist—Kitchens" and "Plan Checklist" in the Appendix.

Designing a kitchen to be practical and efficient yet visually exciting requires creative discipline and the implementation of basic design concepts developed over the years within the industry. With that being said, never let a set of rules dictate your vision for a space. Use guidelines as a way to check the practicality of your design solutions. Remember, kitchens must function well in addition to looking great.

The construction industry, code councils, and appliance, cabinet, and plumbing manufacturers have developed basic standards to help simplify the design and building process. Following are industry standards that design professionals will find beneficial.

Standard Cabinet Dimensions

- Standard modular cabinetry is built in 3" increments (Figure 4-1). Base and upper cabinet widths begin at 9" and increase by 3" widths as you work laterally (12", 15", 18", etc.). See Chapter 6 for more specific information.
- Base cabinets: 6"–54" w, 24" d, 34-1/2" h
- Upper cabinets: 6"–54" w, 12" d, 12"–42" h
- Tall storage cabinets: 9"–48" w, 12"–24" d, 84"–96" h

Figure 4-1 Standard cabinet dimensions.

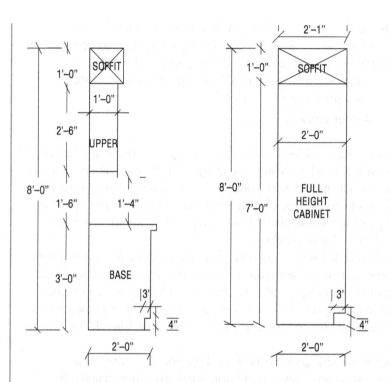

Standard Countertop Dimensions

- Countertop height: 36" finished from floor
- Countertop depth: 25-1/2"
- Backsplash heights: 4"–18" high from countertop

Industry Guidelines for Countertop Work Space

Varied countertop heights may be required because of tasks performed on that surface (Figures 4-2, 4-3).

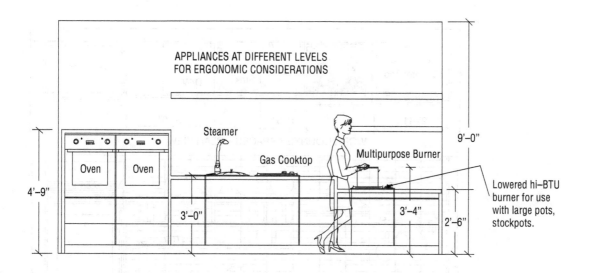

APPLIANCES AT DIFFERENT LEVELS
FOR ERGONOMIC CONSIDERATIONS

Steamer

Oven   Oven

Gas Cooktop

Multipurpose Burner

9'-0"

4'-9"

3'-0"

3'-4"

2'-6"

Lowered hi–BTU
burner for use
with large pots,
stockpots.

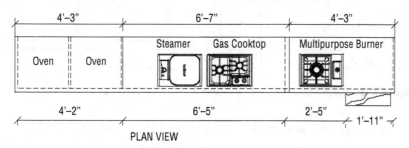

4'-3"   6'-7"   4'-3"

Oven   Oven   Steamer   Gas Cooktop   Multipurpose Burner

4'-2"   6'-5"   2'-5"   1'-11"

PLAN VIEW

Figure 4-2 Today's kitchen designer should plan kitchens based on how the cook and family use the space and the ergonomic profile of the cook.

- Usable counter space between cooktop or range and sink: 18"–36" wide
- Counter space on either side of cooktop or range: minimum 12"–15"
- Counter space on either side of sink: minimum 18"–24"
- Landing space next to refrigerator: minimum 15"–18"
- Counter space between refrigerator and sink: minimum 36"

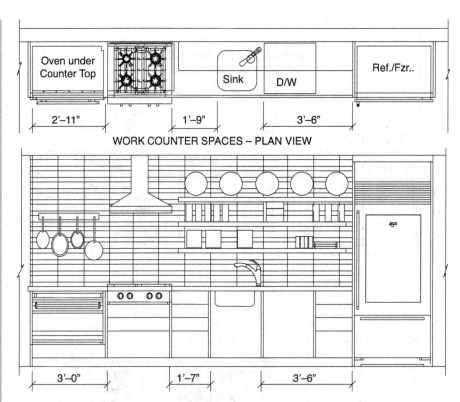

Figure 4-3 Lateral kitchen planned with minimum counter work spaces.

- Counter space next to cooktop or range on island: minimum 12"–15"
- Landing space next to ovens: minimum 12"–15"
- Varied countertop heights

How to Achieve Varied Counter Heights

Different counter heights can be impractical in some kitchen designs, especially small spaces. In those cases, creative solutions are possible (Figure 4-4). For higher counter work spaces, a portable work counter or thick cutting board

Figure 4-4 Courtesy of Poggenpohl, US.

equates to a counter height of 37 to 38 inches. This height helps the user maintain a more erect stance while working at this space.

The top drawer of a bank of cabinets can be equipped to provide a pull-out board. If you put the pull-out board below the split drawer, the height will be 30 to 32 inches. Pull-out boards with locking glides create a stable work surface and additional counter space as needed (Figure 4-5).

Another solution for providing varied work-surface heights is to select a sink with a built-in ledge that supports a removable rack sitting 4 to 5 inches above the sink bottom.

When mixing foods in bowls or pans, this allows you to look into the utensil easily and use your hand in a more neutral position, as well as to use the large muscle sets in your arm as you work (Figure 4-6).

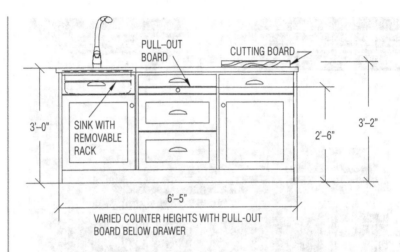

PULL–OUT BOARD

CUTTING BOARD

SINK WITH REMOVABLE RACK

3'–0"

2'–6"

3'–2"

6'–5"

VARIED COUNTER HEIGHTS WITH PULL-OUT BOARD BELOW DRAWER

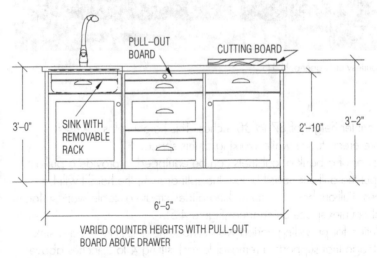

PULL–OUT BOARD

CUTTING BOARD

SINK WITH REMOVABLE RACK

3'–0"

2'–10"

3'–2"

6'–5"

VARIED COUNTER HEIGHTS WITH PULL-OUT BOARD ABOVE DRAWER

Figure 4-5 Cutting boards provide a lower work surface.

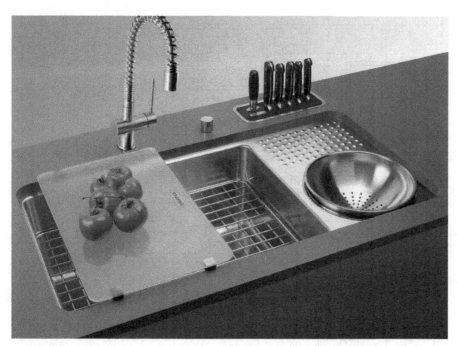

Figure 4-6 Sink with low rack and accessories. (Photo courtesy Franke Kitchen Systems, frankeksd.com)

Scale, Proportion, Balance

Scale, proportion, and balance play an important role in the selection of counter widths and the supporting cabinets. The visual impact of misaligned and unbalanced cabinetry can create a state of disharmony, whereas cabinets that are aligned create a sense of balance and harmony.

Balancing form and function in the kitchen layout will require careful attention to details. Establishing a bisymmetrical or asymmetrical balance can help guide you in spatial allowances (Figure 4-7). For example, the bisymmetrical kitchen will have cabinets of equal width flanking a range (Figure 4-8).

The asymmetrical kitchen will have cabinets of different widths flanking the range yet creating balance within the space (Figure 4-9). Bisymmetry is considered the formal approach and asymmetry informal.

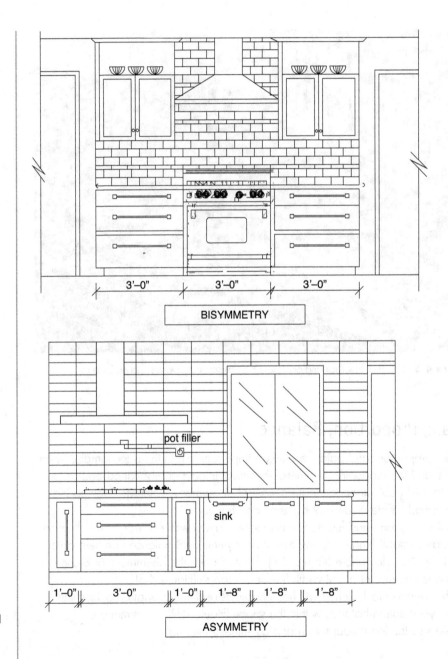

Figure 4-7 Bisymmetrical and asymmetrical balance.

Figure 4-8 Bisymmetrical cabinetry. (Photo courtesy of Northlight Architectural Photography.com, Mary Fisher Designs.com)

Figure 4-9
Asymmetrical layout. (Photo courtesy of Northlight Architectural Photography. com)

Total Integrated Planning

The integrated design of a kitchen brings together ergonomic considerations and the following elements.

A STORAGE PLAN based on:

- First access to stored items
- Frequency of use of the items
- Weight and bulk of items stored

APPLIANCE LOCATIONS planned for:

- Access and use with minimum muscle stress
- Controls at line of sight
- Placement in CoreKitchen™ based on frequency of use
- Relationship, distance, and access to other appliances and fixtures
- Selection of model/features based on cooking style of the home chef

CABINETRY design planned to:

- Accommodate appliance location and provide adequate storage space
- Provide varied cabinet heights for work stations
- Use full-extension hardware for access to all pull-out devices
- Supply adjustable shelving where applicable
- Allow wall space for crown molding returns
- Reflect elements of interior styling

COUNTERTOPS that provide:

- Height variations based on tasks and food preparation techniques
- Depths to accommodate storage and food preparation needs
- Detailing to fit interior styling
- Edge details and overhang to fit space and cabinetry

A flexible LIGHTING PLAN with:

- A minimum of three light systems that function together but are on separate dimmer controls:
  - Ambient
  - Task
  - Accent/indirect
- Dimmer controls on all lighting systems
- Automatic controls whenever possible
- Lighting systems that blend with natural light
- Lighting systems that support task areas during dark hours
- Switch heights that are accessible to all users
- Properly placed motion sensors and timer controls

HARDWARE (cabinetry, windows, and doors) that includes:

- Levers/pulls/knobs that allow hands to grip and operate with ease
- Installation at a level that is easy to reach
- Window hardware that is accessible and functions smoothly
- ADA-required lever handles for doors and pulls for cabinetry

A plan for WINDOWS:

- Locate for minimal strain to muscles when operating
- Note the direction the window opens and how it is accessed
- Ensure that operation of windows does not interfere with cooking and movement
- Select style reflective of the interior and exterior architectural design of the home
- Orient to the view
- Balance with the scale and proportion of kitchen space and walls
- Make windows accessible for cleaning
- Specify quality units for easy operation to prevent muscle strain

A plan for DOORS:

- Locate to enhance the traffic flow from adjacent spaces
- Eliminate interior doors as much as possible
- Select a door style that is consistent with interior design
- Reuse existing interior doors when size and conditions allow
- Make doors wide enough to provide reasonable access and meet local codes
- Outside door, -36" minimum width; interior door, -32" minimum width; arch, -36" minimum width

FLOORS designed for:

- Adequate traction level for safe walking when food or moisture may be present
- Resilience to relieve pressure on the back and legs
- Style consistent with interior design

SPACE PLAN that includes:

- Traffic lanes sufficient for adequate and safe movement
- Layout based on efficiency in movement of people and food preparation tasks

Space Planning

Because the kitchen should not be designed in isolation, lifestyle and interior finishes of adjacent rooms will play an important role in the space planning process. Site considerations affecting the space plan will include:

- Is the kitchen oriented to the view and natural light?
- Is the kitchen open to adjacent spaces?
- Is the kitchen oriented to the social areas of the space?
- To what degree is the kitchen integrated with the rest of the house?

Issues involving sound transmission, ventilation, light (both natural and artificial), and access must be addressed during initial space planning. Ignoring such issues can result in a space lacking in comfort and unity.

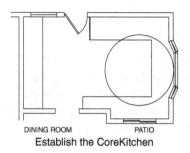
DINING ROOM　　　PATIO
Establish the CoreKitchen

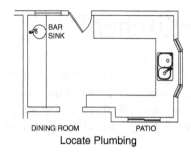
DINING ROOM　　　PATIO
Locate Plumbing

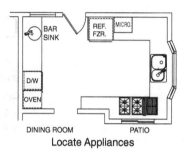
DINING ROOM　　　PATIO
Locate Appliances

SPACE PLANNING STEPS

DINING ROOM　　　PATIO
Locate cabinets and storage

DINING ROOM　　　PATIO
Locate electrical outlets, lighting, and switches

Figure 4-10　Space planning steps.

Balance between visual appeal and function must be considered at each step of the design process. Defining task areas is the first step in planning the space (Figure 4-10).

Space planning steps

- Establish the CoreKitchen™
- Locate plumbing
- Locate appliances
- Locate storage/cabinetry
- Locate electrical outlets, lighting, and switches

CoreKitchen™

Design freedom and flexibility are attained when the CoreKitchen™ formula is employed. The CoreKitchen™ is a defined space identifying the cooking utensils, appliances, and food items that are essential to daily and weekly menus within the overall design. All other cooking equipment and utensils are planned in the next layers of the space and storage outside the core (Figure 4-11).

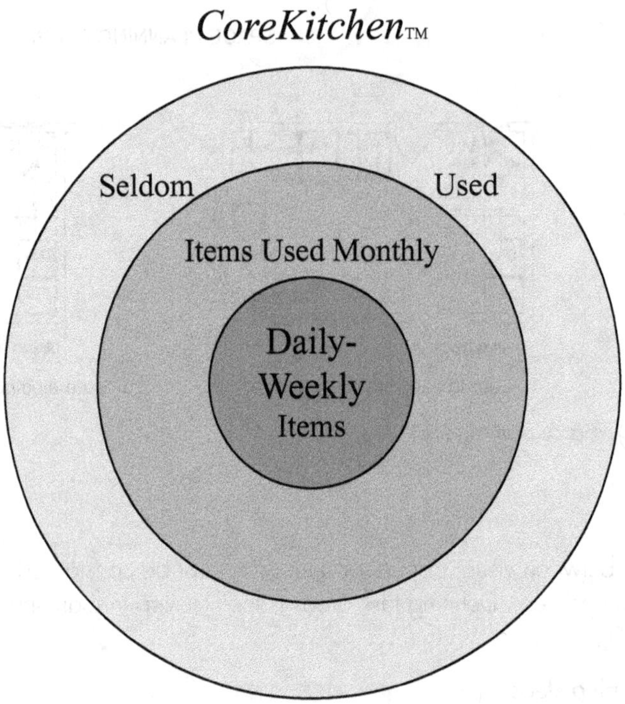

CoreKitchen™

Seldom Used

Items Used Monthly

Daily-
Weekly
Items

The CoreKitchen™ Formula:
Layer One—Daily and weekly items (the essentials)
Layer Two—Items used often but not essential
Layer Three—Seldom-used and seasonal items

Figure 4-11 The CoreKitchen™ formula.

By analyzing daily food preparation and the tools and appliances needed to prepare daily meals, the designer can eliminate nonessential cookware, utensils, and appliances from this primary work space and open the kitchen to the views and adjacent rooms. Upper cabinets often become optional. Daily and weekly essentials are identified, and located and stored accordingly. (Refer to the list of CoreKitchen™ Essentials later in this section.) The essentials will vary with the cook. For example, if the cook is primarily a baker, essential baking equipment used daily and weekly will be included. However, there are basic utensils common to most food preparation techniques, and those make up the list of CoreKitchen™ Essentials.

Identifying a CoreKitchen™ is critical in designing a functional space, whether you are dealing with a small kitchen where space is limited or a mega-sized kitchen where disproportionate space can become a challenge. Planning a complete food preparation work station brings order to any space, large or small. A CoreKitchen™ is made up of four components:

1. Major appliances

2. Plumbing fixtures

3. Cooking tools and tableware

4. Storage systems

Locate the Work Triangle within the Core

An efficient work pattern within the CoreKitchen™ is planned for a flow in which stored food is taken from CoreKitchen™ storage to the work station, washed and prepared for cooking, cooked, and served. This process involves pantry and refrigeration, sink, and a surface cooking appliance. The cook should be able to take a minimum number of steps to accomplish this process.

CoreKitchen™ Formula

The CoreKitchen™ formula consists of three layers of designated work space, storage, and appliance locations (Figures 4-12, 4-13).

Figure 4-12 The best way to illustrate the CoreKitchen™ formula is to view actual projects employing these principles. This unique plan was designed to provide three distinct task areas within one kitchen. Layer One is for the primary cook, Layer Two is planned for family members, and Layer Three is the baking station and auxiliary prep station.

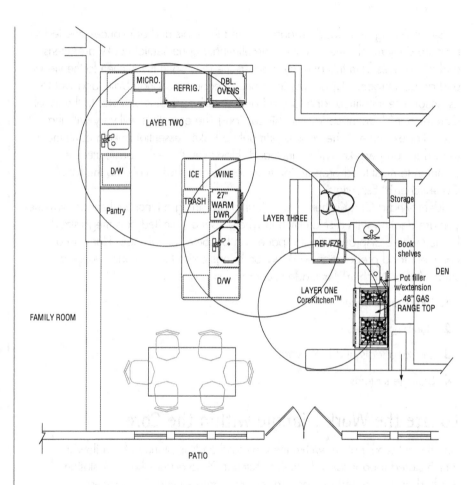

LAYER ONE

Design and equip the core work space to conduct food preparation and service on a daily and weekly basis. Only essential equipment, utensils, and tableware are stored in this core.

LAYER TWO

Tools, utensils, and small appliances used on a monthly basis.

(a) Layer One—Core Kitchen™   **(b)** Layers Two and Three

Figure 4-13 Photos courtesy of Northlight Architectural Photography.com, Mary Fisher Designs.com

LAYER THREE

Infrequently used and seasonal items accessed occasionally. This layer may include adjacent rooms, closets, pantries, basements, or furniture pieces.

CoreKitchen™ Essentials

Home cooks often outfit their kitchens with every gadget made for cooking. In reality, they use a few tools all the time and the others only occasionally, when they remember that they have the tools, where the tools are, and what the tools are for. Good cooks can cook with a basic inventory of tools and cookware, although having special tools and utensils for specific tasks is helpful as well. Deciding what is necessary and what is not can be achieved by analyzing what menus the cook prepares on a daily and weekly basis. The list of essentials is not exactly the same for every cook, although some tools and cookware are common to most food preparation. The following list is a compilation of basic kitchen tools from several resources: chefs, cookbooks, and home cooks. These essentials should be found in the CoreKitchen™. All other tools can be located in the next layer of the kitchen storage plan.

MEASURING/MIXING UTENSILS	FOOD PREPARATION
Measuring spoons	Paring knife
Nested measuring cups	8" chef's knife
2-cup glass measure	Carving knife
6-cup glass measure	Boning knife
Wire whip	Serrated slicing knife
Stainless steel spoon	Whetstone/knife sharpener
Rubber spatula	Vegetable peeler
Stainless steel slotted spoon	Vegetable brush
Stainless steel fork	Garlic press
Tongs	Potato masher
Wooden spoons	Juicer
Pasta fork	Colander
Nested mixing bowls	Large and small strainers
Pastry brush	Can opener
Custard cups	Cutting board
Grater	Kitchen shears
Pancake turner	Pepper grinder
Hand mixer	1-cup ladle
Rolling pin	Stainless steel cooking fork
Funnel	Meat thermometer

POTS AND PANS	OVEN TOOLS
1-quart sauce pan with lid	Cookie sheets
2½-quart sauce pan with lid	Baking sheets
4- to 6-quart sauce pan with lid	Cooling racks
8" skillet with lid	Pie tins
10" skillet with lid	Cake pans
	Loaf pan
	Glass baking dishes
	Roasting pan with rack
	Gratin dish
	Muffin tin
	Casseroles

FOOD STORAGE		**SMALL APPLIANCES**	
Refrigerator containers		Toaster	
Sandwich bags		Mixer	
Freezer bags		Coffee and tea maker	
Waxed paper			
Aluminum foil			
Plastic wrap			
Parchment paper			
Clear airtight containers			

FOODSTUFFS		**MISCELLANEOUS ITEMS**	
Herbs		Cutting boards	
Spices		Hot pads	
Seasonings		Kitchen towels	
Sugar			
Flour			
Baking ingredients			
Coffee/tea			

Locate Plumbing

Place the primary and secondary sinks as you begin your design. The primary sink is used in the food preparation process and is typically located below a window to take full advantage of natural light. Note, though, that this is not always the best location for this sink. Orienting food preparation and cooking to the social areas of the kitchen may require that the primary sink be placed away from the window. When this occurs, the secondary sink can be placed under a window flanked by the dishwasher and recycle center; this will create the clean-up station. Planning a clean-up station outside the CoreKitchen™ can be a very efficient use of space, as it also allows for storage of dinnerware, flatware, glasses, and table service (Figures 4-14, 4-15).

When multiple sinks are planned, each sink should be equipped with a garbage disposer and air switch that turns the disposer on or off. These are located on the sink or countertop, saving wall space and making it more convenient to use.

Figure 4-14 The
CoreKitchen™ core.

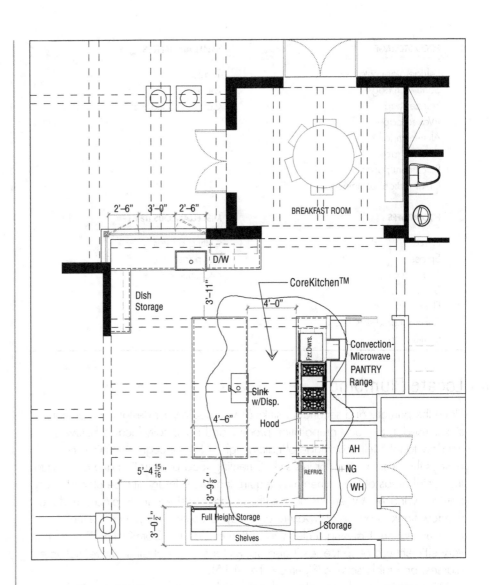

When a single sink is being used, make sure the sink compartment is large
enough to handle how the cook works at the sink. A conflict can occur when
items are being soaked in the single sink compartment and someone wants to

Figure 4-15 Cleanup area outside the CoreKitchen™. (Photo courtesy of Northlight Architectural Photography.com, Mary Fisher Designs.com)

use the garbage disposer. A better choice may be a sink with two different compartment sizes.

Wall-mounted faucets, pot fillers, island sink(s), and faucet locations must be determined early in the design phase. Indicate the height off the finished floor and distance from adjacent walls on your plans for approximate location of faucets and sinks for the island. In locating faucets, be sure there is ample space for installation and operation (Figure 4-16). This will influence the style of fixture you pick.

When placing a sink near an elevated dishwasher, two key elements must be planned: first, the flow of dirty dishes to the dishwasher; and second, the proper counter space between the sink and the dishwasher (Figure 4-17).

Excess counter space between sink and dishwasher encourages water spots on the floor as dishes are rinsed and loaded into the dishwasher (Figure 4-18). (Many dishwashers today are designed to handle small amounts of food left on dishes and utensils, making pre-rinsing unnecessary).

Clients frequently request deep sinks. However, most of the tasks performed at the sink do not require sinks more than 8 inches deep, so the selection of a sink with a grid that elevates the work depth is a great choice. For those clients wanting a deeper sink, 10-inch-deep sinks are available.

Refer to Chapter 8 for specific information on fixture selections.

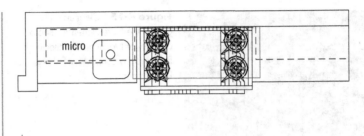

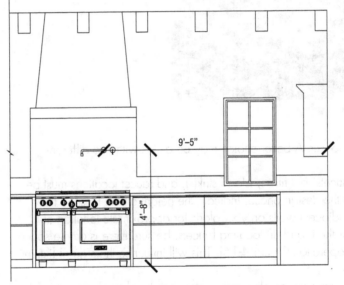

9'–5"

4'–8"

Locate Appliances

The most frequently used appliances should be placed within the CoreKitchen™.
This means a cooktop or range, refrigerator or refrigerator drawers, and sink with
disposer. These three anchor the work triangle within the core. All other
appliances should be placed in locations that support the CoreKitchen™ and
allow efficient work stations for special food preparation. For example, if the
cook regularly braises and then finishes off the food in an oven, a range in the
CoreKitchen™ locates an oven where it is needed; a second oven can be

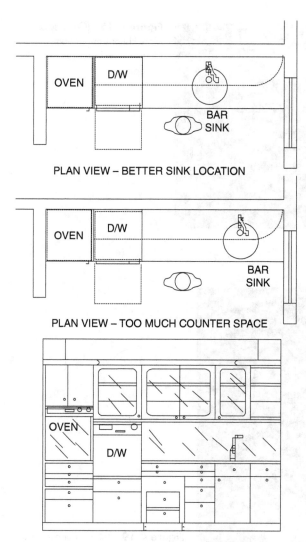

Figure 4-17 Sink location and counter space amounts.

PLAN VIEW – BETTER SINK LOCATION

PLAN VIEW – TOO MUCH COUNTER SPACE

located in the bake center or Layer Two of the design (Figure 4-19). For kitchens where the lack of wall space dictates the use of stacked ovens, placement should be just outside the CoreKitchen™ but readily accessible. It is preferable to install ovens side by side or in two different locations. This ergonomic design

Figure 4-18 (Courtesy of Mary Fisher Designs.com, Northlight Architectural Photography)

Figure 4-19 The smaller oven will be used most frequently, and the larger oven will be used when greater capacity is required. (Photo courtesy of Northlight Architectural Photography.com, Mary Fisher Designs.com)

application accommodates the use of two different-sized ovens placed at the most convenient height for access.

This is a way to use energy more efficiently. (Baking two potatoes in a 30-inch-wide oven is a waste of energy, but is frequently done). Refer to Chapter 5 for detailed information on ovens and other appliances.

Locate Electrical Outlets, Lighting, and Switches

Task lighting is crucial when planning work stations in the kitchen. Task areas must include light over the sink(s); light over counter spaces, with or without upper cabinets; and light over the range/cooktop (Figure 4-20). The physical size and lumen output of the fixture will affect the number of fixtures needed for the space. Eliminating shadows and providing even light for the cook is the goal. When a

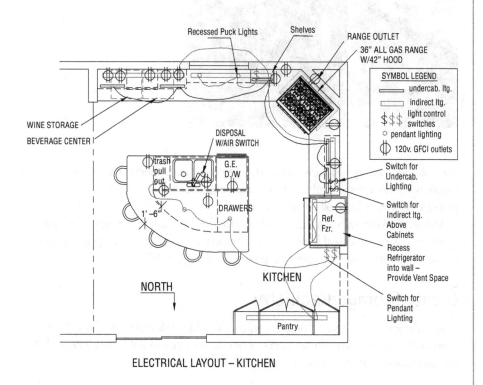

ELECTRICAL LAYOUT – KITCHEN

Figure 4-20 Each lighting system should be on its own dimmer control.

Figure 4-21 When a remodel has insufficient space to install a remodel recessed can, a track lighting system may be the solution. (Photo courtesy of Sub-Zero/Wolf Photograph)

low-voltage lighting system is planned, there are two criteria for selecting a location for the transformer(s): first, access; and second, air circulation (transformers must be well ventilated).

When working with the structural limitations of an existing home, clearance requirements for recessed light cans, access to run new wire, and space available for switches can influence your fixture selections (Figure 4-21).

Locate Storage/Cabinetry

Essential cookware, utensils, and ingredients should be stored in the CoreKitchen™. Select cabinets that provide adequate space for these essential items along with the needed support for proper appliance installation (Figure 4-22).

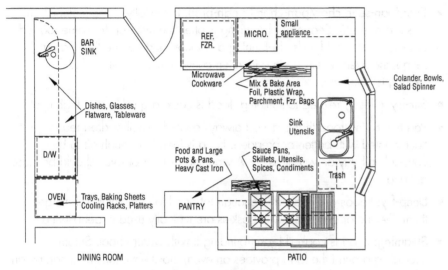

BAR SINK

REF. FZR.

MICRO.

Small appliance

Microwave Cookware

Mix & Bake Area
Foil, Plastic Wrap,
Parchment, Fzr. Bags

Colander, Bowls,
Salad Spinner

Dishes, Glasses,
Flatware, Tableware

Sink Utensils

D/W

Food and Large
Pots & Pans,
Heavy Cast Iron

Sauce Pans,
Skillets, Utensils,
Spices, Condiments

Trash

OVEN

Trays, Baking Sheets
Cooling Racks, Platters

PANTRY

DINING ROOM

PATIO

STORAGE OF THE ESSENTIALS

Figure 4-22 As essential equipment is located in the CoreKitchen™, additional items from Layer Two can be stored in the remaining space of the core. The first priority is placement of the essentials in the CoreKitchen™ storage space.

Food Preparation Techniques

Understanding cooking techniques and terms will help you identify the appliances, plumbing fixtures, counter space, storage, and needed utensils. It is important to note that most food preparation involves more than one appliance. The following defines work centers and cooking techniques performed at those centers.

Cooking Center

This work station is comprised of either a full range or surface cooking only (cooktop or range top). Often-used ingredients should be stored relatively close and a minimum counter space of 24 inches should be available between the surface cooktop and the next appliance or fixture.

Surface cooking is the process in which food is cooked on gas burners or electric units. These methods include:

- **Sauté:** Technique in which food is cooked rapidly in a little fat or oil over relatively high heat.

- **Sear/pan-sear, char/pan-char,** or **pan-broil:** Essentially, these methods are versions of sauté. Searing or browning is often the first step for some roasted, braised, or stewed foods. If planning a cooktop and oven rather than a range, the oven should be in a location convenient for finishing foods when searing is complete.

- **Stir-fry:** Closely related to sautéing; food is cooked quickly over high heat.

- **Pan-fry:** Frying food that is almost always coated, whether dredged in flour, coated with batter, or breaded. Food is fried in enough oil to be covered halfway or two-thirds up. A warming drawer or oven should be close at hand.

- **Deep-fry:** Foods are cooked in enough fat or oil to completely submerge them. Electric or gas fryers with baskets are typically used in deep-frying.

- **Steaming:** Food is cooked by surrounding it with water vapor. Steam circulating around the food provides an even, moist environment. It can be an effective way to reconstitute previously cooked foods.

- **Boiling:** While submerged in an active liquid (usually water or broth), foods may be *blanched*, in a short precooking; parboiled, which partly cooks food prior to frying or roasting; or fully cooked. Other useful equipment for boiling foods includes colanders or strainers for draining; equipment for cooling vegetables cooked in advance; holding containers to keep foods warm; and spoons, ladles, or skimmers for cooking, tasting and serving. A sink to drain the liquid should be located within 24 inches. If foods are frequently boiled, a minimum work counter of 36 inches should be planned. It is important to remember that the sink must be conveniently located for filling or pouring out pots of water.

- **Poaching:** Cooking in a liquid that is just below the simmer point. The surface of the liquid may appear to be rippling. The food should be completely covered by the liquid.

- **Simmering:** Food is cooked gently in a liquid just below the boiling point. The liquid may appear to have a "soft" boiling appearance.

- **Braising and stewing:** Meats or vegetables are cooked by briefly browning in hot fat, adding a little liquid and cooking at a low temperature in a covered pot. One of the benefits of this process is that virtually all the flavor and nutrients are retained. Most braised foods are finished in an oven. Plan a range or locate an oven close to the work center.

- **Grilling:** Cooking by direct exposure to radiant heat (over a gas flame or electric element) or on an iron griddle with parallel metal bars that allow liquids to drain as byproducts.

Oven Cooking

Roasting, broiling, and baking are cooking techniques that do not require constant monitoring and can be located in Layer Two space adjacent to the CoreKitchen™. An exception to this arises when the cook needs to have an oven located close to surface cooking for food that is partially cooked on the surface units and then finished in the oven. In this case, a range or oven close to the surface cooktop is desirable.

Oven cooking processes include:

- **Roasting:** Using dry heat, this method cooks food in an oven or over an open flame.
- **Broiling:** Cooking food under a radiant heat source. This can be either gas flame or an electric element.
- **Rotisserie:** A method of cooking food on a rotating spit that is exposed to a radiant heat source.
- **Baking:** Cooking food in an oven with a bottom heat source or convection hot-air currents circulating in the cavity.

  Provide a minimum 18-inch-wide counter landing space for food from the oven.

Fresh Food Station

Cleaning and preparation of fresh food is normally done at a sink location. Appliances include the refrigerator, sink, garbage disposer, and recycle bins. Utensils needed for cutting, trimming, mixing, and cleaning fresh food are located at this station. This is also the location where wraps and storage containers should be handy. An island can be an alternate location for this task.

Baking Center

Baking center appliances include a refrigerator, sink, mixer, food processor, and oven, as well as convenient access to a surface cooking unit. Plenty of counter space will be needed; a lower counter height or pull-out board is often desirable for rolling out dough and pastries. Utensils and bakeware needed near the oven include baking sheets, baking pans, measuring cups and spoons, bowls, cooling racks, roasting pans, meat thermometers, spoons, pot holders, whisks, and spatulas.

Cleanup Center

Cleaning up after cooking is just as important as food preparation at each center. This cleanup center should contain a sink large enough to soak cookware and baking utensils, a high-arc or pull-out spray faucet, garbage disposer, recycling center or trash compactor, and dishwasher.

Food storage containers, foil, parchment, plastic wrap, and storage bags should be stored in this center.

Food Storage

Food safety and storage are major considerations in kitchen design. Proper refrigeration for perishable foods and appropriate conditions for pantry or food staples must be planned. The refrigerator should be kept at 40°F (5°C) and the freezer at 0°F (−18°C). Both refrigerator and freezer compartments should be easily accessible and food stored with ample room for air to circulate. The size of the refrigerator and freezer should be determined by items to be stored in each and the way the client uses them.

Sufficient air circulation must be maintained to effectively store food in the refrigeration and freezer. Check the existing refrigerator-freezer space as a guide and note whether the space is adequate. It is not always necessary to have the freezer in the kitchen. Because the freezer is typically less often accessed, placing it in a different yet convenient location is acceptable.

The life and freshness of food are greatly affected by how the food is stored. Fresh produce that emits ethylene gas will cause other produce sensitive to the gas to ripen very quickly. Some fruits and vegetables must be stored in the refrigerator immediately, whereas others should be stored on the counter until fully ripened and then moved to the refrigerator. The counter space allotted to fresh produce should be out of direct sunlight and relatively cool. The vegetable drawers in the refrigerator should be humidified.

There should be sufficient refrigeration and work space to ensure that no cross contamination of foods occurs during storage and handling.

FRESH FOODS THAT EMIT ETHYLENE GAS

Apples	Nectarines
Avocados	Onions
Apricots	Pears
Cantaloupe	Plums
Figs	Tomatoes
Mangos	

FOODS AFFECTED BY ETHYLENE GAS

Bananas	Bok choy	Broccoli
Cabbage	Carrots	Cauliflower
Cucumbers	Eggplant	Fresh herbs
Green beans	Honeydew melon	Kale
Kiwi fruit	Lettuce	Lima beans
Parsley	Peaches	Peas
Potatoes	Soft-rind squash	Spinach

Herbs and Spices

Fresh herbs should be stored in the refrigerator in a damp paper towel or standing in a container of water. Dry herbs and spices should be stored in cool, dark, dry locations away from heat sources but within easy reach when needed. The quality of these ingredients is greatly diminished by exposure to heat and light. Spice drawers in the base cabinets or in upper cabinet shelves away from the range or oven are appropriate storage locations.

Pantry Storage

The Food and Drug Administration (FDA) states that shelf-stable food can be safe for long periods of time, but the quality may suffer after extended periods of time

Figure 4-23 Staples or dry foodstuffs should be stored in dark, dry, cool, well-ventilated conditions. (Courtesy of Braxton Builders, Scottsdale, AZ 85262; photo courtesy of Northlight Architectural Photography.com)

in storage. The "best if used by" date on the label of the product is an indication of whether the quality of the food is still good. The FDA does not require an expiration date for shelf-stable foods, because the storage time for these foods is a quality issue, not a food safety concern (Figure 4-23).

A study published by Texas A&M University states, "Ideally, the temperature in the pantry should be 50–70°F. Higher temperatures speed up deterioration. Always store foods in the coolest cabinets away from the range, oven, water heater, dishwasher, or any pipes that emit heat. The area under the sink is not a good place to store potatoes or onions."

Walk-in pantries or pantry cabinets serve this purpose. Surplus or bulk storage is planned for the pantry space. Dry foods that are used on a daily or weekly basis should be stored within the CoreKitchen™.

The designer must determine the amount of space needed for storage and ask the clients what foods they store and how they currently store those foods. If your client stores coffee beans or extra baked goods in the freezer with flour, bread, grains, and nuts in the refrigerator, a refrigerator/freezer large enough to handle the storage must be specified.

Root Vegetables

In the past, root vegetables were stored in "root cellars." These below-grade spaces made the most of natural, stable conditions to hold quantities of food for long periods of time. Root vegetables require cool temperatures and relatively dry and dark conditions.

In today's home, these cool rooms are finding their way back into existence with the cooler cabinet and closet. Some walk-in pantries also accommodate these conditions.

The walk-in cooler shown in Figure 4-24 allows bulk storage of fruit, vegetables, wine, cheese, flowers, and foods prepared in advance for entertaining.

Figure 4-24 (Courtesy of Mary Fisher Designs.com; photo courtesy of Northlight Architectural Photography.com)

Wine

Wine is often used as a cooking ingredient in braising, stewing, and sauces. If a wine storage appliance is not planned, wine can be stored in the pantry at floor level, horizontally (on its side), where it can be kept cool, dark, and immobile.

Pet Food

Considerations when planning storage of pet foods include quantity, size of containers, whether refrigeration is required, and access to stored food. All of these will affect the design. Refer to the "Project Inventory Assessment" in the Appendix.

Plumbing Selections for Kitchens

The plumber may not be completely versed in all of the fixture models available from manufacturers, especially imported fixtures. Your plumbing supply representative is the expert who will make sure you specify fixtures correctly and can review various manufacturer guidelines for installation with you and the plumber. The plumber will specify pipe and fitting sizes.

Sinks

Kitchen sinks come in a variety of shapes and sizes. Single-, double-, and triple-compartment sinks are the most common. However, always consider combining various shapes and sizes to meet specific needs of the cook.

Six basic factors should be considered when selecting the correct sink(s) for the kitchen design:

- How the sink will be used
- Sink location(s)
- Type of installation (top-set, undermount, integrated)
- Dimensions of sink
- Sink material type
- ADA compliance, if needed

SELECTING SINK SIZES

Establishing how the sink will be used is most important prior to selection. A person who washes dishes by hand may want a two-compartment sink. Another may require a large single compartment along with a dishwasher. Sink sizes will vary with number of compartments and features. The standard two-compartment (two-bowl) sink measures 33 inches long by 22 inches wide by 8 inches deep, with both compartments the same size. Today, however, many sizes of two-compartment sinks are available. Selection should be based on how the client will use each compartment. The cutout size of the sink dictates the size your sink cabinet will be.

In addition to the sink size, the number of holes for faucets and sink accessories must be determined before ordering. Identify sink accessories to be used: faucet, air gap, air switch, soap/lotion dispenser, and instant hot water/filtered water faucet all require space and location on or near the sink.

Another important factor is the location of drains and garbage disposer(s). When water purifiers, instant hot water dispensers, or pull-out storage are planned, a sink with drains and disposer located at the back or side of the sink helps free up cabinet space below for the pull-out items. By selecting this sink before even the rough plumbing is done, water supply lines can accurately be set off-center, freeing up cabinet space.

One feature to consider when selecting the sink is whether a rack is to be added to the sink, either on the bottom or on side supports. This provides a work space for the cook that is lower than the counter but higher than the bottom of the sink. See Chapter 3 on ergonomics for further information.

Prior to selecting fixtures, the designer must have some basic information:

- Spatial limitations of room or cabinetry
- How the fixtures will be installed
- If replacing fixtures only, cutout dimensions of the old sink and the distance between centers of faucet and valves
- Desired color and finish

Countertop material, cabinet style, backsplash detail, and the overall decorative scheme will influence your selections.

Any special installation needs must be known prior to finish work. For example, a steam oven plumbed to a water line must have the supply and drain located during rough plumbing and electrical.

Always refer to accurate scaled drawings for clearances and available space and then confirm measurements of the actual areas prior to ordering.

HOW WILL THE SINK BE USED?

The sink is a primary work station of a kitchen. Defining the tasks performed by the cook and matching them to a sink model will result in a proper fit.

Common sink tasks:

- Preparing/trimming food for cooking
- Adding water to food for cooking
- Soaking food
- Rinsing cooking utensils
- Washing pots/pans and dishes
- Obtaining drinking water
- Washing hands
- Arranging flowers

Most sinks can accommodate accessories, which may include colanders, grid racks, fitted cutting boards, and more. Storage for these accessories when not in use must be planned near the sink.

LOCATION OF SINK(S)

Because natural light enhances this work space best, the traditional location of the sink has been under a window—but this may not be the best location with regard to the function of the kitchen. This is when multiple sinks should be considered (Figure 4-25).

An interior kitchen may not have a window; therefore, you will want to orient the sink to the social space of the kitchen.

TYPE OF INSTALLATION

- **Top-set:** Top-set or self-rimming sinks have a finished edge that installs on the countertop. Top-set sinks can be undermounted if properly fitted into the

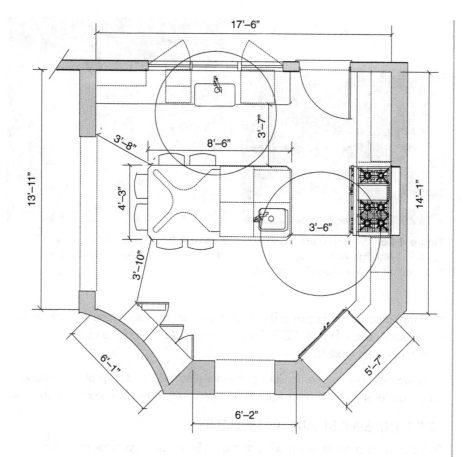

Figure 4-25 More than one sink in a space is desirable when placed where others can access them without interrupting work flow between refrigeration, surface cooking, and the main sink.

rough-top. Coordinate such an installation with the cabinet dealer and countertop fabricator.

- **Undermount:** Installation of a sink under the countertop must be coordinated with the countertop fabricator, cabinet dealer, or builder. This type of installation allows the designer to combine various sink shapes and sizes to fit the client's needs (Figure 4-26).

- **Integrated:** Forming the sink out of the countertop material makes the sink fully integrated.

Figure 4-26 Undermount sink. (Photo courtesy of Northlight Architectural Photography.com, Mary Fisher Designs.com)

Figure 4-27 Front-apron sink. (Photo courtesy of Franke Kitchen Systems, frankeksd.com)

- **Farmhouse or front-apron:** The front of the sink is finished and the sink sits on a cabinet base (Figure 4-27). They are available in single- and double-compartment models.

Undermount or integrated sinks make cleaning the countertop of food residue easy. Top-set sinks have a lip that interferes with wiping food residue into the sink.

MUST THE SINK BE ADA–COMPLIANT?

Manufacturers provide sink models that specifically address clearances for special needs (Figure 4-28). Use the client's ergonomic profile information to help with sink selection.

The drains and/or garbage disposer should be located at the back and to the side of the sink. This will allow more leg space below (Figure 4-29). A client need not be using a wheelchair to enjoy the feature of a sit-down preparation space at the sink.

SINK TYPES AND STYLES

Materials used for sinks are stainless steel, enameled cast iron, solid surfaces, quartz, metals, stone, vitreous china, and fireclay.

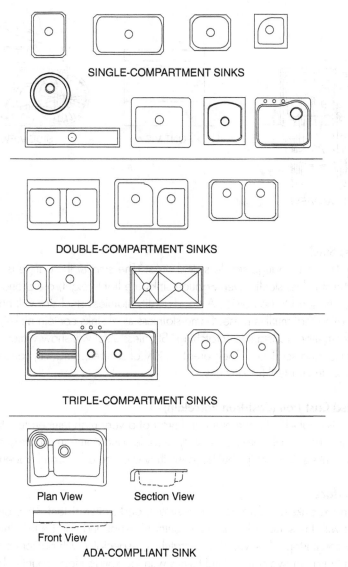

SINGLE-COMPARTMENT SINKS

DOUBLE-COMPARTMENT SINKS

TRIPLE-COMPARTMENT SINKS

Plan View   Section View

Front View

ADA-COMPLIANT SINK

Figure 4-28 Sink models and types.

Figure 4-29 Sink for
seated use—ADA-compliant.

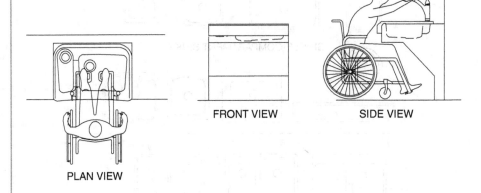

PLAN VIEW   FRONT VIEW   SIDE VIEW

Stainless Steel
Choose 16- or 18-gauge stainless steel sinks. (The *smaller* the gauge is, the
thicker the stainless steel). Twenty-gauge sinks are lightweight, are prone to
denting, and tend to be noisier. A good-quality stainless steel sink will have an
undercoating that muffles noise. Some stainless steel sinks contain nickel, which
makes them more resistant to scratching. Stainless steel will show water marks,
fingerprints, and scratches. Their great variety of shapes, durability, and neutral
color make them ideal for kitchens.

Enameled Cast Iron (Cast-Iron Porcelain)
Cast iron is coated with porcelain and fired at a very high temperature to make
these sinks. These sinks are heavy, very durable, and come in an array of colors.
Cast-iron sinks seldom chip, but because they are coated, it can happen.

Solid-Surface
Solid-surface sinks are durable, heat-resistant, and stain-resistant. They are often
installed with the same solid-surface counter material and can be fully integrated
with the countertop. They will show scratches, especially with darker colors.
When integrating two-compartment sinks with the solid-surface counter, be sure a
spillway is provided between the compartments to allow water to flow into the
sink when the faucet with flowing water is moved from one compartment to the
other.

Acrylic

Acrylic sinks are stain-resistant but susceptible to heat damage. Some are available with antibacterial properties built into the material. They are the least durable of the sink types.

Quartz

Quartz sinks are a composite of quartz and resins. They are durable and come in glossy and matte finishes and a variety of colors and configurations. They are scratch resistant but show some water spotting.

Fireclay

Fireclay sinks are china bisque, poured into a mold and fired at a very high temperature. This produces a very hard, nonporous surface that stands up to heat very well. Fireclay front-apron sinks are a popular choice and come in one- and two-compartment styles. In addition, undermount fireclay sinks in a variety of shapes and sizes are often used.

Vitreous China

Vitreous china sinks are molded clay or liquid bisque poured into a mold and fired at a very high temperature. They are very durable but can chip under some circumstances. Faucets and sink accessories may have to be installed into the countertop, as many of these sinks do not come with predrilled holes.

"Exotic" Metal Sinks

Brass, copper, silver, and zinc are some of the softer metals occasionally used in sinks. Many have hammered finishes to disguise scratches; all will tarnish with use. These characteristics can be desirable qualities in some decorative schemes. They are available in various shapes and sizes but are prone to denting and scratching. The antique finishes are very popular in rustic and "Old World" looks.

Faucets

Three factors influence the selection of a faucet:

1. The location where the kitchen faucet will be installed
2. How the faucet will be used by the cook (and others)
3. The cook's ability to use the faucet

Ergonomic factors, such as weight, ease of operation, and the client's ability to hold a spray arm, are extremely important. If the client cannot reach and operate the faucet, an alternate faucet design and/or location should be selected. Faucets installed on the countertop can be placed at the side of the sink rather than the back, allowing better access.

FAUCET STYLES AND TYPES
There are five basic types of faucets (Figure 4-30):

1. Deck- or wall-mounted pot fillers
2. Wall-mounted faucets
3. Deck-mounted (countertop) and bridge faucets
4. Single-handled, pull-out spray
5. Electronic faucets

Pull-out spray: These single-handle faucets rotate and a spray arm pulls out to fill the sink or a pot. Water temperature is selected and mixed with the same single handle.

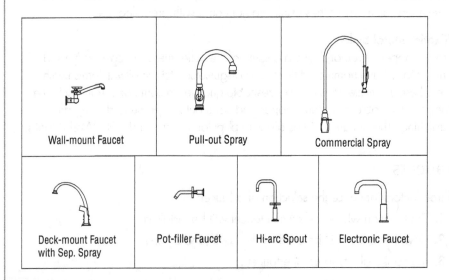

Wall-mount Faucet	Pull-out Spray	Commercial Spray
Deck-mount Faucet with Sep. Spray	Pot-filler Faucet	Hi-arc Spout / Electronic Faucet

Figure 4-30 Faucet types.

Commercial-style pull-down spray: Tall pull-down spray with diverter to allow a constant water flow when needed. Close attention should be paid to the height requirements of this faucet type.

Faucet with side spray: Single-handled faucet with a separate side sprayer.

Bridge faucet: A two-handle faucet raised above the countertop or sink with an exposed bridge connection.

High-arc spout: This practical application provides more room to fill tall pots and use the sink.

Pot filler: Deck- or wall-mounted pot-filler faucets provide water access at the surface cooking area (Figure 4-31).

Figure 4-31 When a pot-filler faucet is planned at a range or range top along with a preparation sink, the pot filler can serve the pots at the range as well as the sink to the side. (Photo courtesy of Mary Fisher Designs.com, Northlight Architectural Photography.com)

Electronic faucet: Automatically controls the flow and temperature of water from the faucet using an electronic motion sensor. User presets the temperature of the water.

Foot-pedal valve: A foot-operated control connects to and controls the faucet. This allows hands free operation at the sink.

ADA: Single-handle faucets and blade- or lever-handle faucets meet the requirements set by the Americans with Disabilities Act.

Appliances

There are two categories of kitchen appliances: freestanding and built-in. Freestanding appliances are finished on all sides and, as the name suggests, can stand alone. These appliances may be ranges, refrigerators, freezers, or microwave ovens. Most older kitchens are equipped with freestanding appliances.

Built-in appliances require cabinetry to house them. The selection or design of cabinets to properly fit the appliance is critical, especially when installation heights of appliances are considered (Figures 4-32, 4-33).

A complete discussion of appliances is found in Chapter 5.

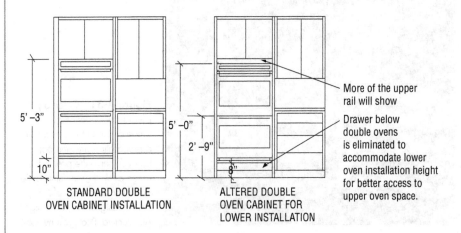

Figure 4-32 When lowering the typical installation height of double ovens to accommodate the height of a client, modular cabinetry may have to be adjusted. Custom cabinetry will be built according to the designer's specification.

STANDARD DOUBLE OVEN CABINET INSTALLATION

ALTERED DOUBLE OVEN CABINET FOR LOWER INSTALLATION

More of the upper rail will show

Drawer below double ovens is eliminated to accommodate lower oven installation height for better access to upper oven space.

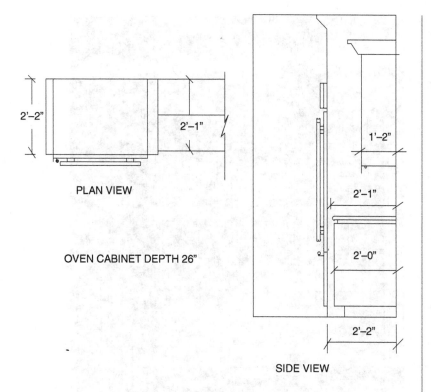

PLAN VIEW

OVEN CABINET DEPTH 26"

SIDE VIEW

2'-2"

2'-1"

1'-2"

2'-1"

2'-0"

2'-2"

Figure 4-33 When refrigeration appliances are built-in, the cabinet should be 26" deep rather than the 24" standard depth to accommodate the edge of the countertop terminating to the side of the refrigerator cabinet.

Counters and Backsplashes

Backsplashes

The backsplash area in a kitchen is the exposed wall surface from the countertop to the upper cabinets and the space behind the range/cooktop and/or sink. Materials typically used include stone, tile, metal, glass, mirror, paint, and water-resistant wallcovering. Backsplashes in cooking and wet areas should be easy to clean, as well as resistant to water and heat (Figure 4-34). Refer to Chapter 11 for detailed information on various backsplash materials.

Figure 4-34 How a backsplash is trimmed out is an important design detail to consider during the initial stages of the design. (Photo courtesy of Mary Fisher Designs.com, Northlight Architectural Photography. com)

For example, glass backsplashes can be backlit, providing a diffused light source for counter work spaces. However, both the electrician and the glass installer need to know what is intended well before they begin work.

If tile is selected for a backsplash, are there trim pieces available to complete the installation? If stone slab is used, how will an exposed edge be finished? Slab material is installed with mastic that creates a small gap between the back of the slab and the surface on which it is applied. In most instances, a grout colored the same as the slab material will be used on any exposed edges.

Countertops

Every material has its own characteristics, and discussions with the tradesperson who is going to fabricate and install the material should be done early in the planning process so accommodations can be made as needed.

Abundant countertop work spaces are one of the most requested features in kitchens. Where and how much counter space should be planned is based on the task that will occur at that location (Figure 4-35).

Close attention must be paid to the counter edge details and how the counter returns to cabinetry, walls, and island corners. The typical counter reaches 25-1/2 inches from the wall to the counter edge, creating a 1/2- to 3/4-inch overhang beyond the base cabinet doors or drawer fronts (Figure 4-36).

A full discussion of counter surfaces appears in Chapter 11.

Figure 4-35 Countertops must be sanitary, easy to clean, and suit the decorative style of the kitchen. (Photo courtesy of Mary Fisher Designs.com, Northlight Architectural Photography.com)

Figure 4-36 Some edge
details, such as a reverse
bevel edge, may extend
more than 1-1/2". (Photo
courtesy of Mary Fisher
Designs.com, Northlight
Architectural Photography.
com)

Cabinetry

Cabinets play many roles in the kitchen. Acting as a bridge between work
centers, cabinets must provide support for appliances and countertops, provide
adequate storage for kitchen gear and service, and set the tone of the decorative
scheme of the space.

Cabinets may be installed to the ceiling, soffit, or with open space above.
The typical height at which upper cabinets finish to a soffit is 7 feet off the
finished floor (Figure 4-37). Cabinetry installed to the ceiling when the ceiling is
higher than 9 feet may be cabinets stacked to fit the height; these systems often
use library ladders to access the upper spaces. When this is the case, the ladder
track and height of the ladder safety rails must not interfere with the opening of
the cabinet doors. When they do, access to the space will be from the side.

Cabinets with open space above can make any space feel larger, because
the eye tends to travel to the wall surface above the cabinet (Figure 4-38).
Staggering the heights of wall cabinets can appear like raised piano keys,
jarring the visual line, if some restraint is not employed.

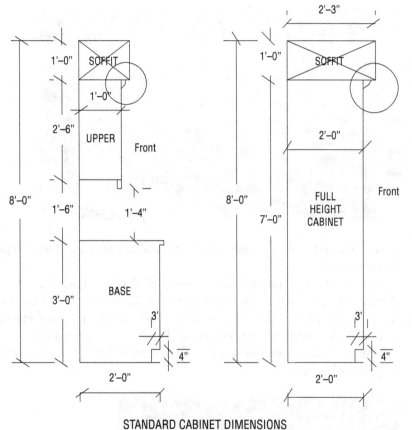

Figure 4-37 When a soffit is built above, be sure the soffit has sufficient depth to allow a crown molding to fit to the bottom of the soffit.

STANDARD CABINET DIMENSIONS
CROWN ALLOWANCE AT SOFFIT

Tall cabinets can act as anchors for a staggered-height design approach. The rhythm set by this design should allow an effortless and deliberate transition for the eye.

In Figure 4-39, the upper cabinet molding was planned to accommodate the ceiling beams. To make a visual statement, cabinets with a furniture look were installed at different heights to draw the eye to the beams and tongue-and-groove (T&G) ceiling. Cabinets were designed with stiles and rails sized to accept

Figure 4-38 (Photo courtesy of Mary Fisher Designs.com, Northlight Architectural Photography. com)

crown molding returns. Consequently, there is an appearance of three separate furniture pieces.

When posts are to be used at the corners of islands, consider how they will affect the storage space in the island (Figures 4-40 and 4-41). The narrow space created by the position of the posts can often be used for storage of individual items. This also occurs when accessing stud cavity space in pantries.

Refer to Chapter 6 and the Case Studies at the end of this chapter for specific cabinet applications.

Figure 4-39 It is important to create a deliberate, well-thought-out plan. (Photo courtesy of Mary Fisher Designs.com, Northlight Architectural Photography.com)

Figure 4-42 Clearances needed for kitchen activities.

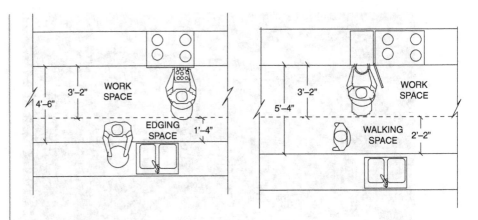

Cabinet Hardware Selection

It is important to select decorative hardware early. When cabinets are installed at right angles, clearance space must be planned in the corner for the depth of the hardware and the thickness of the door or drawer front. (Refer to Chapter 6, Figure 6-12.) Additionally, when an appliance door or handle may interfere with the opening of a cabinet drawer or door, the appropriate clearance must be planned (Figure 4-42). One way to check yourself is to do a clearance sheet of the floor plan, showing the appliances and cabinet doors and drawers when they are fully opened.

Spatial Clearances and ADA Guidelines

ANSI A117.1 804.2.2, 1003.12.1.2: A "U"-shaped kitchen should have a 60" minimum clearance between parallel counters.

ANSI A117.1 304.3.1: A diameter of 60" for a wheelchair turning space should be provided.

ANSI A117.304.3.2: The "T"-shaped turning space for wheelchairs is 60" square overall with 36" arms. This should include knee and toe clearances (Figure 4-43).

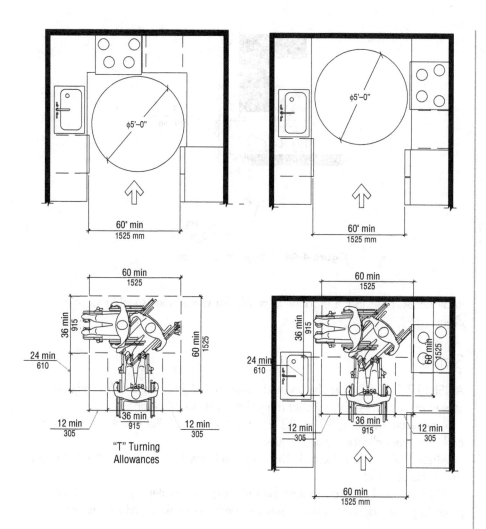

Figure 4-43 Wheelchair clearances.

φ5'-0"

60" min
1525 mm

φ5'-0"

60" min
1525 mm

60 min
1525

36 min
915

24 min
610

60 min
1525

12 min
305

36 min
915

12 min
305

"T" Turning
Allowances

60 min
1525

36 min
915

24 min
610

60 min
1525

12 min
305

36 min
915

12 min
305

60 min
1525 mm

ANSI A117.1 306.2: A minimum 30" wide and 27" high clear space should be planned under the counter, sink, or cabinet space. When a cabinet panel is installed, the slope of the panel starts 11" back from the face and 9" high at the back.

A 9" toe space under a cabinet or appliance allows for wheelchair toe clearance (Figure 4-44). The required toe clearance is typically planned.

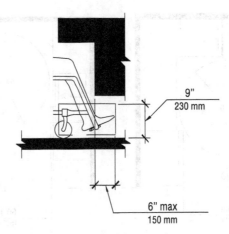

Figure 4-44   Wheelchair toe clearance.

In all cases, refer to the ergonomic profile for dimensions suitable to your client.

Sinks

ANSI 117.1.1002.4.2: The finished minimum height of the sink for someone seated or in a wheelchair should range from 29" to 34" high.

A minimum range of 30" to 32" is typically applied. Refer to the ergonomic profile for your client's specific requirement.

ANSI 117.1 1002.12.4.3: The single sink bowl no more than 6-1/2" deep should be planned.

ANSI A117.1 606.6: Insulate the sink's exposed water supply and drain pipes to protect against contact. Surfaces under the sink should be smooth.

Food Preparation Station

ANSI A117.1 8.04.3, 1003.12.6.3: At least one 30"-wide counter space, ranging from 29" to 36", should be planned (Figure 4-45). A movable cabinet can be placed under the counter provided the finished floor extends under the cabinet.

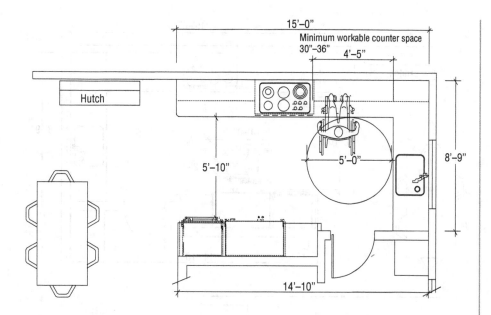

Figure 4-45 Wheelchair-usable counter space.

Figure labels within image:
15'-0"
Minimum workable counter space
30"-36"
4'-5"
Hutch
8'-9"
5'-10"
5'-0"
14'-10"

Appliances

REFRIGERATOR

ANSI A117.1 804.6.6, 1003.12.6.6: Plan a 30" wide by 48" long clear space for a parallel approach to the refrigerator/freezer (Figure 4-46). The center line of the appliance should meet the 24" maximum offset of the clear space.

MICROWAVE ABOVE COOKTOP

IRC M 1901.1: A 30" minimum clearance is required between the cooking surface and an overhead unprotected, combustible surface (Figure 4-47).

IRC M 1504.1: Follow manufacturer's specifications when a microwave hood combination is installed over the cooking surface.

OVEN

ANSI A117.1 804.6.5.1: A counter space should be planned on the handle side of a side-hinged door oven.

Figure 4-46 Parallel approach to refrigerator.

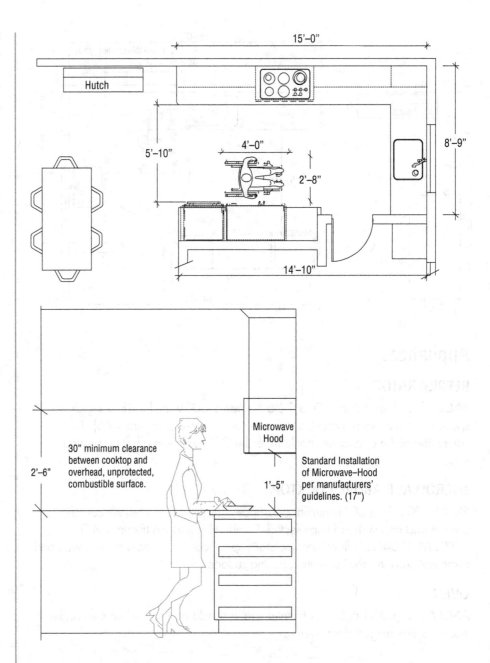

Hutch

15'–0"

8'–9"

5'–10"

4'–0"

2'–8"

14'–10"

Microwave Hood

30" minimum clearance between cooktop and overhead, unprotected, combustible surface.

2'–6"

1'–5"

Standard Installation of Microwave–Hood per manufacturers' guidelines. (17")

Figure 4-47 Above-cooktop clearances.

REACH OF WHEELCHAIR USERS

ANSI A117.1, 308.2.1, and 308.3.1: When an unobstructed forward or side reach occurs, a 48" high maximum and 15" minimum low reach off the finished floor should be planned (Figure 4-48).

   ANSI A117.1, 308.2.2: When the forward or side reach is hindered by an obstacle such as a countertop, a high reach should be 44" maximum off the finished floor.

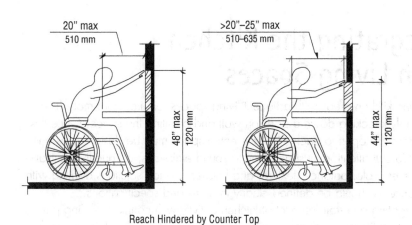

Reach Hindered by Counter Top

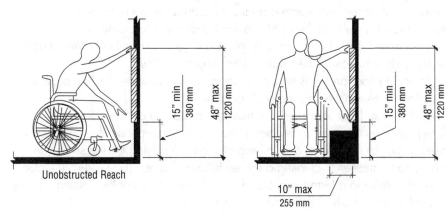

Unobstructed Reach

Figure 4-48   Reach of wheelchair users.

Food Preparation Flow

A very deliberate, organized flow exists in preparing food for service. It begins with food storage (refrigerator-freezer, pantry), then moves through retrieval of stored food and ingredients for prep work (sink); cooking the food (cooktop, range, ovens); service to the eating area; delivery of dishes, glasses, and service to the cleanup area for washing; and, finally, storage of tableware after cleaning. When properly planned, this process moves along smoothly.

Integrating the Kitchen with Living Spaces

Integrating kitchen areas with adjacent living spaces requires a lot more finesse than merely knocking down a partition wall and outfitting the space. Once the two spaces are open to each other, the entire space must be designed as one space. Careful attention must be given to sound emissions, air quality, ventilation, light sources, color balance, texture, and finishes. Design solutions dealing with these concerns should be defined clearly in plans and specifications.

Segregating a certain amount of kitchen activity with counters, sliding panels, half-height partitions, or island units is often a good solution for defining work areas. Cooks often appreciate a degree of separation or enclosure from other family activities in the kitchen that enables the designer to create the CoreKitchen™. Island and peninsula plans are good ways of controlling traffic within a kitchen/eating area without hindering traffic flow.

Extending floor and wall finishes throughout a multipurpose kitchen provides a visual link between the cooking and social areas.

Color, form, function, and décor must be considered as they relate to the living space as a whole, rather than to each space independently. Color can be used as both a defining and a unifying element, identifying the transition from one area to another or creating a unified feeling of space (Figure 4-49). Color can add vitality to a bland space and is an important part of the lighting scheme of the kitchen or bath. Balance must be achieved.

CASE STUDY ONE
Sustainable Design

Figure 4-49 If the basic surfaces are made of the same material, a change of color can highlight a change of use or mood. (Photo courtesy of Mary Fisher Designs.com, David Zilly Photography, Scottsdale, AZ)

The same strategy works by using a monochromatic color scheme while varying the materials to provide just enough visual consistency to unify the room. This monochromatic approach is especially effective in small spaces.

Carefully examine designs of kitchens that work effectively and look great.

CASE STUDY ONE
Sustainable Design

GOALS:

1. Enlarge window to bring in more natural light.
2. Make the kitchen more functional.
3. Keep desk in same space in front of window.

4. Remove sink and convert bar to a dry bar/buffet. Provide cabinet furniture designed to hold bottles in drawers at a convenient height for access.
5. Maintain eating space in the kitchen for two people with space for overflow if needed.

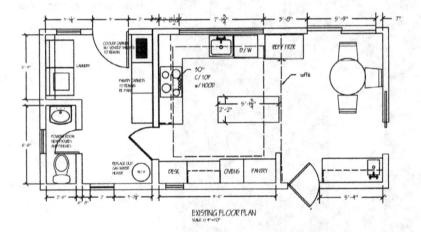

EXISTING FLOOR PLAN
SCALE: 1/4"=1'0"

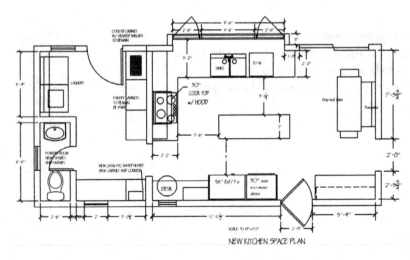

NEW KITCHEN SPACE PLAN
SCALE: 1/4"=1'0"

Figure 4-50 Old and new space plans.

SOLUTIONS:

1. A new 8'-0" x 3'-6" window was installed at the sink location. This required the engineering and installation of a new header. The window design selected had two operating casements on either end with a stationary center pane that was centered on the sink. This provides natural air circulation when open. Because of the length of the window, an island vent was installed. Typical drain vent installation would have sent the vent pipe up on an angle and then up and out next to the studs. This could not occur because the window was brought to the counter level and an appropriate angle could not be attained. The window was installed so that the countertop surface met flush with the sill of the window (Figure 4-51).

2. A wall protruding by the door to the dining room was removed to accommodate the new location of the refrigerator-freezer. By locating the refrigerator and ovens on the interior wall, window and doors could be planned in the exterior wall of the kitchen. An island was installed to act as landing space for the ovens and refrigerator. A large, single-compartment sink was undermounted at the window flanked by the dishwasher and "Essentials" storage.

3. The desk is counter height, providing additional work space when needed.

4. The sink in the old bar location was removed. A center line of tall drawers was built to fit the bottle storage and keep it at a convenient height for access.

5. Providing an eating area in this small kitchen required the use of a banquette and drop-leaf table. The proximity to the island and sink counter space made minimum clearances critical. Although seating for two people is the norm for daily use, having the option to seat more was still provided.

Figure 4-51 The bottom of the window frame must be calculated at the rough framing stage. (Courtesy of Judy Svendsen, ASID, Raven Interiors/Mary Fisher Designs.com; Photo courtesy of Don Milici Photography)

Figure 4-52 "Found" Asian screens were found and used as doors of upper cabinets. This space serves as both a dry bar and buffet. (Courtesy of Judy Svendsen, ASID, Raven Interiors/Mary Fisher Designs.com)

6. EnergyStar® appliances were selected to outfit the kitchen. A flow-restrictor faucet and catalytic water heater were installed as water-saving features.

7. Surfaces and materials were selected for their color, texture, and sustainable qualities. Clean lines and organic colors are found throughout. Honed black granite countertops were sealed with a penetrating sealer. The honed finish cuts down on the glare occurring from the natural light streaming into the room. A 4-inch-high backsplash of honed granite finishes the counter at the wall. Tile behind the cooktop was recycled and set the color of the selected wallcovering. Bamboo is the island counter surface. It is hard and a practical work surface. Hot items coming from the ovens are placed on a trivet to protect the bamboo. Stained cork is used as the floor surface. It is practical, easy to clean, and a resilient surface on which to stand. Resilient materials ease stress on legs and back as one works in the kitchen. Natural reed blinds were set into the window alcove in three parts. This provides control of light, air flow, and privacy at each window space.

8. Lighting consists of five different systems: (1) Recessed cans with color-corrected fluorescent bulbs are installed as general light to enter the room. (2) Smaller recessed cans with color-corrected fluorescent bulbs provide task light over the sink and counter space. (3) Xenon under-cabinet lighting is the third system. (4) Three pendants over the island provide both task and decorative light. (5) Two pin lights and a horizontal drop fixture light the eating area. All light systems are on their own dimmer controls.

9. Cabinet details were designed for specific purposes. Adjustable shelving is located in all upper cabinets. A pull-out shelf housing the toaster was designed to provide access by the client when at the table (Figure 4-53).

The island is located so dishes can be unloaded easily from the dishwasher (Figure 4-54).

The upper cabinets to the right of the hood are hinged on the right-hand side to allow direct access while working at the sink or cooktop. Had the cabinet door next to the hood been hinged on the left-hand side, as is typically done, access to stored items would be impeded by the cabinet door.

Figure 4-53 An electrical outlet located in the cabinet interior allows the toaster to be used easily while seated at the table. (Courtesy of Judy Svendsen, ASID, Raven Interiors/Mary Fisher Designs)

Figure 4-54 Drawers fully extend in the island to house dinnerware. (Courtesy of Judy Svendsen, ASID, Raven Interiors/Mary Fisher Designs.com)

Figure 4-55 A pull-out trash container is easily accessed from the sink or cooktop. (Courtesy of Judy Svendsen, ASID, Raven Interiors/Mary Fisher Designs.com)

10. The laundry-pantry was repainted to update the finish to fit with the new kitchen. The old storage-tank water heater was replaced with an energy-efficient catalytic water heater (Figure 4-56).

The existing pantry cabinets were kept, utilizing the slotted shelves in the cooler section of the cabinetry. This feature, found in many older homes, is a great asset for storage of staples, root vegetables, and citrus.

Figure 4-56 New cabinet storage and counter surface were created in space previously lost to the water heater tank. (Courtesy of Judy Svendsen, ASID, Raven Interiors/Mary Fisher Designs.com)

CASE STUDY TWO
Southern France

GOALS:

1. Create a kitchen oriented to the view and outdoor living space and open to the living room (Figure 4-57).

2. Make clearance spaces ample width to accommodate breathing equipment. Provide an island that looks like furniture and still has space for seating and display.

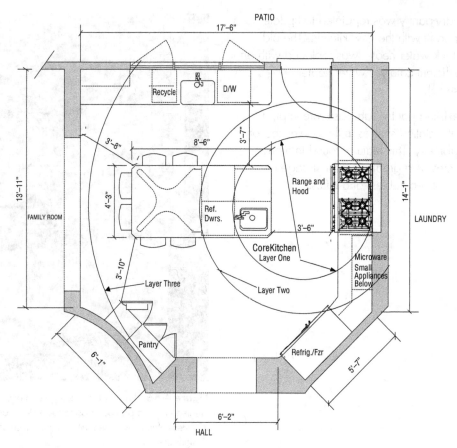

Figure 4-57 CoreKitchen™ space plan.

3. Create a custom hood compatible with a sunny Mediterranean interior.

4. Install a beamed ceiling.

5. Select professional-style appliances that are easy to use.

6. Hide small appliances.

SOLUTIONS:

1. A large window installed at the secondary sink provides ample natural light during the day (Figure 4-58). A door leading out to the patio kitchen is located for easy entry to interior kitchen work stations. The refrigerator was placed for convenient access from the CoreKitchen™ and by other family members. Small appliances were stored behind pocket doors that hinge and slide out of the way. The cabinet was recessed into space in the adjacent room and placed under the microwave, which is only 15 inches deep.

A front apron sink was selected to accommodate larger cookware and racks. An air switch to the left of the faucet controls the disposer. Because only one upper cabinet was installed on this wall, glass doors and side panel lessen the mass of the cabinetry. The toe kick is set back 6 inches, accommodating furniture feet on each cabinet, including the dishwasher.

Figure 4-58 The window was set deeper into the wall to allow installation of custom shades. (Photo courtesy of Mary Fisher Designs.com, Northlight Architectural Photography.com)

Figure 4-59 Photo courtesy of Mary Fisher Designs.com, Northlight Architectural Photography.com

2. Passage aisles are 42 inches wide to accommodate easy access and circulation. The island was designed to have a furniture look, ample storage for cooking utensils, and use of every inch of accessible space. When posts are used at the corner of an island, shallow spaces are created—and they should be used. Drawers with bowls, utensils, and mixing gear are located to the right-back of the faucet. At the seating end of the island, a sculpted bottom shelf allows chairs to slide in and still provide display space for collectibles. The limestone countertop was acid-washed, polished, and then treated with a penetrating sealer until the stone would accept no more of the liquid. It stands up to work beautifully. The eased edge eliminated sharp edges. The iron lighting fixture provides downlight as well as ambient light in the room. The beamed ceiling was waxed to finish the wood. Cabinets were held down from the beams to accommodate the ceiling (Figure 4-59).

Kitchen pantry storage (Layer Two) contains foods used daily, weekly, and monthly. Additional storage space was located down the hall. Planning bulk storage in a Layer-Three location makes often-used items available when needed. Note the narrow space holding flat containers (Figure 4-60). Adjustable shelving should be planned to eliminate wasted space above stored items.

Figure 4-60 Full-extension roll-out shelves make lower storage accessible without strain on the body. (Photo courtesy of Mary Fisher Designs.com, Northlight Architectural Photography.com)

CASE STUDY THREE
Contemporary

GOALS:

1. Plan an efficient working kitchen with a coffee center and eating area.
2. Keep existing tile floor.
3. Create an open space between the kitchen and living/family room.
4. Keep existing windows and doors.

SOLUTIONS:

1. A peninsula was eliminated to create and open up the work space. The sink was centered on the window at the previous location. The freezer was placed next to the coffee center, allowing more counter space in the surface cooking area (Figure 4-61). An induction cooktop was selected and vented by a hood that looks like sculpture. Because the hood can be seen from the living/family room, it needed to appear as an art piece yet still function well.

2. An arched opening between the kitchen and living/family room provided more light into the kitchen and a visual connection while entertaining (Figure 4-62).

3. The refrigerator and freezer were separated for better access by family members and as used in the CoreKitchen™ (Figure 4-63).

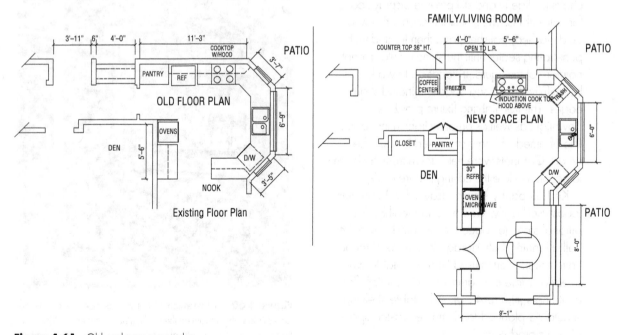

Figure 4-61 Old and new space plan.

Figure 4-62 The granite countertop on the kitchen continued as the surface for the dry bar on the living/family room side of the arch. (Photo courtesy of Mary Fisher Designs.com, Northlight Architectural Photography.com)

Figure 4-63 Oven and microwave oven were installed just outside the core and, along with the refrigerator, were encased in stainless steel to unify the look of the cabinetry. (Photo courtesy of Mary Fisher Designs.com, Northlight Architectural Photography.com)

Figure 4-64 Ceiling light placement must always be carefully designed when ceiling fans are being used. (Photo courtesy of Mary Fisher Designs.com, Northlight Architectural Photography. com)

4. Recessed xenon lighting was installed as task lighting over the sink and ambient lighting throughout the ceiling. A small stainless steel fan with downlight was located so that, when engaged, it does not create a strobe flicker of light (Figure 4-64).

   The coffee center was located in the transition space from the hall to the kitchen (Figure 4-65).

Figure 4-65 To provide landing space for the center, a pull-out board that locks into place was installed below the coffee center. (Photo courtesy of Mary Fisher Designs.com, Northlight Architectural Photography.com)

Figure 4-66 Cabinetry for the dry bar was anchored to the wall at every stud to carry the weight of the cantilevered cabinetry and granite countertop. The 3-inch, reversed-bevel counter edge detail adds additional impact to the look of the space. (Photo courtesy of Mary Fisher Designs.com, Northlight Architectural Photography.com)

CASE STUDY FOUR
Loft Space

GOALS:

1. Create a serene, efficient kitchen space that is part of the loft space as a whole.
2. Use finishes and materials that anchor the space and create unity.

SOLUTIONS:

1. The designer planned varied counter heights to accommodate available space and gear tasks to ergonomic height considerations (Figure 4-67).

2. The compact use of space includes a drawer refrigerator, convection oven, cooktop and hood, sink, and dishwasher.
3. Essential cookware, dishes, glasses, and tableware can all be stored within the CoreKitchen™.
4. Horizontal shelves provide linear storage as well as drawing the eye along the wall.

Figure 4-67 Balance and efficiency mark this well planned kitchen. (Courtesy of Barbara Houston, Vancouver, B.C.)

CASE STUDY FIVE
Sunriver Project

GOALS:

1. Space allotted by the architect for the kitchen was limited by sliding doors to a deck, position of the dining room, and entrance from the stairs to the living room.

2. The homeowners wanted to capture views to the east and west, limiting wall space and location of upper cabinetry.

3. Two fully equipped work stations were desired, to allow multiple-cooks in the kitchen simultaneously.

4. Family member heights ranged from 5'-3" to 6'-9". All of them cook.

5. The primary cook is eighty years old and more physically limited than other family members.

SOLUTIONS:

1. Entrance to the kitchen was placed on an angle, creating separation from the dining room.

2. The primary sink was placed in cabinetry separating the kitchen from the dining room with an unobstructed view to the dining room, living room, and western exposure.

3. An island complete with sink and halogen cooktop created the second work station.

4. Counter heights ranged from 36" to 40" (island). Pull-out boards throughout the kitchen that lock into place provided additional countertop space 34" high.

5. The CoreKitchen™ was located along the south wall and equipped for the older cook to use when the family is not in residence.

Figure 4-68 CoreKitchen™ area.

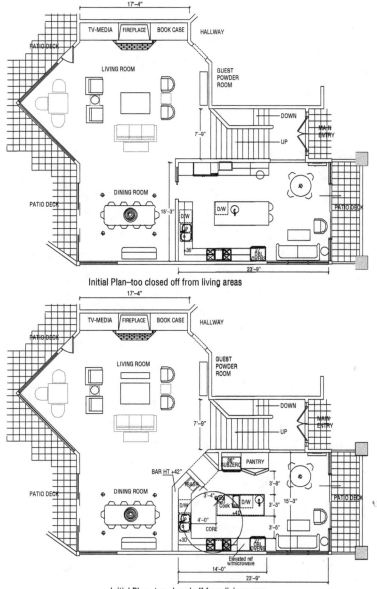

Initial Plan–too closed off from living areas
Plan as built–open to outside views and entertainment spaces.

Figure 4-69 Kitchen and dining room floor plan.

Appliances

5

Today's appliances are engineered to be energy-efficient, easy to use, and adaptable in design. Convenience and healthful living continue to be high priorities for consumers. Refrigerators blend into cabinet schemes; integrated dishwashers are neither seen nor heard; restaurant-style ranges and cooktops separate from ovens are a few of the available options. Multitasking appliances are in great demand. Combination steam-convection ovens, speed ovens, induction cooktops, convection-microwave ovens, and deep fryers that can also poach and steam are some restaurant cooking applications that have been redesigned for the residential kitchen. With so many choices, confusion is certain to follow. The designer must become familiar with the clients' cooking habits, their skills in food preparation, and the amount of kitchen space that can be devoted to appliances. Typical questions to be answered are:

- What appliances best meet the needs of the client?
- Which appliances fit the concept of the kitchen design?
- How much is too much equipment for a kitchen space?
- What task is the appliance to perform?
- What features does the cook desire?
- Are the scale and proportion of the appliance conducive to the space?
- Does the appliance fit the ergonomic profile of the primary cook(s)?
- What is the environmental impact of the appliance on energy, water, and air quality?

The most basic kitchen fixture/appliance package consists of a range, refrigerator, and sink. These three appliances have formed the anchor points of the kitchen work triangle for years. In today's kitchen design, appliances are selected to complete work centers throughout the space (Figure 5-1). Different work stations require different appliances and utensils (Figure 5-2).

The two categories of appliances are:

- Freestanding appliances (Figure 5-3)
- Built-in appliances (Figure 5-4)

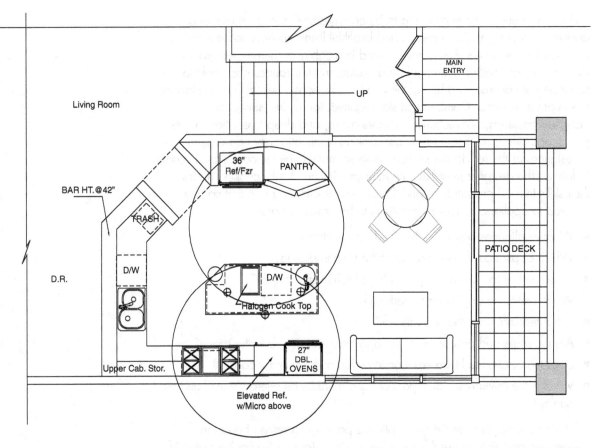

Living Room

UP

MAIN ENTRY

36" Ref/Fzr

PANTRY

BAR HT.@42"

TRASH

D.R.

D/W

PATIO DECK

D/W

Halogen Cook Top

Upper Cab. Stor.

27" DBL. OVENS

Elevated Ref. w/Micro above

Figure 5-1 When appliances are located carefully and thoughtfully, appliances may be shared by one or more cooks at separate work centers.

Refrigeration

The refrigerator-freezer is the most important appliance for keeping food fresh and preserved. Its primary function is to provide a cooling system that will inhibit the natural growth of bacteria found in food. According to the USDA, bacteria grow most rapidly in temperatures ranging from 40° to 140°F. The refrigeration

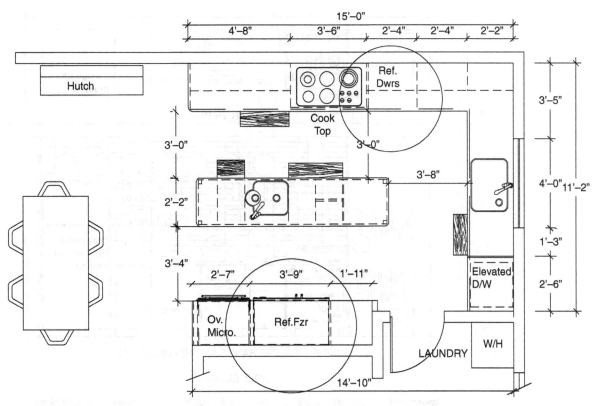

Figure 5-2 When a refrigerator-freezer is placed outside the CoreKitchen™, providing refrigerator drawers in the core space will complete the work center and allow the full-sized refrigerator-freezer to be placed where it is accessible by others.

space, at a regulated temperature of 32°–40°, protects most foods (Food Safety and Inspection Service, www.fsis.usda.gov).The refrigeration process works by the extraction of heat from an enclosed space by a compressor, refrigerant, and evaporator coil (Figure 5-5).

In a refrigerator-freezer, the refrigeration compartment must hold produce, proteins, fats, grains, nuts, and perishables for relatively short periods of time; the freezer compartment stores a variety of foods and prepared meals for much longer periods. It is important that you take stock of what and how much is

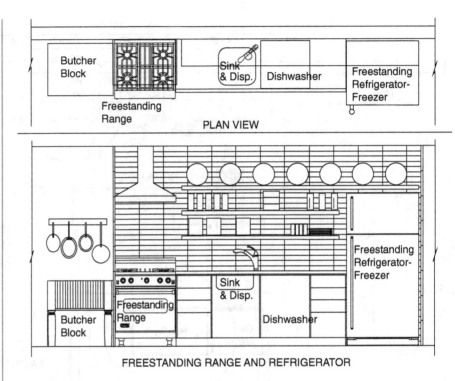

Butcher
Block

Freestanding
Range

Sink
& Disp.

Dishwasher

Freestanding
Refrigerator-
Freezer

PLAN VIEW

Freestanding
Refrigerator-
Freezer

Sink
& Disp.

Freestanding
Range

Dishwasher

Butcher
Block

FREESTANDING RANGE AND REFRIGERATOR

WALL ELEVATION

Figure 5-3 *Freestanding* appliances are finished on all sides and engineered to stand alone.

normally stored and match the appliance size to the storage need. It is not
unusual for a person living alone to need as much freezer space as a family
of four. If a person living alone stores raw nuts, coffee, bread, butter,
cooking ingredients, and prepared meals, along with the usual frozen
foodstuffs and leftovers, the freezer compartment has to be large enough to
meet this need.

Water filtration for ice makers, automatic defrosting, and microprocessors
that maintain constant temperatures throughout the interior space are some of
the technical innovations and benefits in energy-efficient refrigerators and
freezers.

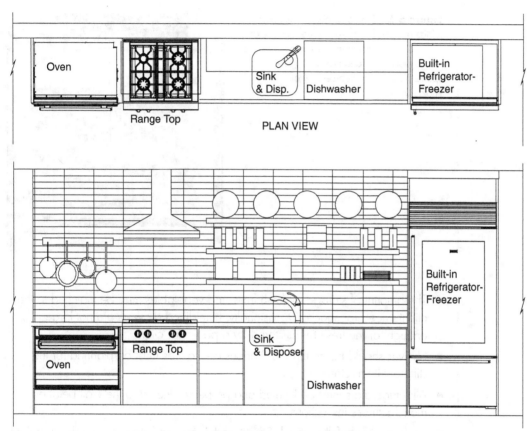

Oven

Range Top

Sink & Disp.

Dishwasher

Built-in Refrigerator-Freezer

PLAN VIEW

Oven

Range Top

Sink & Disposer

Dishwasher

Built-in Refrigerator-Freezer

BUILT-IN RANGE, OVEN AND REFRIGERATOR
WALL ELEVATION

Figure 5-4 *Built-in* appliances are designed and engineered to be built into cabinetry or support structures.

Considerations when selecting a refrigerator-freezer:

- Match accessible storage space to the physical characteristics of the client. Can the client reach and see the top shelf? Can the back of the shelf be reached?

- A built-in refrigerator with the compressor located at the top of the unit makes storage space below more accessible.

Figure 5-5 The compressor compresses the refrigerant gas that moves through a valve and evaporator coil absorbing heat from inside the refrigerator-freezer and thus cooling the interior space. (Courtesy of Sub-Zero/Wolf Photograph)

- The amount of storage for fresh fruits and vegetables must be matched to the client's need for space. Occasionally, humidified drawers are not large enough for the fresh foods stored by a particular client.
- Shelves should be adjustable. Various clearances must be planned for the different items stored.
- All refrigerators must be leveled and properly secured to the wall per the manufacturer's instructions.
- Drawers should fully extend. Some models feature full-extension roll-out shelves.
- The freezer compartment in a bottom-mount model should extend fully.
- Interior finishes of refrigerators should be easy to clean.
- Interior lighting should illuminate all the refrigerator space.
- It should be easy to change the light bulbs. Many units now use LED light sources, which last much longer than traditional lamps/bulbs.
- How much storage space is lost because of the ice maker?
- Filtered water connections, whether remote or built-in, should be accessible for when the filter must be changed.
- Does the manufacturer allow connection to a reverse-osmosis system?

Freestanding Refrigerator-Freezer

Though typically sized 32"–48" wide, 67"–70" high, and 34" deep, refrigerator-freezer models come in a variety of configurations (Figure 5-6). Models include:

- Top-mount freezer
- Bottom-mount freezer
- French door models

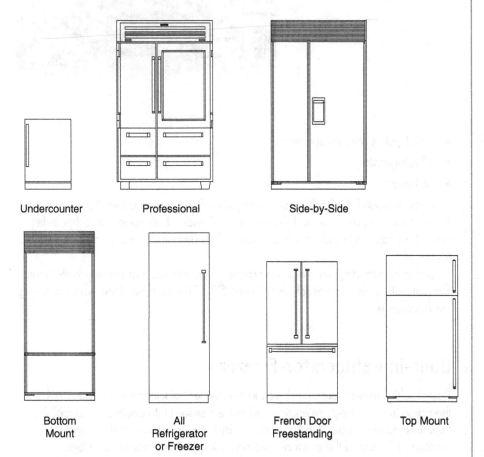

Undercounter	Professional	Side-by-Side

Bottom Mount	All Refrigerator or Freezer	French Door Freestanding	Top Mount

Figure 5-6 Refrigerator types.

Figure 5-7 Freestanding unit with trim kit. (Photo by Don Milici Photography: Courtesy of Judy Svendsen, ASID, Raven Interiors, Mary Fisher Designs.com)

- Side-by-side refrigerator-freezer
- All refrigerator
- All freezer

If you surround the freestanding refrigerator-freezer with cabinetry to give it a built-in look, you must allow 1/4 inch to 1/2 inch of air space on either side and at the top and back of the appliance. The manufacturer's guidelines must be followed.

Some freestanding units can be ordered with trim kits that allow you to blend the units into your cabinet scheme (Figure 5-7). This must be done when ordering the appliance.

Built-in Refrigerator–Freezer

Built-in refrigerators were introduced to the residential kitchen in the late 1940s. As the name implies, they are engineered to be installed into cabinetry; hence, they lack finished side, back, and top panels. Built-in refrigerators with compressors located at the top of the unit make storage space below more accessible.

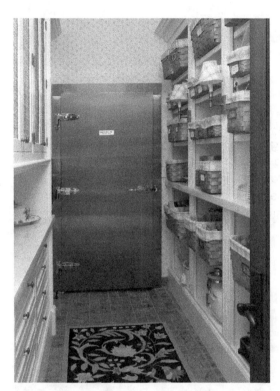

Figure 5-8 Built-in refrigerators and walk-in coolers were a feature of estate homes around the turn of the twentieth century. They are a popular feature in today's upscale homes as well. (Photo courtesy of Northlight Architectural Photography.com, Mary Fisher Designs.com)

All refrigerators and freezers must be anchored and leveled per manufacturer's instructions to assure that the unit is correctly secured to the wall. This also ensures proper operation of the appliance.

Model dimensions vary:

- Widths: 18"–48"
- Heights: 72"–84"
- Depths: 24"–26" deep

Models include:

- Bottom-mount freezer
- Side-by-side refrigerator-freezer

- French-door model
- All refrigerator
- All freezer

WATER AND AIR FILTERS

Air filtration removes bacteria, airborne viruses, odors, and (in some manufacturer's models) ethylene gases (Figure 5-9). Water filters include built-in models, in-line filters, and remote filters.

Not all ice makers can be attached to reverse-osmosis systems; manufacturers' guidelines must be followed. The critical issue with reverse-osmosis systems is maintaining a consistent water pressure when other water appliances are in use.

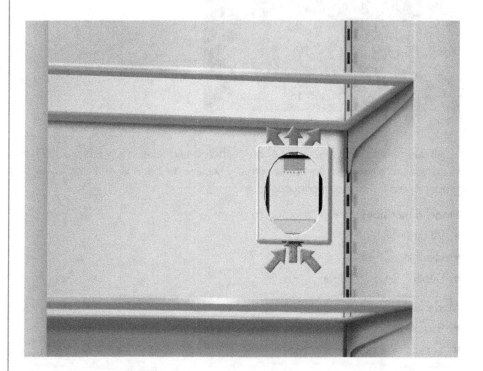

Figure 5-9 Cutaway illustrates the filtered air flow of this refrigerator. (Photo courtesy of Sub-Zero/Wolf Photograph)

WALK-IN COOLERS

Walk-in coolers are air-conditioned spaces that frequently are planned in high-end custom homes. The room is framed and insulated with a rigid foam insulation panel (these panels are available in white, gray, or chrome finish). An insulated door with rubber gasket is provided by the refrigeration contractor. The exterior of the door can be covered in stainless steel or wood. The mechanics of the system include a condenser within the space, a condensate line that runs outside to a condensation drain, and a compressor located outside. A ceiling-mounted lighting fixture lights the interior. Custom sizes and shapes can be built by contractors experienced in this application; be sure to use experienced professionals, as such a unit must meet local building code constraints. (See Figure 5-8.)

Undercounter Refrigeration

As you read through this section on appliances, you will occasionally see "(E)" next to a phrase, illustration, or photograph. This mark alerts you to an ergonomic application of an appliance or design option.

STANDARD MODELS

Most undercounter models are installed under the countertop at the point of use (Figure 5-10), but may be raised for easier access. However, this application is not recommended if needed counter space must be sacrificed for the improved access.

Typical dimensions:
Widths: 15"–30"
Depth: 24"
Height: 34-1/2"

REFRIGERATION DRAWERS

Refrigerator drawers allow cold storage space to be located at the point of use. Therefore, you can zone your cold storage needs. When a full-sized refrigerator is planned in a location outside the primary work space or CoreKitchen™,

Figure 5-10 Consider the ergonomic option (E) of elevating the unit to a height that allows access to the cooled space without bending over. (Courtesy of Mary Fisher Designs.com)

refrigerator drawers can be placed in the design to supplement the needed cooling of foods within the core space to be used by the cook (Figure 5-11).

BEVERAGE CENTERS

Beverage centers feature wine storage, a freezer compartment, and refrigerated storage (Figure 5-12). They are a good alternative to separate refrigerators and ice makers.

Typical dimensions:

Widths: 24" and 27"

Depth: 24"

Heights: 34-1/2", double drawer; 25-1/4", single drawer

Figure 5-12 A beverage center provides storage for beverages and snacks outside the food preparation center and frees up space in the main refrigerator.

Figure 5-11 Models available include two-drawer all-refrigerator, all-freezer, and combination refrigerator-freezer drawers. A single refrigerator drawer from Fisher-Paykel, also referred to as a cooler drawer, is available. (Photo courtesy of Sub-Zero/Wolf Photography)

COMMERCIAL REFRIGERATORS

Some upscale kitchen plans include commercial refrigerators (Figure 5-13). However, they tend to be noisy and not as energy-efficient as residential refrigerators.

Mounting the compressors in remote locations can reduce sound emissions. The distance of these locations must be calculated and approved by the manufacturer. Some commercial refrigeration manufacturers now make a residential version, often called the "Professional Series." These have been calibrated to fit within the home kitchen and are much more energy-efficient than

Figure 5-13 Commercial refrigerators.

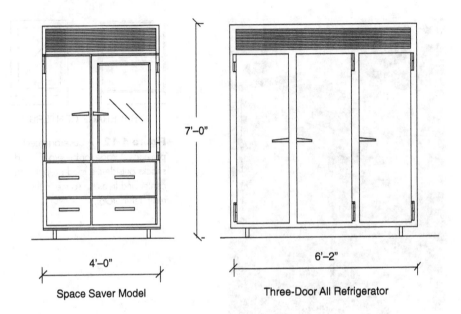

7'–0"

4'–0"

Space Saver Model

6'–2"

Three-Door All Refrigerator

COMMERCIAL REFRIGERATION

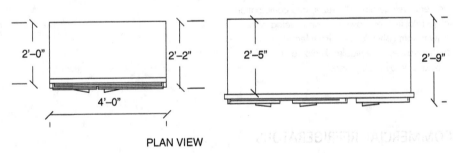

2'–0"

2'–2"

4'–0"

2'–5"

2'–9"

PLAN VIEW

the corresponding commercial units. State and local building codes affect their use in residences.

Typical dimensions:

Widths: 30"–100"

Depths: 24"–36"

Height: 84"

Freezers

Freezers come in two forms: upright and chest models (Figure 5-14).

Freezers may be either freestanding or built-in models. Standard-defrost models are typically chest-type freezers; self-defrosting models are typically upright units.

Freezer selection considerations:

- What types of food does the client store in the freezer?
- Is the freezer used in the food preparation process?
- What is the storage capacity of the freezer?
- Is the interior storage arrangement designed for the type of storage the client needs?
- Is the ice maker easily accessed?
- Is the air filtered?
- Are the shelves adjustable?
- How easy are the drawers to use?

Wine Storage

Proper storage of wine involves control of air temperature, reduction of exposure to light, and minimizing agitation of the bottles during storage (Figure 5-15).

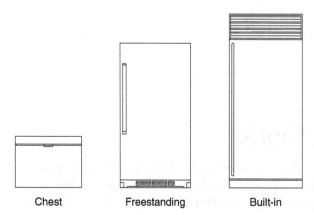

Chest   Freestanding   Built-in

Figure 5-14 Freezer types.

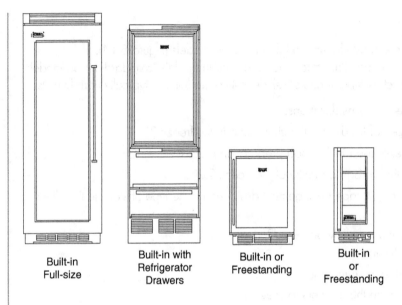

Figure 5-15 A large selection of freestanding and built-in wine storage units is available.

Built-in
Full-size

Built-in with
Refrigerator
Drawers

Built-in or
Freestanding

Built-in
or
Freestanding

Today's wine storage units come with one, two, or three temperature-controlled zones. Most have tinted glass to block ultraviolet rays of light and keep them from damaging the wine. Some models also have humidity control for wine preservation. It is important to review the manufacturer's features and specifications when selecting the correct model for a particular design.

Typical dimensions:

Widths: 15"–30"

Depths: 24"

Heights: 34-1/2"–84"

Cooking Methods

Cooking methods are generally dry or moist. Dry-heat cooking occurs in baking, grilling, broiling, and rotisserie methods. Moist-heat methods include boiling, pressure cooking, steaming, scalding, simmering, poaching, stewing, and braising

Figure 5-16 Always consider how to integrate the various cooking methods into your design. (Photo courtesy of Mary Fisher Designs.com, Northlight Architectural Photography.com)

techniques. Most cooking, however, is a combination of processes. Ranges, cooktops, ovens, steamers, and steam ovens provide many options to the designer when the designer is selecting cooking equipment for the client (Figure 5-16).

Cooking Appliances

Cooking occurs when heat is transferred to food via an energy source. Three basic methods used are conduction, convection, and radiation.

CONDUCTION COOKING

Conduction cooking is the process in which an energy source comes in contact with a cooking vessel, allowing heat to be conducted to the contents of the pan.

Figure 5-17 When a surface unit is active, the sensor extends and begins to sense the temperature from the pot. When cooking is finished, the sensor retracts. (Photo courtesy of BSH Home Appliances Corporation, Thermador brand)

Sensor cooking is surface cooking controlled by a laser beam (Figure 5-17). The sensor measures an infrared or laser beam reflected from the pot and compares the actual temperature of the pot with the programmed temperature and regulates the heating element accordingly. The elements cycle on and off, maintaining a constant temperature via a relay switch.

CONVECTION COOKING

Convection cooking occurs when air is heated, causing expansion of the air molecules (Figure 5-18). This expansion creates a rapid movement of the air.

RADIATION COOKING

Radiation cooking occurs when the energy source emits waves that come into contact with the food, causing cooking to occur. Examples include broiling, grilling, and rotisserie techniques.

Induction cooking (E) is a process in which the energy source, a special electric element, induces energy into the food by creating an electromagnetic

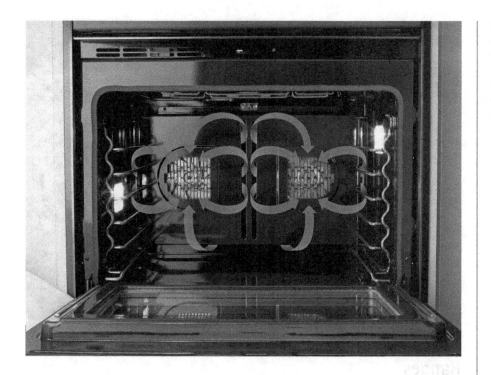

Figure 5-18 Convection occurs both naturally (boiling water) and mechanically (oven fan) when hot air is forcefully circulated in an enclosed space. (Photo courtesy of Sub-Zero/Wolf Photograph)

field between the element and special ferrous metal cookware (Figure 5-19). When the cooking vessel is moved from the surface of the cooktop, the magnetic energy field is broken and energy transfer ceases.

In induction cooking, the cooktop remains cool. The surface area of the pot or pan that comes into contact with the induction cooktop is the cooking zone, so a pan smaller than the induction cooking surface will receive energy only through the bottom surface area that is in contact with the surface. This makes induction cooking very energy-efficient and safe.

Microwave ovens emit electromagnetic waves from a magnetron, and these waves penetrate the food mass at a high rate of speed. The friction and transfer of energy caused by this penetration heats the water molecules in the food, which in turn cook the food.

Figure 5-19 This cutaway illustrates how induction works. Where a magnetic field is created with the metal cookware, cooking takes place (melting chocolate), yet the surface where no energy is created remains cool and the chocolate remains a solid. (Photo courtesy of BSH Home Appliance Corporation, Thermador brand)

Ranges

The range is a complete cooking appliance containing oven(s) and surface cooking units (Figure 5-20). Ranges are available as freestanding, slide-in, or drop-in units.

In kitchens where space is at a premium, the range provides the complete cook center in one location. A variety of range configurations give the designer the opportunity to select the correct size, shape, and features for the client and space. Models include all-electric, all-gas, and dual-fuel models (which have electric ovens and gas burners). Gas ranges are powered by natural gas or liquid propane (LP). The type of fuel must be specified when the appliance is ordered.

In addition to the fuel source, the designer must choose between an open or a sealed burner. Open burners have air space surrounding the burner where it sits in the drip pan. With a sealed burner, the drip pan abuts to the base of the burner, eliminating the open space surrounding it.

Figure 5-20 A range installation. (Photo courtesy of Mary Fisher Designs. com, Northlight Architectural Photography. com)

Many range ovens have been designed for improved access to the oven interior. One manufacturer's bottom rack slides out completely onto the door; many other manufacturers offer full-extension slides for the oven racks.

Full access to the racks is important when you need to tend to food during the cooking process as well as to remove cooked foods. This is the reason a minimum clearance space of 42 inches should be planned in front of the range.

Back guards can be ordered in 6-, 9-, 10-, and 24-inch (high-shelf) heights and island trims that are flush with the range top. The purpose of the back guard is to vent the oven heat up and out to an overhead hood.

When a high shelf is specified, the oven vents out to the hood from the top of the back guard or back of the range. The air flow from cooking utensils on the back burners is impeded and must work its way past the shelf to be vented out (Figure 5-22).

Figure 5-21 When basting a roast, you can clearly see the food and complete the process without having to lift the food and container to the top of the range or counter. (Photo courtesy of BSH Home Appliances Corporation, Thermador brand)

Figure 5-22 The high shelf can become a warm surface when the range is being used. It is a great place to warm plates before serving, but is not the place to store herbs and spices. (Photo courtesy of Sub-Zero/Wolf Photograph)

Professional-style ranges must have overhead venting. Most manufacturers do not recommend downdraft vents for these ranges.

The surface cooking elements of the range include open gas burners, sealed gas burners, electric elements, and a smooth glass surface.

Typical dimensions:

Widths: 24"–60"

Depths: 24"–27"

Height: 36"

Model configurations available include:

All burners

Burners with griddle and grill

Burners with griddle or grill

Burners with French top

Range Top

A *range top* is the surface cooking area only, without ovens below (Figure 5-23). It must be supported by cabinetry with the counter surface abutting to the edges of the range top. Typically, the knobs are located on the front of the appliance.

Typical dimensions:

    Widths: 24"–60"

    Depths: 22"–26"

    Heights: 8"–10"

Figure 5-23 The advantage of the range top over the full range is the option of placing the range top at the proper height for the cook. (Photo courtesy of Mary Fisher Designs.com and Northlight Architectural Photography.com)

Figure 5-24
Surface burner
options.

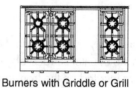

Burners with Griddle or Grill

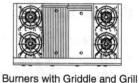

Burners with Griddle and Grill

All Burners

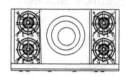

Burners with French Top

Model configurations (Figure 5-24):

All burners

Burners with griddle and grill

Burners with griddle or grill

Burners with French top

COOKTOP

The cooktop or modular cooking unit is surface cooking installed in the countertop (Figures 5-25 and 5-26). Cook tops come in a variety of sizes, and

Figure 5-25 (Photo courtesy of Sub-Zero/Wolf Photograph)

Kitchen and Bath Design

Figure 5-26 Modular cooktops place the surface cooking units exactly where needed. (Photo courtesy of BSH Home Appliances Corporation, Gaggenau brand)

typically the controls are on the top. However, Gaggenau, a German manufacturer, makes some models with controls that can be mounted on the cabinet face or in the adjacent countertop.

Separate cooking stations for performance of a particular task can be designed with these appliances. Installing a cooktop at a comfortable height (E) for the performance of that task can be easily achieved with modular units.

Countertop steamers (E) eliminate the need for large boiling pots of water. When you are finished cooking the food, you simply turn the control and the water empties into the drain.

Typical dimensions:

Widths: 12"–45"

Depth: 22"

Heights: 34"–36"

MODULAR COOKTOPS

Modular surface units come in a variety of forms and energy sources.

Gas: Natural gas or liquid propane

Electric: Glass top, coil element, induction, halogen

Steamer: Electric

Teppan cooktop: Electric

Grill: Electric or gas infrared

Griddle: Electric

Fryer: Electric

Induction (E): Electric

Considerations when selecting surface cooking units:

- What kind of food is prepared?
- How many cooking surfaces are needed?
- What types of cooking surfaces should be planned?
- If modules are being installed laterally rather than in a standard fashion, can the user read and access the controls properly?
- What will the energy source be? Gas, LP, electric, electric induction, or a combination of fuel sources?
- What is the ergonomic profile of your client?

Ovens

Ovens operate with heated air, microwaves, and/or steam. Energy sources include natural gas, liquid propane, electricity, or a magnetron tube. Wood and/or natural gas is typically used in pizza ovens.

Care in selecting and placing ovens in the kitchen design can yield many benefits, both ergonomically and practically. Analyze the client's oven use, size of family, and space available for equipment. Not all families need two large ovens (Figure 5-27).

Baking two or four potatoes in a large, 30-inch oven does not make sense. The designer could suggest a smaller-capacity oven, partnered with a larger oven, for those times when more space is needed, to make energy use more efficient. Cooking techniques should match the types of oven-cooked foods done on a regular basis. A 30-inch and 27-inch convection oven could be paired with a convection-steam oven and a small microwave.

Figure 5-27 Different-sized ovens that accommodate entertaining and daily use prove to be a more energy-efficient way of oven cooking. (Photo courtesy of Sub-Zero/Wolf Photograph)

Oven doors hinged on the side (E) make access much easier, especially for someone seated in a wheelchair (Figure 5-31). Another ergonomic feature found in many ovens today is full-extension slides for racks (Figure 5-29). This brings food, in traditional oven styles where doors hinge on the bottom, out to be safely handled by the cook.

Considerations when selecting ovens:

- What foods are cooked in the oven?
- How often the oven is used.
- Is the cook a baker?
- What is the ergonomic profile of the cook?

Figure 5-28 By placing the ovens side by side, access to the ovens can be designed to fit the cook's ergonomic profile. (Photo courtesy of NY LOFT.

Figure 5-29 (Photo courtesy of BSH Home Appliances Corporation, Thermador brand)

- How often is the oven used when the client is entertaining and how much food is prepared?
- Is there space within the kitchen for more than one or two ovens?
- What specialty ovens should be planned?
- What cleaning system is used, pyrolytic or catalytic?

ENERGY DISTRIBUTION

Energy is distributed within the oven cavity through a variety of methods:

Conventional: An electrical element or gas flame at the bottom of the oven heats the air within the oven cavity to a predetermined temperature. The heated air naturally rises within the oven chamber to cook the food. Food placed closer to the heat source cooks faster.

Convection: Heated air is moved throughout the oven to evenly cook food (Figure 5-30).

Others, often referred to as "true convection" or "European convection" ovens, heat the air on the outside of the oven and import the air into the oven through one or two fans in the back.

Figure 5-30 Some models heat the air inside the oven and move the heated air with a fan at the back of the oven. (Photo courtesy of BSH Home Appliances Corporation, Thermador brand)

Convection/microwave: This single oven offers three methods of cooking: pure convection, microwave, or the combination of convection and microwave simultaneously.

Microwave: Microwaves are produced by a magnetron tube that is powered by electricity. The microwaves penetrate the food, agitating the water molecules in the food; the friction-induced heat created by this agitation cooks the food. Microwave ovens are available as built-in models, over-the-counter models, over-the-range models, countertop units, and microwave drawers. The drawer model is a perfect solution if you wish to place a microwave in a base cabinet. Microwave oven-hoods provide two appliances in one, both microwave oven and ventilation. The best of these models are vented to the outside.

Steam: One of the most nutritious methods of cooking is steam. Steam ovens are available as plumbed-in models, in which water is pumped directly into the unit when needed; or as models with a manual-fill water tank, where you fill the water vat from the tap. This latter model permits installation without the need for a water connection.

Convection/steam: A combination steam-convection oven offers three cooking methods in one appliance. You can cook with only steam or only convection heat, or the combination of both steam and convection heat (Figure 5-31).

Lift (E): This wall-mounted oven by Gaggenau is engineered with a descending oven chamber for easy access by the cook (Figure 5-32). Heated air rises naturally, and so remains in the oven cavity, with minimal heat loss, while the oven platform descends to the cook. When installing this model, it is critical to follow the manufacturer's instructions carefully. When placed adjacent to upper cabinets, a 3-inch clearance on either side must be maintained. The oven should be installed prior to the installation of adjacent cabinetry. Installers have developed and recommended this procedure after having done several installations. You must plan correct vertical space allowance for the oven platform to lower.

The lift oven is finished on all sides and can be installed without cabinetry on either side. This oven is ideal for placing the oven at the most convenient height for users, whether they are short, tall, or in a wheelchair. This oven design is ADA-compliant. This appliance can be placed in any space for entertaining.

TurboChef oven: This speed-cook oven utilizes patented Airspeed Technology™ to cook foods in seconds and minutes rather than minutes and hours. It is an enhanced version of a combination of convection currents and microwaves.

Figure 5-31 A combination steam-convection oven allows you to bake, steam, roast, and reconstitute food in one chamber. (Photo courtesy of BSH Home Appliances Corporation, Gaggenau brand)

Pizza oven: Fueled by wood, gas, or electricity, pizza ovens are a popular feature in high-end kitchens, whether indoors or outdoors. Careful planning must be done concerning weight, ventilation, heat output, and air conditioning. Footings may be necessary to handle the weight of the oven. It is important that you synchronize your design with the manufacturer's representative and/or qualified installer.

OVEN CLEANING PROCESSES

Pyrolytic self-clean: A typical electric oven cycles the heating elements and heats up slowly to a very high temperature, burning the food soils in the oven chamber. When the cleaning cycle is complete, an ash may remain in the bottom of the oven but can be removed with a damp sponge. Oven racks are removed during this process.

Figure 5-32 (Photo courtesy of BSH Home Appliances Corporation, Gaggenau brand)

Catalytic cleaning: Often referred to as "continuous clean," catalytic cleaning is so called because it uses a chemical that is bonded to the oven interior and reacts to food soils and heat as they come in contact with each other. This method is most often found in gas models.

Warming Drawers

Warming drawers offer a holding station for food prior to service (Figure 5-33). Temperatures range from 85° to 200°F. Dough can be proofed at the low setting; vegetables and proteins can be held at the higher setting. Plates and serving pieces are often heated in these drawers prior to serving.

Typical dimensions:
  Widths: 24", 27", 30", 36"
  Depth: 24"
  Heights: 10", 11"

Considerations when selecting warming drawers:

- How will the warming drawer be used and how many should be planned for?
- Where will the drawer(s) be installed?
- Will the warming drawer(s) be integrated into cabinetry?

Ventilation

As homes become more airtight, with energy-efficient building construction, effective ventilation is critical. Removing steamy air, laden with the vegetable and protein oils that are byproducts of cooking, and odors and heat are the most important factor when designing a ventilation system. When hoods and ventilators are not used, the hot, moist air circulates throughout the house and collects on the closest cooler surface it can find. In a short time, a tacky film is felt on cabinets; odors and dust collect on fabrics and surfaces. When people do not use their hoods because they are noisy and ineffective, it is usually a sign that the wrong hood was specified and the hood was not properly sized. Calculation of the correct cubic feet per minute (cfm) rating for the hood is based on the cooking appliance to be vented. Oversizing the hood with too high a cfm rating is just as problematic as undersizing the vent. A more extensive discussion of this, along with makeup air and interior air quality, appears in Chapter 10. Sound control and decibel ratings are also covered.

Capture area refers to the all-important ability of the hood to capture the hot, moist air and vent it out (Figure 5-34). For this reason, manufacturers typically

Figure 5-34 The most important aspect in the selection of a ventilation system is the capture area. (Photo courtesy of Mary Fisher Designs.com, Northlight Architectural Photography.com)

suggest that the designer specify a hood that extends 3 inches beyond the edge of the cooking surface on each side. If, however, you are designing for a very tall person, you will need to increase the height of the space between the cooking surface and the bottom of the ventilation unit. Increased cfm will be required and a larger capture area designed in width and length. This is covered extensively in Chapter 10.

One tip given me by a distributor's representative was to have the client turn the ventilation system on the lowest setting before surface cooking begins. This will establish a convection current that moves the air into the ventilation system as cooking begins. In many cases, if the client does this, the ventilator setting will not have to be increased during the cooking process.

Aesthetics are an important consideration in choosing a hood (Figure 5-35).

Overhead drafting is the most efficient method of venting cooking equipment. Most manufacturers recommend that the hood width extend 3 inches beyond each side of the range or cooktop (Figure 5-36).

Figure 5-35 When it is the focal point and is seen from more than one space, the sculptural nature and visual appeal of the hood is as important as its function. (Photo courtesy of Mary Fisher Designs.com, Northlight Architectural Photography. com)

Figure 5-36 Hood width and capture area.

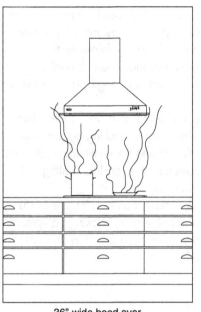

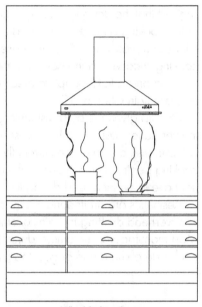

36"-wide hood over
a 36"-wide Cooktop

42"-wide hood over
a 36"-wide Cooktop

Hood liners give the designer the option of creating custom hoods that may be architectural features of the kitchen. The liner is the complete ventilation system built into the custom façade.

Downdraft ventilation extracts air from the cooking surface and vents it down and out of the building. This system of ventilation is commonly used in designs with islands or peninsulas where an overhead hood is not practical (Figure 5-37).

Most downdraft vents are located at the back of the cooktop and are controlled by a switch that raises and lowers the unit. Because of the natural flow of heated air, overhead ventilation is always the most efficient choice.

In-line blowers are typically installed in attics, located between the hood and exterior wall or roof vent cap. They may be suspended with a chain-mounting kit, lessening the noise and vibration that often accompany ventilation systems.

Figure 5-37 The most efficient downdraft system is one that fits between the cooking units. (Photo courtesy of BSH Home Appliances Corporation, Gaggenau brand)

Microwave oven/hoods are dual-purpose appliances. They provide both microwave cooking and ventilation of the cooktop below. Venting to the outside is the best installation of these units. However, if that is not possible, recirculating systems using filters are available.

Refer to Chapter 10 for a more detailed discussion of ventilation.

Considerations when selecting a ventilation system:

- What cooking equipment must be vented?
- How tall are the cook(s)?
- Are the control locations convenient for all users?
- Is there convenient access to lights and filters for servicing?
- Is it easy to clean the filters?
- What type of hood canopy is planned (manufactured or custom)?
- If a custom hood is designed, is it in proportion to the space and mass of the kitchen?
- What amount of space is available for the ventilation system?
- How will ductwork be installed?

- What is the length of the duct run?

- How many bends will there be in the duct run?

- What type of blower is to be used in the hood canopy (in-line blower, remote blower)?

Hoods are heavy, and adequate structural support must be provided. They must be secured to framing members of the wall and ceiling. Metal ductwork should be installed in the straightest possible route to the outside. Ductwork and transition pieces should be ordered at the same time as the hood.

Dishwashers

Full-sized dishwashers (bottom-hinged door) come in widths of 18 inches, 24 inches (standard), and 30 inches. Selection of the correct model for a kitchen design involves knowing how the clients use their existing dishwasher. Standard dishwashers offer basic features with one or two water sources. Higher-grade models feature adjustable racks, silverware trays, removable parts to accommodate larger items, and three water sources. Miele is now offering a commercial dishwasher with a short, 10-minute cycle for residential use. These units produce more noise than their quiet residential models.

Full-sized dishwashers may offer upper-rack-only washing cycles for small loads.

Typical dimensions:

Widths: 18″, 24″, 30″

Depth: 22″

Height: 34-1/2″

One of the most important features to homeowners is quiet operation. Quiet dishwashers are fully insulated and often have rubber mounts to control sounds emitted by vibration.

Elevating the dishwasher (E) is an ergonomic application that should be employed in kitchens whenever possible, but may not be possible in every plan (Figure 5-38). An important consideration is the loss of counter space that occurs

Figure 5-38 Elevated dishwasher. (Photo courtesy of Mary Fisher Designs.com, Northlight Architectural Photography.com)

with this design feature. How the countertop will terminate at the elevated dishwasher also must be considered (Figure 5-39).

Bosch offers dishwashers with a unique molded base. This helps insulate the dishwasher from emitting sound downward, an important consideration when elevating a dishwasher. An aqua-stop feature prevents leaking by sensing when water is present and automatically shutting off the water, a positive feature when a dishwasher is installed above storage in cabinetry below.

(a)

(b)

Figure 5-39 a & b If the cabinet containing the dishwasher is a standard 24-inch depth, you may need to dog-ear the counter edge. The cabinet stiles will have to measure the distance of the edge detail overhang plus 1/4 inch. (Photo courtesy of Asko, Inc.)

If you select a dishwasher that is not insulated on the bottom, sound board can be installed on the top of the base cabinet on which the dishwasher is mounted and will absorb downward sound emissions.

Design considerations when planning an elevated dishwasher:

- The type of cabinet construction, depth of countertops, and location to the sink all play important roles in a successful installation.
- A minimum of 12 inches of counter space and a maximum of 24 inches between the sink and the elevated dishwasher should be planned. This allows dishes to be loaded and unloaded without water damage to the floor below.
- If the counter edge is to die into the elevated cabinet side, the base cabinet depth must be 26 inches.

Considerations when selecting dishwashers:

- What size of dishwasher fits the design?
- What finish should be specified for the dishwasher (integrated into cabinetry or appliance finish)?
- What is the sound level of the selected model?
- Can the dishwasher door open fully if the dishwasher is elevated and built into cabinetry?
- How good is the interior rack adjustability? (Some manufacturers supply three racks.)
- How many water sources are there within the unit?
- Where is the filter located?
- What number of dishwashers is needed?
- Does the full-sized dishwasher offer separate washing cycles to enable a small wash when the dishwasher is not fully loaded?
- How much water does the dishwasher consume?
- Is a water heater built in?
- Is a vacuum breaker built into the unit? If there is, no air gap will be needed at the sink.

DISHWASHER DRAWERS (E)

A single dishwasher drawer (Figure 5-40) placed on either side of the sink is an ergonomic solution that reduces stress to the back when you are loading and unloading the dishwasher, and also enables you to keep valuable counter space on either side of the sink. Combining one full dishwasher with a single dishwasher drawer can be a successful solution to provide efficient daily use and the extra capacity needed when entertaining.

Dishwasher drawers are available in single- and double-drawer models. In the double-drawer models, each drawer works independent of the other.

Typical dimensions:

Width: 24"

Depth: 22"

Height: 16"

Both types of dishwasher drawers are available as fully integrated (controls hidden from view) models, allowing the designer to fully integrate the front of the appliance into the cabinetry and furniture.

Figure 5-40 (Courtesy of Fisher & Paykel Appliances, Inc.)

Trash Compactors

Trash compactors (Figure 5-41) are designed to compress trash to a manageable size for disposal. Currently, recycle bins are being designed into kitchens more often than trash compactors. It is important to review the client's trash-handling and recycling needs and local requirements.

Typical dimensions:

Widths: 15", 18"

Depth: 22"

Height: 34-1/2"

Considerations when selecting a trash compactor:

- Will the compactor be freestanding or built into cabinetry?
- Will the compactor be fully integrated with the cabinets?
- Where is the best location for the compactor?
- What kind of trash will be compacted?

Figure 5-41 Trash compactors can be specified to receive cabinet panels or finished fronts. (Photo courtesy of Mary Fisher Designs. com, Northlight Architectural Photography.com)

Water Appliances

Instant Hot Water

A compact dispenser spout mounted next to or in the sink can provide filtered cold and hot water. Hot-only models are available with or without a water filter. For instant hot water, a compact tank that holds up to 1 gallon of water sits under the sink connected to the cold water supply and provides hot water on demand. Water is heated to a temperature of up to 200°F, although the temperature can easily be adjusted.

It is very important to consider all plumbing applications that use space in the sink cabinet. The plumber needs to install all the equipment—disposer, air switch and controller, faucet, air gap (if applicable), instant hot water and water filtration systems—before installing sink-cabinet storage accessories. When the dispenser also filters water, a "T" connection can be run to the ice maker. It is important to know whether the ice maker or ice maker in a freezer has a built-in filter system.

Water Treatment

Water filters can be added to appliances as needed in the kitchen. These are considered *in-line* filters. The plumber should be consulted about the correct placement of an in-line filter. Easy access to change the filter is of prime importance.

Home water treatment systems are discussed thoroughly in Chapter 12.

Disposers

New technology and better engineering have made food-waste disposers more efficient and quieter. Models with full insulation and rubber mounting gaskets lower sound levels and absorb vibrations. Models are available in 1/2 horsepower (h.p.), 3/4 h.p., and 1 h.p. The two types normally seen are *continuous-feed* units, in which operation of the disposer is controlled by a switch; and *batch-feed* units, in which operation is controlled by turning the handle on the top of the cover. A model made for septic systems is available from Insinkerator. It injects a solution with microorganisms that break down food wastes when the disposer is activated.

Disposers can be activated by air switches. A button installed beside the faucet on the sink or in the countertop activates the disposer when depressed. This is the best application for sinks located in islands and under windows and is a safer, more practical alternative to the traditional toggle switch.

Considerations when selecting water appliances:

- Will the client need a combination of instant hot water, cool water, and filtration?
- If there are multiple sinks, where will the instant hot water unit be located?
- Does the space in the sink cabinet allow for installation of the equipment and periodic filter changes?
- Is there a power source for the appliance?
- Have you verified the size of water filtration equipment prior to locating it in the kitchen design?
- Can this filtration system be connected to other water sources such as ice makers?
- If a reverse-osmosis system is selected, does the manufacturer of the refrigerator-freezer allow connection to the ice maker?
- What type of garbage disposer will be used—continuous-feed or batch-feed?
- Does the disposer drain to a sewer or septic system?

Coffee Brewing Systems

Automatic Coffee Machines

Two types of coffee centers are available. One model is plumbed to a water source; for the other, water is supplied manually to a water reservoir. Most manufacturers offer a cup-and-plate warming drawer that installs just below the coffee center. This is a very useful accessory (Figure 5-42).

If the coffee machine is installed in a location lacking adjacent counter space, a pull-out board with locks should be planned.

When designing a coffee center, you should also plan storage for coffee supplies, a small refrigerator for dairy products and other ingredients, a tapping bar and collector for processed grounds, and storage for mugs, cups, and serving pieces.

Typical dimensions:
> Width: 23"
> Depth: 20-1/4"
> Height: 18"

Built-in Coffee Maker

Coffee makers built into the stud cavity of the wall and plumbed to a water source are also available. The designer must make sure that a water source and 110-volt outlet are accessible. These models offer coffee and tea brewing, and are also a source of instant hot water for instant beverages and soups (or other uses).

Typical dimensions:
> Width: 24"
> Depth: 21"
> Height: 18"

Considerations when selecting coffee systems:
- What kind of hot beverages will the owner be brewing?
- How many cups will be brewed at one time?
- Are a water source and power available?
- Is there a need to add an in-line water filter?
- What coffee machine design should be planned, built-in or freestanding?
- Can the kitchen design accommodate a coffee center or should the center location be planned in an adjacent space?

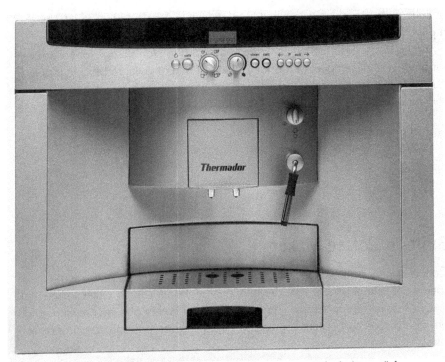

Figure 5-42 Built-in coffee systems provide complete brewing options for frothing milk for cappuccino or latté, and grinding whole beans for coffee and espresso. (Photo courtesy of BSH Home Appliances Corporation, Thermador brand)

Summary

Before doing any space planning of a kitchen, you must make a careful analysis of appliance needs and options. The client's cooking skills, ergonomic profile, and foods that will be prepared must all be identified before you put pencil to paper or mouse to CAD drawing. A design assessment must be made to ensure that appliance selections are appropriate to both food preparation requirements and available space of the kitchen plan.

Keeping current with appliance choices, modifications, and new features is a major responsibility of the kitchen designer. Familiarity with all manufactured brands and the options available, as well as installation procedures, is extremely important. Seeking the advice of certified appliance installers regarding the installation of particular appliances can give insight into design options available to you.

Establishing good communication with appliance manufacturers' representatives and appliance dealers can enhance your product knowledge. Personally guiding your client through appliance selection and purchase protects your design and reduces the confusion felt by overwhelmed consumers. Attend showroom appliance demonstrations whenever possible.

Finally, allow yourself to visualize appliances in practical yet unconventional ways. Elevating or lowering models to fit the client's physical characteristics and/ or locating modules laterally rather than in traditional front-to-back installations can allow you to present several alternatives for the client to consider and choose from.

Cabinetry

6

Cabinets set the tone for kitchen and bath design. Cabinets must provide support for appliances and counter surfaces, connect work stations, and allow storage of equipment and utensils. The layout of cabinetry should create an efficient work space, allow adequate circulation space and reflect the style of the interior décor. The cabinets may become the focal point of the kitchen.

Cabinetry is sold through cabinet dealers and local cabinet builders. Price levels vary, based on materials and features. This provides the designer with flexibility in making cabinet selections appropriate to the client's budget. Prefinished cabinetry in standard modular sizes will be the most affordable option. Special interior hardware and accessories will add to the cost of the "stock" cabinet but are well worth the additional expense.

All designers should understand the basic cabinet construction types.

Cabinet Construction Types

Construction methods vary in cabinetry. The type of cabinet construction should be determined early in the design process, because it influences countertop edge returns, finished counter heights, and plumbing fixture and appliance installation, as well as the decorative style of the kitchen or bath (Figure 6-1).

Stock/modular: Preset cabinet dimensions, features, and finishes. Typically a framed cabinet with a set number of standard finishes. Dealers will have stock readily available.

Semi-custom: Modular cabinet offering custom sizes and interior appointments; mixes a selection of standard and some custom finishes. Standard and custom storage accessories are available. Semi-custom offers many more options.

Custom: No preset parameters. Built and finished to the designer's specifications.

Framed (also called face frame): Traditional cabinet manufacturing where box frame is exposed (Figure 6-2). Doors and drawer fronts are surface mounted, full overlay, or inset. This style limits access to the vertical space of

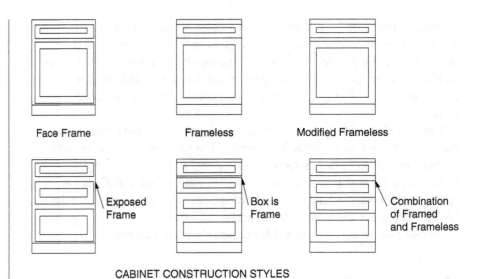

Face Frame   Frameless   Modified Frameless

Exposed Frame

Box is Frame

Combination of Framed and Frameless

CABINET CONSTRUCTION STYLES

Figure 6-1 Knowing each construction category will enable you to select the right cabinet for the look and function of your space.

Figure 6-2 Flush-inset, face-frame cabinets. (Photo courtesy of Mary Fisher Designs.com, Northlight Architectural Photography.com)

the cabinet interior because of the rails (horizontal frame member) between drawers.

Frameless (also called 32 millimeter): First introduced by European cabinet manufacturers, in this style the cabinet box is the perimeter frame (Figure 6-3). Doors fronts are mounted to the sides of the cabinet box and drawers line up with doors.

Modified frameless: A combination of both framed and frameless styles of construction. The modified frameless cabinet contains a rail above and below the top drawer but no rails between the drawers. This keeps the line of cabinet door tops and drawers in alignment in base cabinetry (see Figure 6-1). There can be a net gain of 2 to 3-1/2 inches vertical space over a face-frame cabinet.

Figure 6-3 The advantage of the frameless construction style is access to cabinet interior space. (Photo courtesy of Mary Fisher Designs.com, Northlight Architectural Photography.com)

Standard Cabinet Dimensions

The standards established for cabinetry are based on the materials used in the manufacturing of cabinets. Typically, 4-foot by 8-foot panels of material are cut to fit the standard 24-inch depth of base cabinets and 12-inch depth of uppers. When cabinets are designed deeper or higher than the standard base and upper cabinet sizes, the manufacturer will consider them custom and adjust the building method and pricing accordingly. Because of the demand for deeper wall cabinets, some manufacturers are now offering 15-inch-deep upper cabinets as a standard upgrade.

Base cabinets: 24" overall depth; 34-1/2" overall height; widths begin at 6" and increase by 3" increments.

Upper cabinets: 12" overall depth; 12"–42" heights vary to fit design and ceiling height; overall widths vary from 6"–54", depending on wall spaces. See Figure 6-4 for standard cabinet dimensions for base and uppers.

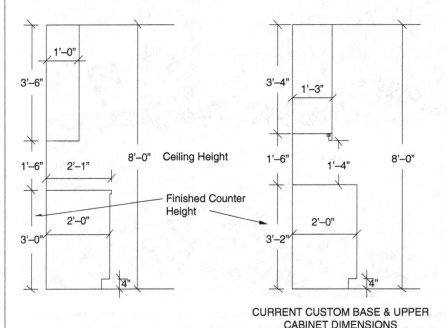

Figure 6-4 Standard cabinet dimensions.

CURRENT CUSTOM BASE & UPPER CABINET DIMENSIONS

Standard bath cabinet dimensions are:

Base cabinets: 18"–21" overall depth; 29"–34-1/2" overall height (countertops are added to that dimension to yield the finished height). Current trends in bathroom vanity heights are to finish at 36". This promotes a more erect stance at the sink. Widths begin at 12" and increase by 3" increments to 72"-wide vanity cabinets.

Upper cabinets: 12" overall depth; 12"–42" heights, varying to fit design and ceiling height; overall widths vary from 6"–54", depending on wall spaces. See Figure 6-5 for standard vanity cabinet dimensions.

Cabinet Terms

Box: Framework of individual cabinet.

Rail: The horizontal cabinet frame member.

Stile: The vertical cabinet frame member.

Toe kick: Horizontal recessed space where the cabinet sits on the floor.

Upper cabinet: Wall cabinet, typically 12" depth.

Lower cabinet: Base cabinet, typically 24" depth.

Drawer bank: A base cabinet containing drawers.

Tall cabinet: Tall (floor to ceiling) cabinet, typically 24" depth; often houses appliances.

Crown: Molding finishing the top of the cabinet uppers or talls.

Filler strip: Spacer to allow return at corners and end of cabinet run.

Cabinet run: Continuous span of cabinets along one wall.

Rough top: Underlayment on top of cabinet box; acts as support for counter material.

Cabinet door designs (Figure 6-6):

Full overlay door: The full overlay door covers the cabinet frame.

Half overlay door: The half overlay door covers half of the cabinet frame.

Flush inset door: The inset door fits flush with the outside edge of the cabinet frame.

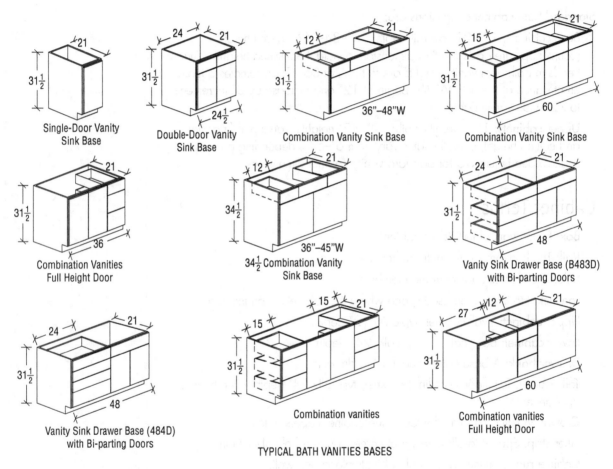

Single-Door Vanity
Sink Base

Double-Door Vanity
Sink Base

Combination Vanity Sink Base

Combination Vanity Sink Base

Combination Vanities
Full Height Door

$34\frac{1}{2}$ Combination Vanity
Sink Base

Vanity Sink Drawer Base (B483D)
with Bi-parting Doors

Vanity Sink Drawer Base (484D)
with Bi-parting Doors

Combination vanities

Combination vanities
Full Height Door

TYPICAL BATH VANITIES BASES

Figure 6-5 Bath vanity bases.

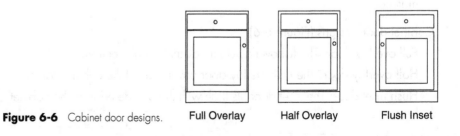

Figure 6-6 Cabinet door designs.

Full Overlay   Half Overlay   Flush Inset

Interior Cabinet Hardware

Full-extension slides (E): Drawer or roll-out shelf slides that travel 100 percent out of the frame box, allowing full access into the drawer or roll-out shelf.

3/4-extension slide: Travels 75 percent out of the frame box, limiting access to drawer and roll-out shelf space.

Bottom-mount slide (E): Slide hardware installed on the bottom of the drawer or roll-out shelf. Typically these slides are "soft-closing," limiting the emission of sound caused by uncontrolled closing.

Side-mount slide: Slide hardware mounted on the side of the drawer or roll-out shelf.

Nylon roller slides: Hardware mounted on the exterior bottom corner of the drawer box or roll-out shelf. Full-extension and 3/4-extension slides are available.

Electronic openers (E): Hettich International's Easy system allows drawers and cabinets to open automatically by the press of a finger on the cabinet door or drawer. This ergonomic feature would work well for someone who has restricted arm and hand muscle use.

Concealed hinges: Hidden hinges; these are available for full-overlay, half-overlay, and inset panel doors.

Most high-grade cabinetry uses bottom-mount slides that are hidden from view. They decrease the vertical clearance slightly but increase the horizontal space by 2 to 3 inches. Side-mounted slides are visible when the drawer extends but allow the maximum amount of vertical space available. Side-mount or bottom-mount slides that fully extend are an important ergonomic feature, providing full access to the drawer and roll-out shelf space. Full-extension slides may or may not be standard with selected cabinet lines, so it is important to clarify the hardware selection prior to specifying a particular cabinet.

Modular or Stock Cabinetry

Modular cabinets provide a simple format for selecting sizes and features from cabinet manufacturers. A standardized language for cabinet identification exists. For example, a three-drawer base cabinet is listed as:

> B33-3D (base 33" wide, 3 drawer bank)

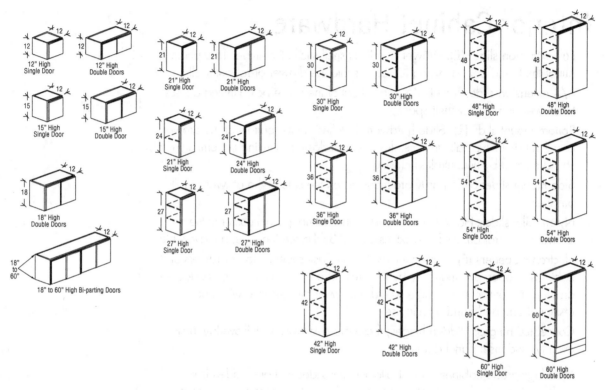

Figure 6-7 Wall cabinet dimensions.

Wall cabinets (Figure 6-7) are also identified in code. For example, a wall cabinet 18 inches wide and 36 inches high would be listed as a "W1836."

As features are added to a cabinet, the codes reflect those supplementary items. Guidelines from manufacturers set a procedure the designer must follow when ordering cabinetry. Working with a cabinet dealer will simplify the process, as it is the dealer's responsibility to make the final order and correctly specify the desired features and model numbers.

Custom Cabinetry

Designing the cabinet style, interior fittings, and access to space from toe to crown is true custom cabinetry. Designing custom doors and furniture applications becomes part of the process. Typically, the designer and cabinet shop work together in making the designer's plan a reality. With knowledge of cabinet construction, the designer can create a complete kitchen or bath design and take it to the cabinet shop to be manufactured. When this procedure is followed, it is critical that the cabinet shop produce detailed shop drawings for approval by the designer *before* materials are ordered and the cabinets are manufactured. Shop drawings should include detailed drawings of cabinet construction, door and drawer front styles, hinge and slide selections, interior fittings and materials to be used in the manufacture of the cabinets, finishes, and decorative hardware.

Each cabinet shop has a particular style of manufacturing. It is extremely important that the designer and cabinet shop have clear and open communication during the entire process.

Most cabinet shops have stains for wood cabinets that they have developed. Whenever possible, select from their stains to save money. However, if the designer has a particular finish or finishes in mind, it is the designer's responsibility to provide a large enough sample of the desired finish so the cabinet finisher can re-create the look. Most custom shops have finishers on staff. It may be necessary for the designer to work with an independent cabinet finisher. If this is the case, it is critical that the finisher and cabinet shop build a relationship and have open dialogue prior to the delivery of cabinetry to the finisher.

Another specialist often found in custom cabinet shops is the wood carver. In the Southwest region of the United States, hand-carved cabinet doors are a staple in custom homes (Figure 6-8).

When adding custom features to cabinet doors (glass, iron, metal panels, lattice, fabric, etc.), it is necessary that the frame of the cabinet door and the hinges holding the door to the box be adjusted to allow for the custom panel (Figure 6-9). For example, glass for cabinet doors can vary from 1/8 inch to 1/4 inch thick. Additional weight of the glass must be factored into the door

Figure 6-8 Designers often provide a detail sketch of a design to the carver, who interprets the design in wood. (Photo courtesy of Mary Fisher Designs.com, David Zilly Photography, Scottsdale, AZ)

Figure 6-9 Decorative iron panels must fit door frames or vice versa. (Photo courtesy of Mary Fisher Designs.com, Northlight Architectural Photography.com)

hinges, and the thickness of the glass must fit within the framework of the cabinet door.

Some cabinet shops make their own doors to accommodate these custom applications. If the cabinet shop itself does not make the doors or drawer fronts but instead uses an outside supplier, the designer must create designs and select materials that fit the parameters of the supplied cabinet doors.

Adjustability in Cabinetry

Conventional upper cabinets may come with two or three shelves with predefined heights.

Contemporary cabinetry of all price ranges typically comes with adjustable shelf systems in the upper cabinets. The benefits to the user are substantial:

Stationary shelves:

- No flexibility in use of space.
- Too much air (lost) space above items.
- Items must be nested to use space.

Adjustable shelves:

- Flexibility for specific items to be stored; can change locations easily.
- Shelves can be placed where needed to use space most efficiently.
- Can store items based on size and weight.
- Drilled holes for shelf supports should be 1-1/4" on center beginning 6" above the bottom to within 6" of the top of the cabinet sides.

Appliances and Standard Cabinetry

Appliance manufacturers set standard dimensions compatible with stock cabinetry manufacturers. When selecting a cabinet for double ovens, for instance, the designer finds that the cabinet manufacturer offers an oven cabinet that fits the 24-inch, 27-inch, or 30"-inch wide ovens. Should the design call for

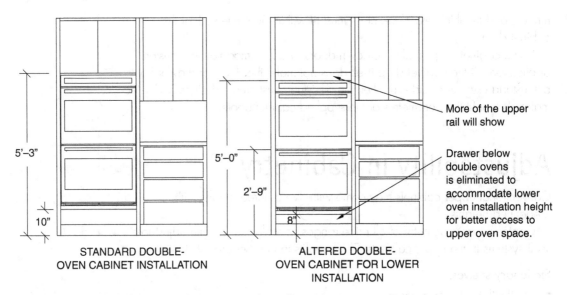

5'-3"

10"

STANDARD DOUBLE-
OVEN CABINET INSTALLATION

5'-0"

2'-9"

8"

ALTERED DOUBLE-
OVEN CABINET FOR LOWER
INSTALLATION

More of the upper
rail will show

Drawer below
double ovens
is eliminated to
accommodate lower
oven installation height
for better access to
upper oven space.

Figure 6-10 Always refer to the appliance cutout and overall size (dimensions supplied by the manufacturer) when selecting cabinets to house them.

installation of double ovens lower than the standard cutout offered, it may be necessary to order a semi-custom cabinet (Figure 6-10). Typically, manufacturers offer cabinets with some space for adjustments. This becomes an issue, though, when the design, for ergonomic reasons, places double ovens 3 to 6 inches lower than the standard installation.

The standard dimensions of appliances provide the designer with preset space allowances by which to make the cabinet selection.

- Determine the style wanted (traditional, contemporary, rustic, urban, etc.).
- Select the cabinet construction type that fits that style.
- Consider cabinet storage systems and details when selecting your cabinet type (Figure 6-11).

Access to corner cabinet storage can be achieved with a standard blind-corner cabinet with a single shelf, lazy susan, half-shelf units, 45°-angled door, or blind-corner access cabinet. If the corner space is going to be accessed from the opposite side, two cabinets at right angles will be planned (Figure 6-12).

Figure 6-11 When upper cabinets vary in height, the crown molding must return to a cabinet side or face frame. If you select a frameless style of cabinet, the termination point of the crown must be altered or a filler must be installed to terminate the crown molding. (Photo courtesy of Mary Fisher Designs.com, Northlight Architectural Photography.com)

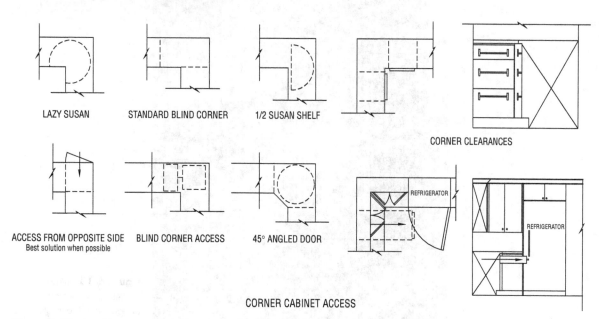

LAZY SUSAN

STANDARD BLIND CORNER

1/2 SUSAN SHELF

CORNER CLEARANCES

ACCESS FROM OPPOSITE SIDE
Best solution when possible

BLIND CORNER ACCESS

45° ANGLED DOOR

REFRIGERATOR

REFRIGERATOR

CORNER CABINET ACCESS

Figure 6-12 It will be necessary to plan corner stiles that will accommodate the distance the hardware protrudes.

Whether planning custom or custom modular cabinetry, always work with the cabinet dealership or cabinet builder early in the design process.

When custom features, such as stainless steel wrapped cabinet doors and drawers, are combined with wood cabinetry, careful attention must be given to the finish details of the appliances and hardware.

Figure 6-13 (Photo courtesy of Mary Fisher Designs.com, Northlight Architectural Photography. com)

Kitchen and Bath Design

Bath Design Basics

7

Designing a bathroom occurs through a series of steps and procedures. Understanding the client's goals for the space, while incorporating considerations for hygiene, safety, ergonomics and storage, is the designer's goal. Building construction integrity and code compliance must be achieved. Accomplishing this requires an organized approach to gathering pertinent information, simplifying the decision-making process, and setting priorities.

There are five basic steps in bath design:

1. Gathering client and project information

2. Setting priorities

3. Researching and selecting products

4. Doing design and layout (space planning)

5. Drawing up a plan checklist before submitting a design

Information Objectives

Following is a description of information objectives to be set before space planning begins.

Project Information. A thorough assessment of the infrastructure of an existing space, or a set of drawings from an architect or builder on a new construction project, is your point of departure. Use the "Project Inventory Assessment" and "Plan Checklist" forms in the Appendix to help you draw up a comprehensive list.

Client Profile. Using the "Ergonomic Profile" forms in the Appendix, list the client's physical characteristics and abilities that influence space use and interaction. Because color preferences and style influence the client's feeling of well-being, be sure this information is included in the profile.

Design Goal. Establish a visual style and functional goal for the space. Space planning decisions and product selections will be made based on this goal.

- *Space planning.* Analyze the overall space and possible design options for the bath. Bubble layouts for larger spaces identify various areas of activity within the room and begin the space planning process.

- *Principles and elements of design*. Carefully examine volume, form, line, texture, and light, as well as scale, proportion, balance, contrast, and unity.

- *Plumbing fixtures*. Plumbing fixture selections should reflect the client's ergonomic profile, style, and function within the space.

- *Installation criteria*. Reviewing the manufacturer's product installation guidelines with the plumber and contractor prior to laying out final plans enables you to note practical information in the plans and specifications. The plumber and contractor can often anticipate and identify installation problems that may be avoided through design. If the contractor has not been selected by the client, a good working relationship with a licensed plumbing contractor and a manufacturer's representative will allow you to take advantage of their practical knowledge.

- *Mechanical systems*. Before any construction is started, or final plans are complete, carefully consider what must be done with the home mechanical systems. The location of air-conditioning/heating ducts and registers, return air grills and chases, vents, water supply lines, and drain pipes must be established.

- *Lighting*. A functional space that blends natural and artificial light is the goal of the lighting system. A lighting plan consisting of four layers of light is best in the bathroom:

  1—**Ambient light** for safe passage into and out of the bath.

  2—**Task light** for specific grooming and hygiene activities.

  3—**Accent light** for decorative features in the space.

  4—**Natural light** for mixing with artificial light when the bathroom has a natural light source.

  It is the designer's responsibility to research and apply any lighting codes to the design, even when a lighting designer is involved.

- *Textures and surfaces*. The way(s) in which materials may impact the space visually and practically upon installation must be anticipated at the beginning of the design phase, so that allowances for material weight and installation can be made. A stone or tile wall is a good example (Figure 7-1).

Figure 7-1 (Photo courtesy of David Dalton, Inc., Los Angeles, CA 90019; www. daviddaltoninc.com)

Codes, Clearances, ADA and Universal-Design Bathrooms

The International Code Council (ICC) and the American National Standards Institute (ANSI) are two bodies that produce technical standards and design guidelines for making buildings and sites accessible to all people. ANSI A117.1 standards apply to the design and construction of new buildings and the remodeling or alteration of existing construction. Americans with Disabilities Act (ADA) guidelines fall within this realm.

ANSI–ADA Standards

PASSAGEWAYS

IRC P 2705.1.5: The clearance space in front of lavatory, toilet, bidet, or tub should be a minimum of at least 21" (Figure 7-2).

Figure 7-2 Plan for clearance spaces.

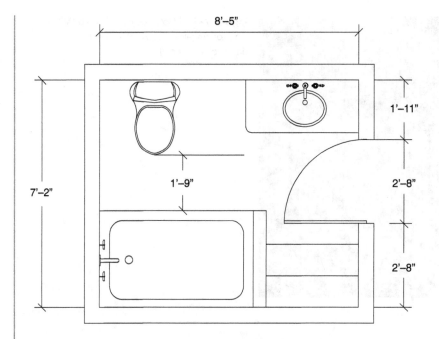

IRC R 307.1: A clearance space of at least 24" must be planned in front of a shower entrance.

ACCESS STANDARDS

IRC P 2705.1.5: A clear floor space of at least 30" x 48" should be planned at each fixture. These spaces may overlap (Figure 7-3).

ANSI 304.3.1: A wheelchair turning space with a diameter of at least 60" should be provided. This can include knee and toe clearances.

ANSI 304.3.2: A wheelchair turning space could utilize a T-shaped space, which is a 60" square with two 12" wide x 24" deep areas removed from two corners of the square (Figure 7-4).

This leaves, at a minimum, 36" wide arms. T-shaped wheelchair turning spaces can include knee and toe clearances.

GROOMING

ANSI 1002.10.1: Clear floor space should be centered on the lavatory.

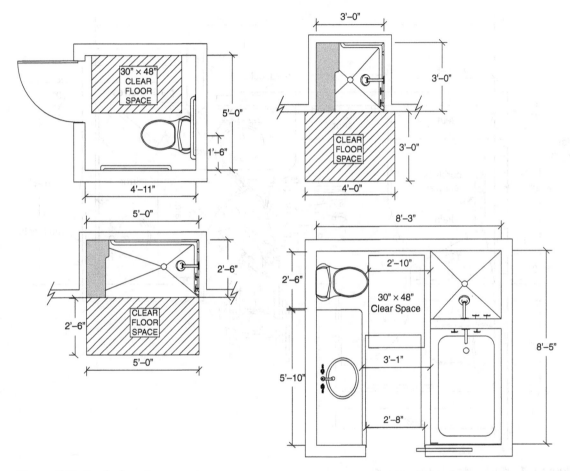

Figure 7-3 Plan for floor clearances.

BATHTUBS AND SHOWERS

ANSI 607.2: The clearance space in front of bathtubs should extend the length of the bathtub and be a minimum 30" wide.

ANSI 607.2: When a permanent seat is installed at the head of the bathtub, the clearance should extend a minimum of 12" beyond the wall at the head end of the bathtub.

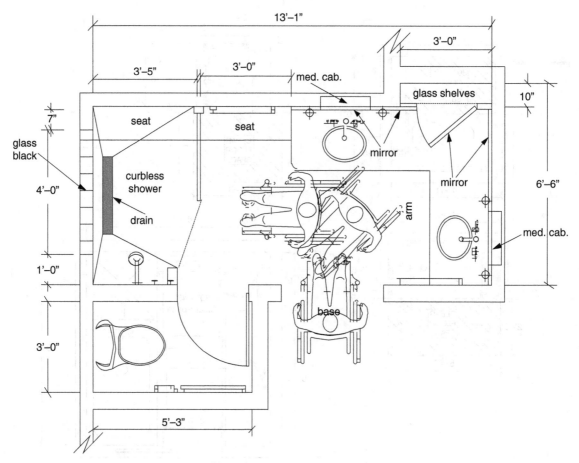

Figure 7-4 Plan for wheelchair turning space.

ANSI 608.2: The clearance in front of the transfer-type shower compartment should be at least 48″ long, measured from the control wall, and 36″ wide.

ANSI 608.2: The clearance in front of an accessible shower compartment should be at least 60″ long next to the open face of the shower compartment and 30″ wide (Figure 7-5).

IRC P 2708.1, IPC 417.4: The minimum interior size of a shower is 30″ x 30″ or 900 square inches.

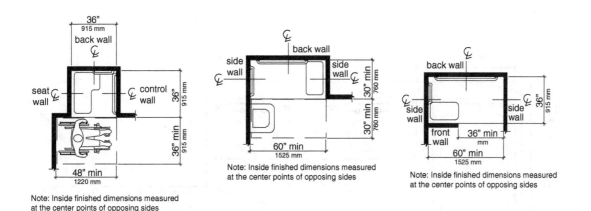

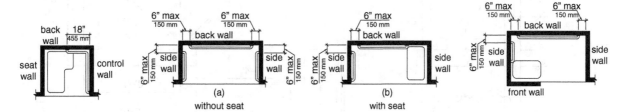

Figure 7-5 Plan for bathtub/shower clearances.

ANSI 608: Accessible shower compartments should have an inside finished dimension of 36″ and have a minimum of 36″ wide entry on the face of the shower compartment. Provide a seat in the 36″ x 36″ area (Figure 7-6).

ANSI 608.2.2: An accessible shower compartment should have a minimum finished interior dimension of 30″ wide by 60″ deep, and have a minimum of a 60″ wide entry on the face of the shower compartment (Figure 7-5a).

ANSI 309.4: Door/drawer pulls and tub/shower controls should be operable with one hand and require only a minimal amount of strength for operation; they should not require a tight grasp.

ANSI 607.5(a): Controls should be on an end wall of the bathtub between the rim and grab bar, and between the open side of the bathtub and the midpoint of the width of the tub (Figure 7-8).

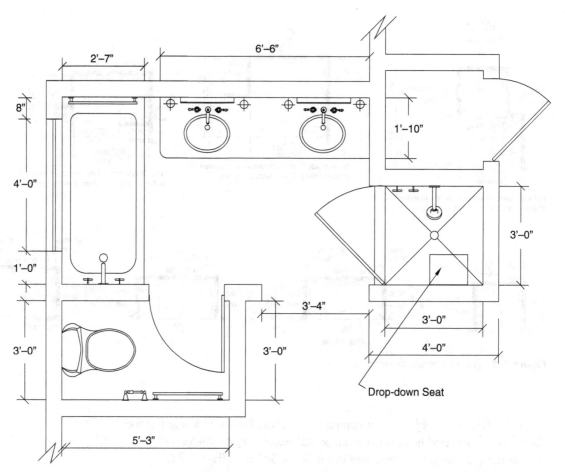

Figure 7-6 Plan for accessible shower and drop-down seat.

ANSI 608.5(b): Controls in roll-in showers should be above the grab bar, but no higher than 48" above the shower floor. In accessible shower compartments, controls, faucets, and the shower unit should be on the sidewall opposite the seat between, 38" and 48" above the shower floor (Figure 7-9).

ANSI 608.6: A handheld spray unit with a hose at least 59" long can be used as a fixed showerhead and as a handheld shower. In accessible showers, the controls and shower unit should be on the control wall within 15" of the centerline

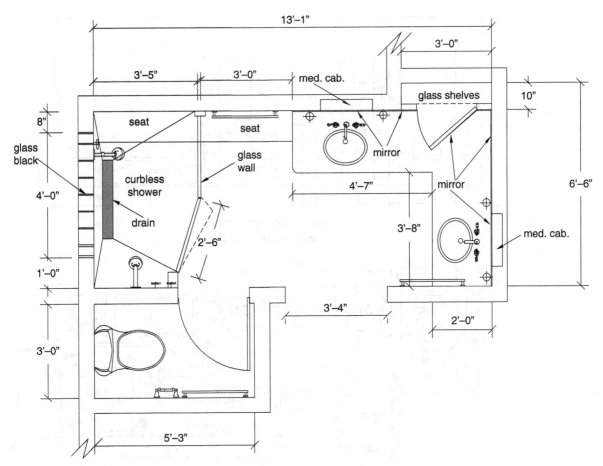

Figure 7-7 Plan for an accessible shower. Glass wall and door can be removed for wheelchair access.

of the seat. In accessible showers, hand shower units mounted on the back wall should be no more than 27" from the sidewall. An adjustable-height showerhead mounted on a vertical bar should not obstruct the use of the grab bars.

IRC P 2708.3: Shower and tub/shower control valves must be one of the following: pressure-balanced, thermostatic mixing, or thermostatic/pressure-balanced mixing valves.

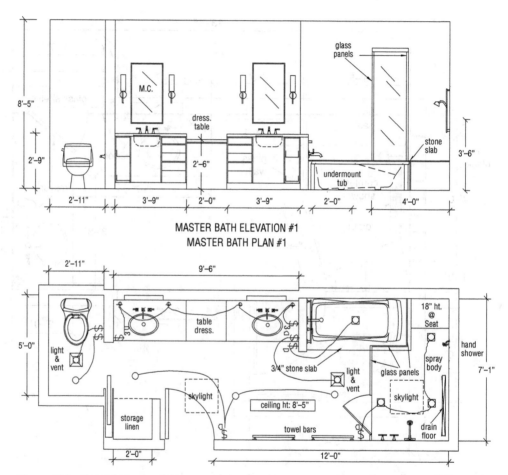

MASTER BATH ELEVATION #1
MASTER BATH PLAN #1

Figure 7-8 Plan including control locations.

IRC P 2708.1: When designing a shower seat, it must not infringe on the minimum interior size of the shower (30" x 30").

ANSI 610.2: A permanent tub seat should be at least 15" deep and positioned at the head end of the bathtub. The top of the seat should be between 17"–19" above the bathroom floor. A removable seat should be 15"–16" deep and able to be secured in place.

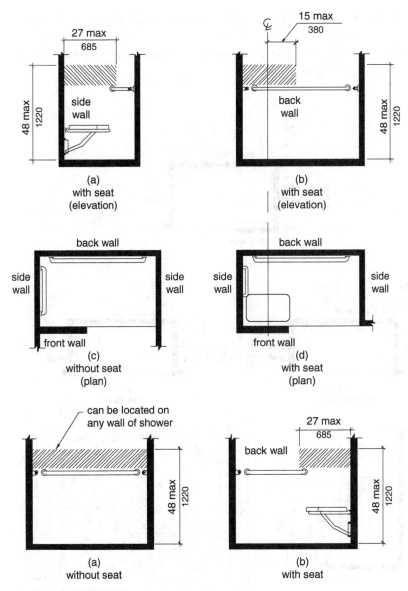

Figure 7-9 Plan for roll-in showers.

ANSI 610.3: Where a seat is provided in an accessible shower, it should be a folding seat and installed on the wall adjacent to the controls. The top of the seat should be between 17" and 19"above the bathroom floor and within 3" of the shower entrance (Figure 7-10).

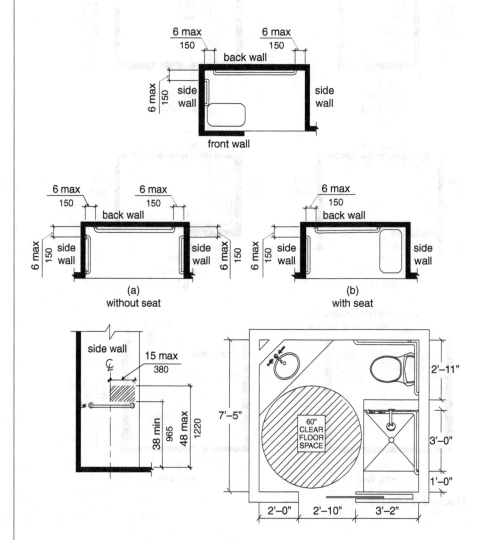

Figure 7-10 Plan for accessible showers.

ANSI 610.4: The shower and/or bathtub seat must support a minimum of 250 pounds of pressure.

IPC 417.4.1, IRC R 307.2: The wall area above a tub or shower pan must be covered in a waterproof material extending at least 3" above the showerhead rough-in.

Universal Shower

Seating: Build a bench in the shower or install a fold-down seat.

Sprays and controls: An adjustable handheld shower spray gives maximum flexibility. It can go where it needs to be, whether the person in the shower is tall or short, standing or seated. Put the controls where they can be reached from the shower seat and from outside the shower. Choose a lever or other style that is easy to grasp and turn.

Thermostatic valves: Use a valve that protects from scalding.

Shampoo niches: Plan for two wall niches—one for children and one for adults.

Flooring and walls: Specify nonslip flooring, such as tumbled stone or nonglossy ceramic tiles. Grout lines are good, as they add texture, but keep them thin.

Lighting: Overhead lighting in the shower need not be dead center.

Grab bars: Locate grab bars at the shower entry, at the optimum heights to provide secure handholds. Plan for additional support blocking while the walls are being framed (Figure 7-11).

The anthropometric data you have gathered regarding your client(s) will be invaluable in making clear decisions in the ergonomic phase of your design. You

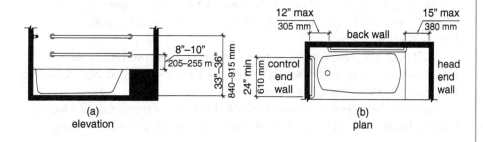

Figure 7-11 Tub grab bars.

will have a format from which you can make valid decisions in selecting and placing plumbing fixtures, appliances, and all the components making up the kitchen and bath. This format for gathering data has proven to be one of the most useful (and valid) tools I have used in more than four decades of designing kitchens and baths for hundreds of clients. Resources on anthropometric data are listed in the Bibliography.

GLASS SHOWER DOORS AND ENCLOSURES

IRC R 308.1: Glass used in tub or shower enclosures or partitions must be tempered and must be permanently marked as such.

IRC R 308.4.5: If the tub or shower surround has glass windows or walls, the glazing must be tempered glass or an approved equivalent when the bottom edge of glazing is less than 60" above any standing or walking surface.

ANSI R308.4.2: Any glass whose bottom edge is less than 18" above the floor must be tempered glass.

ANSI P 2708.1: Hinged shower doors shall open outward.

ANSI 608.7.303: Shower compartment thresholds should be no more than 1/2" high. Changes in level of no more than 1/4" high are permitted, but changes in level between 1/4" high and 1/2" high should be beveled in a slope not steeper than a ratio of 1:2.

GRAB BARS

ANSI 607.4.1: Install grab bars at the tub, shower, and toilet according to the following:

Bathtubs with permanent seats: Two horizontal grab bars should be provided on the back wall, one between 33" and 36" above the floor and the other 9" above the rim of the bathtub. Each grab bar should be no more than 15" from the head end wall or 12" from the foot end wall. A grab bar 24" long should be provided on the foot end wall at the front edge of the bathtub (Figure 7-11).

ANSI 607.4.2: For bathtubs without permanent seats: two horizontal grab bars should be provided on the back wall, one between 33" and 36" above the floor and the other 9" above the rim of the bathtub.

Each grab bar should be a minimum 24" long and not more than 24 inches from the head end wall or 12" from the foot end wall. A grab bar 24" long

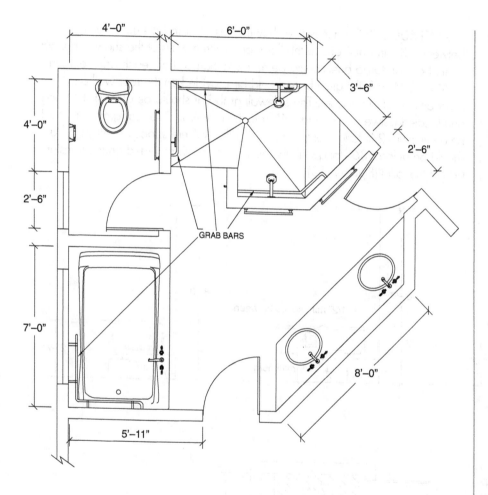

4'-0" 6'-0"

3'-6"

2'-6"

4'-0"

2'-6"

GRAB BARS

7'-0"

8'-0"

5'-11"

Figure 7-12 Plan showing grab bars.

should be provided on the foot end wall at the front edge of the bathtub. A grab bar 12" long should be provided on the head end wall at the front edge of the bathtub.

ANSI 608.3.1: For transfer-type showers, install grab bars horizontally, between 33" and 36" above the floor, across the control valve wall and across the wall opposite the valve controls, and across the back wall to a point 18" from the control wall (Figure 7-11).

ANSI 608.3.2: For accessible showers, install grab bars horizontally, between 33" and 36" above the floor, on all three walls of the shower, but not behind a seat. Grab bars should be no more than 6" from each adjacent wall.

ANSI 604.5: Toilet grab bars should be provided on the rear wall and sidewall closest to the toilet. The sidewall grab bar should be at least 42" long and located between 12" and 54" from the rear wall. The rear grab bar should be a minimum 24" long, centered on the toilet. Where space permits, the bar should be at least 36" long with the additional length provided on the transfer side of the toilet (Figure 7-13).

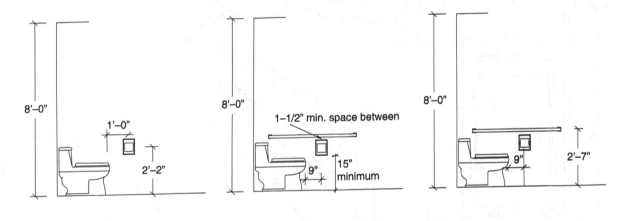

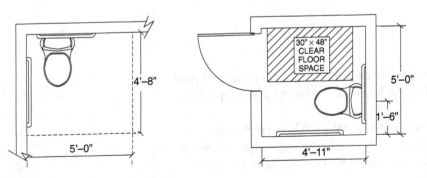

Figure 7-13 Plan for toilet grab bars.

TOILETS AND BIDETS

ANSI 604.3.1, 1002.11.5.2.3: When both a parallel and a forward approach to the toilet are provided, the clearance should be at least 56" measured perpendicular from the rear wall, and 60" measured perpendicular from the sidewall. No other fixture or obstruction should be within the clearance area.

IRC R 307.1, IRC P 2705.1.5, IPC 405.3.1: A minimum distance of 15" is required from the centerline of the toilet and/or bidet to any bath fixture, wall, or other obstacle (Figure 7-14).

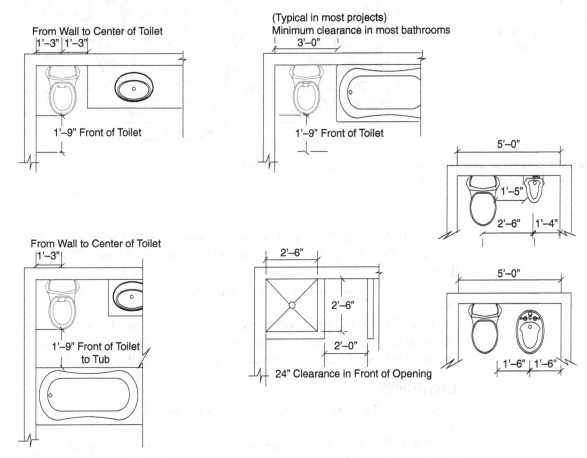

Figure 7-14 Minimum fixture clearance.

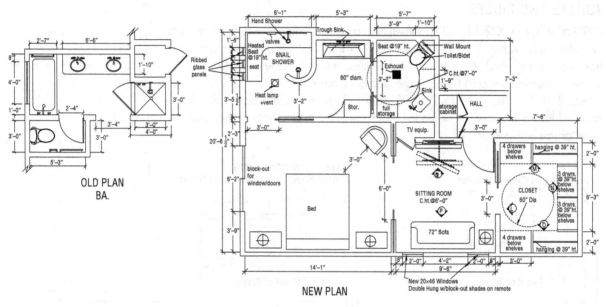

Figure 7-15 Master suite remodeled to provide wheelchair access in the bath and closet. The new plan expanded the closets and sleeping areas.

ANSI 1002.11.5: The toilet should be centered 16"–18" from a side wall.

ANSI 1002.11.5.3: The toilet seat should be between 15" and 19" from the floor.

IPC 405.3.1: The minimum size for a separate toilet compartment is 30" x 60".

ANSI 604.8.1.1: Wheelchair-accessible compartments should be a minimum 60" wide and 56" deep for a wall-mounted toilet and at least 59" deep for a floor-mounted toilet measured perpendicular to the rear wall (Figure 7-15).

LAVATORIES

IRC 405.3.1: The minimum distance from the centerline of the lavatory to a wall is 15".

IRC R 307.1: The minimum distance between a wall and the edge of a freestanding or wall-hung lavatory is 4".

IPC 405.3.1: The distance between the centerlines of two lavatories should be a minimum of 30".

IRC R 307.1: The minimum distance between the edges of two freestanding or wall-mounted lavatories is 4".

ANSI 606.3: The lavatory sink front edge should be no more than 34" above the floor, measured to the higher of the fixture or counter surface.

ANSI 309.4: Lavatory controls should be operable with one hand and not require tight grasping, pinching, or twisting of the wrist.

FLOOR COVERINGS

ANSI 403.3: Plan a slope for the bathtub or shower drain with a maximum slope ratio of 1:48 pitch (1/4" per foot).

ACCESS TO FIXTURE MECHANICALS

IRC M 2720.1: All equipment, including access panels, must be installed per manufacturers' specifications.

IRC P 1307.1: All manufacturers' instructions must be available for installers and inspectors and left for homeowners.

REACH OF WHEELCHAIR USERS

ANSI 308.2.1 and 308.3.1: When the forward or side reach is unobstructed, the high reach should be 48" maximum and the low reach should be 15" minimum above the floor.

ANSI 308.2.2, 308.3.2: When the forward or side reach is obstructed by a 20"–25" deep counter, the high reach should be 44" maximum (Figure 7-16).

BATH ACCESSORIES

Mirrors
ANSI 603.3: Mirrors above lavatories should have the bottom edge of the reflecting surface no more than 40" above the floor.

Toilet Paper Holders
ANSI 604.7: The toilet paper holder should be 7"–9" in front of the toilet bowl and between 15" and 48" above the floor. There should be clearance of at least 1-1/2" below or 12" above the grab bar.

Figure 7-16 Reach
requirements for a
wheelchair user.

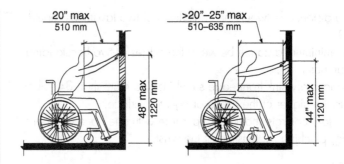

Reach Hindered by Countertop

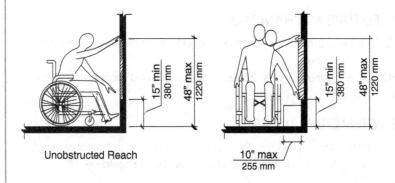

Unobstructed Reach

10" max
255 mm

Plumbing Codes

Plumbing codes regulate the materials that may be used, as well as the methods
of installation performed by the plumber within the building structure. State and
local codes have jurisdiction over the project. If you are designing a bath
remodel, you may find that local codes will require existing plumbing within the
structure to be brought up to current code standards. An example of this would
be the need to upgrade sewer drains when the location of a toilet is changed. It
is imperative that you check this with the plumber before finalizing your design. It
has a major impact on the budget of a project.

A primary element in bath design is water supply and pressure. Larger shower systems, spa tubs, and other water appliances typically require a 3/4-inch supply line to the system or fixture. You must check these requirements with the respective manufacturers and design accordingly.

The water supply line from the street may have to be increased to accommodate the new plumbing plan. Water pressure should be checked by the plumber, especially when the bath is located in an upper floor of the residence. Fluctuations in water pressure can lead to scalding showers. A good test of water pressure for an existing bath water supply is to turn on the shower and flush the toilet. If the shower pressure decreases significantly, adjustment of the supply may be necessary to allow for proper operation and safety.

Pressure-balanced, thermostatic valves in the showers should be planned, especially if a dip in water pressure occurs when more than one water appliance is in use. Most local codes now require that pressure-balanced valves be installed in bathrooms. Additional details about pressure-balanced and thermostatic valves can be found in Chapter 8.

Electrical Codes

The National Electrical Code (NEC), along with state and local codes, sets the minimum standard for electrical applications. The number, type, and placement of electrical fixtures are dictated to ensure a safe environment. These are minimum standards and should be regarded as such; that is, the design should exceed them.

When remodeling older homes, outdated wiring and inadequate electrical service panels will have to be replaced and brought up to code. This adds cost to the project but is vital in creating a safe environment.

The International Residential Code requires that one 20-ampere circuit be dedicated to the lighting and electrical outlet needs of the bathroom. In larger bath suites, additional fixtures may require specific circuits for operation. A spa tub must have a dedicated circuit, as must a steam shower system or a sauna. Manufacturers' specification and installation sheets detail the amperage required for the specific use. This information should be included for the electrician in your specification books.

Review this information with the contractor and electrician to ensure complete compliance with all regulations.

Ground fault circuit interrupters (GFCIs, also shown as GFI on plans) are required in kitchens and baths where the receptacles are located within 3 feet of the outside edge of a sink. All power outlets in the bathroom are controlled by this circuit interrupter. If the GFI outlet is tripped, it immediately interrupts the flow of electrical energy to the outlets. They are easily reset by pushing the reset button.

In addition to traditional wiring in the bath, low-voltage, WiFi systems, and cable bundles for televisions are frequently planned in bathroom designs. Wireless remote controls and air switches are options to be considered.

The electrical code mandates the following:

- Receptacles may not be installed within the tub or shower space.
- No switches may be located within the reach of a person standing in a tub or shower. In some instances, air switches may be used.
- The exception to this is when the switch is a control for a shower or spa/whirlpool system or steam shower control that has been approved by the UL (Underwriter's Laboratory) for its application.

Following is a list of appliances and features found in modest-size and large bathrooms:

- Lighting systems
- Point-of-use water heaters
- Heated floors
- Towel warmers
- Refrigerators or beverage centers
- Touch-pad controls for multiple shower systems
- Warming drawers
- Washers and dryers
- Televisions (encased in shower walls and behind mirrors)
- Sound systems for audio and television

- Space heating system
- Radiant heaters
- Ventilation
- Ceiling fans
- Bidet-toilets
- Toilets with heated seats
- Recharging stations

A detailed electrical layout must be made that accounts for distribution of electrical use. (Refer to the electrical terms in Chapter 9.)

When laying out the electrical plan, be sure to note whether the receptacles will be installed horizontally or vertically. Receptacles are typically installed vertically because the outlet box is attached to the adjacent stud. When they are to be installed horizontally, stud blocking must be provided to support the outlet box.

Basic Bathroom

A basic bathroom will be equipped with a toilet, vanity sink, and tub-shower. The designer must arrange these fixtures and design the interior finishes of the space to be functional, safe, and relaxing.

Children's Bathroom

Designing a bath that children can continue to use into their teens is a special challenge, but it can be accomplished with some "built-in" accommodations. The most apparent change is in their height; the plan must ensure that the child can always have comfortable access to the vanity sink and faucet. For example, a lower drawer can be fitted to convert to a step.

Faucets are usually single-handle valves installed at the back of the sink, but can be placed to the side of the sink if needed for better access. The upper drawers are to accommodate everything the child users need. Stacked towel bars should be provided.

Master Suite Bath

Bathing in a master bath is just one of the activities that may take place in the space; plan for additional amenities. A television, exercise equipment, lounging furniture, and a kitchenette and coffee/beverage center are just a few of the features that may be included in the master bath suite (Figure 7-17). A retreat-like or spa-like

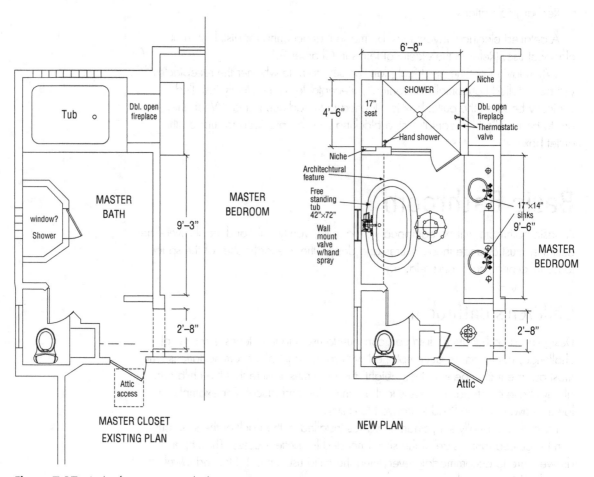

Figure 7-17 A plan for a new master bath.

atmosphere is currently the most requested feature for a master suite bath. This space may even include refrigeration space for cosmetics and pharmaceuticals.

Wet Rooms

Harking back to ancient times when Roman baths were a popular aspect of daily life, the "wet room" has come to the forefront in luxury bathroom design. Massage tables, soaking tubs, steam shower rooms or saunas, and chromatherapy tubs are frequently featured in this type of bath. The wet room is characterized by floor-to-ceiling tilework, ample floor space for varied activities, wall-mounted fixtures, a freestanding tub, and a feeling of serenity created by use of subtle finishes and colors. The openness of the space creates the spa experience for the home bather.

Certain design aspects must be considered:

- The floor plan should be generous and spacious, making the room feel open.

- Finish materials and "furniture" should all be water resistant. Woods such as teak, certain bamboo products, and mesquite resist water and could possibly be used. However, most other woods should be avoided. Always check with a reliable wood source before specifying.

- Flooring should be slip-resistant.

- Drainage should be sized to handle water flow with surfaces sloped to account for water volume. A vanity counter should be designed with a back-to-front taper to avoid water pooling and yet allow grooming aids to remain in place.

- Placement of the shower space is the critical starting point for your space planning. Locating it on the wall across from the sink and toilet and designing it larger to accommodate overspray is one successful approach.

- Installing wall-mounted sinks and toilets/bidets allows water from an open shower to drain under the fixtures without pooling. This water is removed by the floor drain.

- Spa features such as sound systems, two-way mirrors, towel warmers or warming drawers, chromatherapy lights, massage tables, aromatherapy dispensers, a small refrigerator for cosmetics, and beverage centers with ice dispensers all have a place in the wet room.

Planning Checklist for Bathrooms

ANALYZE HOW THE SPACE RELATES TO ADJACENT ROOMS

In bath design, access and privacy are as important as the style and finish materials. Locating plumbing fixtures to minimize sound emissions and providing good access to the space are very important.

ANALYZE SPACE USE

Obviously, personal hygiene is the primary consideration for any bath design. However, when larger spaces are being designed, other features come into play as well. Who will be using the space, and will it need to serve other purposes? Does the space do double duty, such as a guest bath that also serves as a powder room?

SELECT PLUMBING FIXTURES

Ergonomic and spatial considerations play important roles in the fixture selection process. If existing space is being redesigned, check the size of fixtures to make sure they will fit through doorways for installation.

LAY OUT SPACE PLAN

Keep the rough plumbing connections close together whenever possible. Implement ergonomic planning principles.

VERIFY SPACE CLEARANCES

Clearances in the bathroom are of primary concern in allowing proper movement and comfortable and safe use of the space.

PLAN LIGHTING LAYOUT

Placement of fixtures and controls must be planned early. Effective lighting systems are carefully planned using the space plan with all the plumbing fixtures in place. Fixture location and controls require careful consideration. Locate the height and placement of lighting fixtures on wall elevations (Figure 7-18).

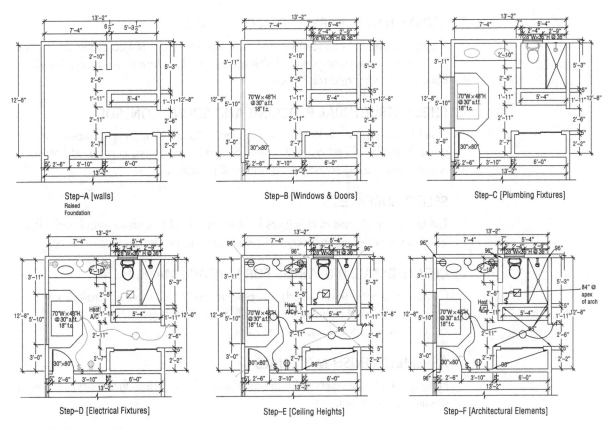

Step–A [walls]
Raised
Foundation

Step–B [Windows & Doors]

Step–C [Plumbing Fixtures]

Step–D [Electrical Fixtures]

Step–E [Ceiling Heights]

Step–F [Architectural Elements]

Figure 7-18 Space-planning steps.

LOCATE VENTILATION

Ventilation in the bathroom is one of the highest priorities in effective
design of the space. Air quality, moisture control, and air temperatures are
all affected. Vents should be placed to exhaust humidity created by bathing
and odors from toilet areas. Bathroom vents should be very quiet and
sized by proper calculation of the cfm required for the square footage of the
space.

LOCATE TOWEL BARS AND ACCESSORIES

A frequent oversight concerns towel bars: often they are not considered until the space plan is near completion. Wall space must be planned to accept towel bars, towel rings, and robe hooks.

CHECK STRUCTURAL BLOCKING AND SOUND CONTROL

Stud blocking in the walls must be planned initially. Wrapping for pipes and ducts should be called out at this time. Sound control issues can be addressed with a design using sound board and wall insulation.

SELECT SURFACES

The kinds of materials and finishes for the bath should be determined early. This will allow any necessary spatial considerations to be designed into the plan.

CREATE DETAIL DRAWINGS FOR SURFACE MATERIALS

Counter thickness, edge details, tile patterns and trims, molding projections, casing widths, and flooring thickness all affect the design of fixtures and cabinetry in the room (Figure 7-19).

ASSEMBLE FINISH MATERIALS

Having samples of selected finish materials on hand makes the design process of details more efficient.

PREPARE COLOR BOARDS

Color boards should display all finishes being designed into the space. One board should be on site during construction and another available for ready reference.

MAKE UP SPECIFICATION BOOKS

Manufacturers' specification and installation sheets are beneficial to the trades involved in execution of the design. Your specification books should be as complete as possible. Designers seldom allot the time needed to select materials and make up these books. Do yourself, your clients, and your trade workers a favor: Take the time.

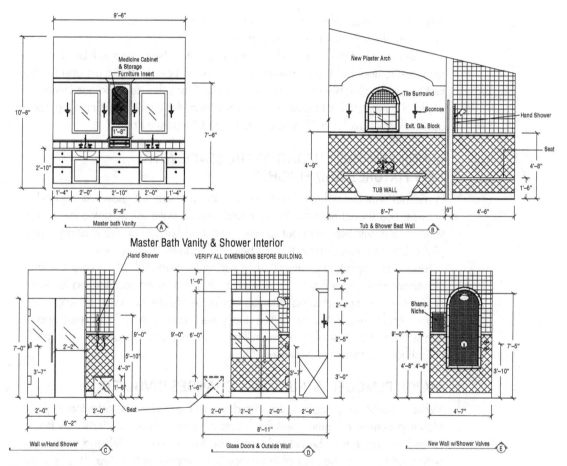

Figure 7-19 Plan for master bath vanity and shower interior elevations.

Bathroom Space Planning

Existing Bathroom Remodel

Remodeling of an existing bathroom involves an established set of design parameters. The shape and dimensions of the space, installed plumbing fixtures, lighting and electrical locations, and type of construction all influence the decisionmaking parts of the design process.

One of the first decisions to be made is whether the project will be a complete remodel of the space (teardown), or an update of fixtures and finishes that keeps the plumbing in the same location. Once this decision has been made, the next step is to gather information from the client for planning purposes. See the Appendix for a "Planning Procedure Checklist—Baths."

MINOR REMODEL: UPDATING THE SPACE WITH NEW FIXTURES AND FINISHES

In a minor remodel, where the space is to be updated with new fixtures and finishes, you should note the location and size of water inlets, sink drains, and vents, along with electrical outlets, switches, and lighting on the existing space plans. List the dimension width and height of installed fixtures.

These are important elements when setting the budget for the project. Minor alterations of the space may include changing from overhead lighting to wall sconces, centering plumbing fixtures to balance the design, and/or replacing faucets and valves with new units in the same location. A well-designed space can withstand the test of time and still allow for periodic decorative changes for a fresh look at minimum expense.

MAJOR REMODEL: STRUCTURAL CHANGES INVOLVED

When an existing space is to be torn down to the stud walls, additional space planning options become available—and evident. Fixture locations may be moved, or space may be added to enlarge the bathroom. Defining and setting priorities for the uses of the space is an important first step. This list may include larger vanities or shower, a separate tub and shower, a steam bath, and/or a separate room for the toilet. This is the time to specify additional frame blocking for accessibility features, such as grab bars, thermal insulation, sound barrier materials, ventilation system, lighting, and the modification of doors and windows (Figure 7-20). The list should include all elements of the space that are to remain. It is most important to listen to the client and make thorough notes or record this session with a digital voice recorder. Photographs of the room and adjoining spaces can be very valuable for reference during the design phase.

Figure 7-20 Traffic patterns to and from the space will be affected by a major remodel, and must be carefully planned to determine the feasibility of expansion. (Photo courtesy of David Dalton, Inc., Los Angeles, CA 90019; www. daviddaltoninc.com)

The planning procedures include:

Review of planning information

Ergonomic profile

Priority list

Construction assessment

Selection of plumbing fixtures

Architectural elements

Elements and principles of design

Entry (door size, swing range, and hinging or pocket)

Spatial clearances

Cabinetry and storage

Lighting and electrical layout

New Construction

Developing the bathroom plans for a new home typically means working from a set of plans provided by an architect or builder. Although the space has already been defined, many design options can be considered. Preparing a variety of overlay sketches will help in the process of creating the best space plan for the client.

Interior and exterior elevations are affected when changing or adding door and window locations. It is necessary to present and explain your design options to the architect and builder. Building a positive relationship with the architect and builder serves your client best.

Planning procedures will be the same as for a major remodel.

How to Get Started

Review of Planning Information

1. List priority items identified in client meetings. This will act as a checklist as you develop your design.

2. Note any design elements affecting the space planning of the bath.

3. Appraise any construction constraints and evaluate how they impact your design. Any obvious compromises must be discussed and settled as early as possible.

Selection of Plumbing Fixtures

It is essential to match the physical characteristics of the client with the right fixture. Visit showrooms with your client to allow a hands-on experience of the latest fixtures available. The choices are innumerable.

Tubs, tub-showers, shower interiors, toilets, bidets, urinals, and sinks should be comfortable for the client(s) to use. The fixture proportions and scale must fit within the overall scheme of the room. Easy-care finishes are a must with homeowners. A guest powder room, however, may use less practical finishes selected for their visual impact alone.

Architectural Elements

The use of windows, doors, and architectural features such as pillars, posts, soffits, light wells, molding, and counter returns must be evaluated early in the planning stage. Changing the location of a door to make the space work better or relocating a window to improve the natural light source should be done in the early stage of the space plan. The primary task, though, is to determine the location of the shower, tub, toilet, and vanity, as they will directly influence the location of these other elements. Blocking for accessibility features, thermal insulation, sound insulation, and any other structural feature of the space should be specified.

Elements and Principles of Design

The scale and proportion of fixtures should balance with the size and shape of the room. Oversized or underscaled fixtures will create a sense of imbalance within the room. A variety of shapes and textures will add interest to the room, while harmony within the color palette will create a feeling of serenity in the space.

Access and Flow

Movement into and within the space must be carefully planned. The size of the doorway and clearance space at each task area should meet or exceed minimum spatial requirements.

Doorways to bathrooms should have a minimum of 32 inches of clear space. This is typically achieved with a 34-inch-wide doorway (accounting for the stop and thickness of the door when open 90°). This dimension should accommodate a person using a cane, crutches, walker, or wheelchair. Because mobility aids vary in size, as do the persons using them, accurate measurements of how the

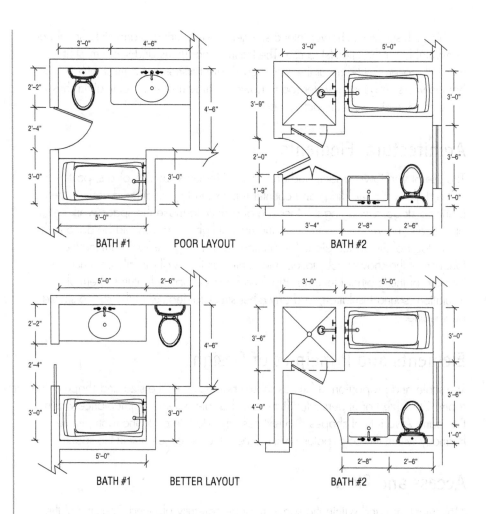

Figure 7-21 Compare the design solutions in these plans, especially with regard to doorways and access.

BATH #1   POOR LAYOUT   BATH #2

BATH #1   BETTER LAYOUT   BATH #2

clients use their aids and noting their agility in and out of the space will yield the correct access dimension (Figure 7-21).

Pocket doors can solve access issues in bathrooms with limited space if the wall space is available.

The number of people using the bathroom at one time influences the location of fixtures and clearances needed when the space is occupied. A recommended minimum clearance of 30 inches is typical. If the person is tall and has larger body mass, 36 to 42 inches may be required.

Clearances

Standard clearances are a critical part of the bath space planning process. Building codes and industry standards ensure a safe environment and functional design and are accepted minimum guidelines from which to begin. This section presents a range of measurements from minimum to maximum clearances, with recommended dimensions suggested. However, the reason you gather the client's ergonomic information is to enable you to custom-design the space to fit the physical characteristics of the client and family. These spatial guidelines will benefit the design process by eliminating the need for time-consuming research into passage requirements.

Code References and Recommended Industry Standards

BATH ENTRY DOOR

IRC P2705.16 states that the door should open into the bath without interfering with bathroom activities. A person should be able to move into the task areas without the door interfering with the use of cabinetry or fixtures.

Doors placed 6 inches or less from the adjacent wall must have sufficient space allowance for the projection of the door knob when the door is standing open 90° (Figure 7-22).

Bathroom doors have traditionally been between 24 and 28 inches wide. If you are designing an existing bathroom with such a door and the door is not changing location, the existing width can be maintained by code. Currently, acceptable door widths range from 32 inches to 36 inches. Always check state and local codes governing the location of your project.

Minimum and Recommended Door Widths

IRC	INDUSTRY	ADA	RECOMMENDED
32″	32″–34″	36″	34″–36″

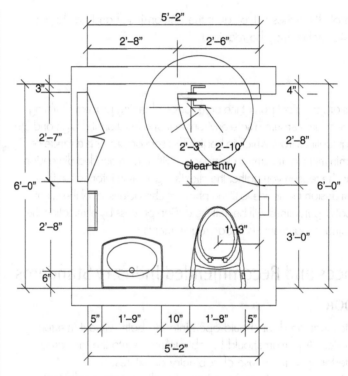

Figure 7-22 Plan with good entry clearance.

BATH WINDOWS

The IRC states that the glazing area in a bath window must be no less than 3 square feet with one-half of that space operable. An exception is allowed when mechanical ventilation and artificial light are used.

TRAFFIC FLOW

The bathroom design must allow at least minimum clearance for fixture use and traffic flow (refer back to Figure 7-14).

Check minimum clearances for:

Width of toilet space

Width between toilet and bidet or urinal

Towel bar placement
Width of vanity for one sink
Width of vanity for two sinks
Width of tub
Interior of shower
Height of shower controls:
  With a seat
  Without a seat
Shower seats
Shower door openings
Floor space clearances:
  Floor space in front of vanity/sink
  Floor space between tub or shower and opposite wall or cabinetry
  Floor space for wheelchair use (circle diameter of 60" or T-turn space allowance)
Ceiling height
Blocking for grab bars
Counter heights

Aesthetically, centering the sink(s) on the cabinet is preferred. Depending on a person's right- or left-hand orientation, locate the sink to allow arm movement by that person. Recommended counter space is 12 inches to the side of the sink edge. A range of 4 to 15 inches is adequate.

If there is only a 30-inch-square clearance in the shower interior, your elbows will hit the shower walls while bathing. Thus, 36 inches should be considered a minimum; 42 inches allows comfortable bathing, and 42 x 48 inches allows abundant space.

A 60-inch turning circle should be included somewhere in the bathroom. If this turning circle is not possible, a 36" x 60" x 36" T-turn is a possible solution.

When planning grab bars for a shower, add additional space (projecting space) for seats and walls where the grab bar protrudes.

Tub-showers provide length for showering when the width of the tub is less than 36 inches.

Bathroom Electrical

Traditional wiring in the bathroom is often supplemented with low-voltage applications, WiFi systems, and cable bundles for televisions and sound systems. Wireless remote controls and air switches are options often considered. Air switches connect to a controller, which must have power to engage. Another bathroom feature that requires electrical power is the bidet toilet seat, which must have an outlet near the toilet to operate.

A detailed electrical layout must be designed that accounts for each electrical use. As mentioned earlier, when laying out the electrical plan, be sure to note whether the receptacles will be installed horizontally or vertically. Receptacles are typically installed vertically, because the outlet box is attached to the adjacent stud. When they are to be installed horizontally, stud blocking must be provided to support the outlet box. Bathroom light should flatter the face as well as provide levels of light needed for grooming.

Plumbing Fixtures

PRODUCT INFORMATION

Manufacturers provide plumbing fixtures to meet just about any design criteria. Selecting the right fixture for a specific application can be very confusing without product knowledge of their applications and limitations. Following is a summary of products and their features.

Toilets

Toilet dimensions and features vary widely. Toilets come as one-piece or two-piece, standard height and comfort height. Comfort-height toilets are ADA-approved in most instances; the seat height typically measures 18 inches above the finished floor. Standard toilet seat height is 15 to 16 inches above the finished floor.

Pressure-assist toilets have a container within the tank of the toilet that receives water from the cold water line. As it fills, the air space in the container is compressed; when it reaches 35 pounds per square inch (psi), it is ready to flush. When the handle is engaged to flush, the air pressure assists the reserved water into the toilet to flush away waste. This process uses less water but can be noisy.

Toilet-bidets tend to be larger than traditional toilets. Some bidets have heated seats and warm-air drying cycles, which require a 110-volt GFCI electrical outlet to operate. Remote-control panels are available on some models.

When remodeling an existing bathroom, selecting a wall-mounted toilet will require structural alterations to the drain and water supply (Figure 7-23). If a new toilet is to be installed in the current location, measuring the location of the sewer drain and water supply is critical because you must select a toilet that will match the location of the drain. Another factor that influences the replacement of an existing toilet is the new wall treatment behind the toilet and the thickness of a new floor. The thicknesses of the new materials must be taken into account.

Water consumption in the operation of a toilet has been reduced from the 3–4 gallons used by old toilets to 1.6 gallons per flush (g.p.f.) as mandated by code. Current technology in toilet water use provides fixtures using 1.28 gallons or less. These are often referred to as high-efficiency toilets (HETs) and have

Figure 7-23 Wall-mounted toilets provide adjustability in installed heights and protrude less from the wall—a great feature for tight spaces. (Photo courtesy of Geberit)

earned the EPA's WaterSense label. A dual-flush system operates with 1.6 g.p.f. for solid waste and 0.8 g.p.f. for liquid waste.

Another important element is the flushing mechanism and its location. Typically you will find the handle on the right or left side of the tank. Buttons located on the lids of the water tank and remote panels are available in wall-mounted units. It is important that the flush handle be readily accessible and easy to reach.

Bidets (E)

The bidet is an important part of hygiene in the bath. Often considered only as a feminine hygiene fixture, in reality benefits for the entire family can be realized when a bidet or bidet-toilet is selected. When separate toilets and bidets are planned, quite often the bidet goes virtually unused and valuable bathroom space is misused or wasted. An alternative choice would be a bidet-toilet and urinal, offering a mix of hygiene features in the same allotted space.

It has been my experience that one reason the bidet is seldom used in the United States is that one must move from the toilet appliance to use the bidet. When one is wearing slacks, one must literally partially undress to use the bidet.

Nevertheless, no matter what age a person may be, but especially as a person ages, the health benefits of the bidet are considerable. Cleansing and drying cycles offer complete hygiene without unnecessary movement.

The most efficient way to take advantage of this hygiene system is to specify a toilet-bidet. This combines the benefits of personal hygiene with the space-saving features of an all-in-one fixture.

Manufacturers provide bidet-toilet seats to retrofit existing toilets. A GFCI outlet must be provided for the electronic system of the unit, whether it is a new fixture or a seat retrofitted to an existing toilet.

If a separate bidet is planned without an air-dry feature, a towel bar within easy reach is a necessity.

Urinals (E)

Often an overlooked bath fixture, the urinal is now coming into its own in residential construction. Shapes and dimensions vary by manufacturer and must be considered prior to design. Installing a urinal 15 to 18 inches on center from the adjacent wall, cabinetry, or fixtures is recommended. Front stance clearances

Figure 7-24 As an alternate fixture to the bidet, a urinal should be considered to provide convenient use to men. (Photo courtesy Mary Fisher Designs.com)

should be a minimum of 21 inches, but 30 to 36 inches is recommended. The proper installed height of the urinal can be determined by acquiring the inseam trouser size of the adult male and subtracting 3 to 4 inches from that figure; this is the installation height off the finished floor for the front lip of the urinal. This measurement will need to be noted on the wall elevation of your plans as well as in your specifications (Figure 7-24).

When the urinal is installed in a powder room, the recommended height for the lip of the urinal is 24 to 26 inches.

Showers

Minimum measurements for shower interiors, by code, are 30 inches by 30 inches finished. Corner showers, as well as round showers, are available in ready-to-install shower pans from various manufacturers for very small bathrooms.

Large showers are a top priority with many homeowners. Space and location of the shower are critical and one of the first steps in space planning. Tub-showers are discussed later in this section. Barrier-free showers do not have a curb to negotiate, making access easier for all users. Some shower pans are available for such flush-floor installations.

Shower Heads and Valves

Select and install shower heads and valve functions that are easy to use. Standard shower heads and valves are typically wall-mounted and controlled by one or two valves. Additional water outlets can be added to the system but will require additional ports for valves and/or diverters.

Electronic shower systems provide the convenience of preset temperature control. They are easy for all to use and can be installed in the wall or in the tub skirt, or be remote.

Pressure-Balanced and Thermostatic Valves

Pressure-balance valves, now required by code, monitor and control fluctuations in water pressure and maintain a consistent water flow to the shower head. The most desirable pressure-balanced valve control is the pressure-balanced thermostatic valve, which controls both the water pressure and the temperature of the water. These should be used in all shower applications for safety and comfort.

Shower valves are selected on the basis of the number of components (e.g., shower heads, body sprays) being planned and the gallons per minute (gpm) of water flow. The plumber can tell you the flow rate capacity available at the valve opening based on the pressure (in psi). Verifying the water pressure from the street and throughout the house is critical when designing a larger shower with multiple water components.

Valve controls should be designed to fit the user's ergonomic profile. The ability to grasp and operate with wet soapy hands must be considered.

Handheld Shower Heads

Handheld shower heads installed on a vertical rod provide adjustability for varying user heights. When locating a hand shower near a seat or bench for use while seated, plan for the right- or left-handed person (Figure 7-25). (When a glass wall hinders this application, know that the user will adapt to the other

Figure 7-25 A wall-mounted, handheld shower head. (Photo courtesy of Mary Fisher Designs.com, Northlight Architectural Photography.com)

side.) Make sure the water hose does not hit the floor when the handheld shower head is in the lowest position. Also, make sure the hand shower fits the user's grasp.

Stationary Shower Heads

Stationary shower heads should be installed high enough to wash the tallest body. Code dictates a minimum height of 80 inches above the finished floor.

Rain Shower Heads

Rain shower heads or ceiling shower heads are often combined with an adjustable handheld shower head. A diverter valve allows the choice of either one or both heads. The height of the shower ceiling and height of the user will dictate the distance the shower head can be hung from the floor.

Barrier-free, accessible, or curbless showers require a drain large enough to handle water flow and a shower floor sloped to direct water to the drain. Long, rectangular lateral drains are great solutions for this shower application and allow a minimal slope to be used. Certain construction constraints must be met. In new construction, floor slope is accounted for in the framing or slab work. It is much more complicated in a remodeling project. When designing an accessible shower, the floor joists must be altered (cut into to lower the space for the floor material, which may be tile or stone) requiring that the foundation and floor joists be re-engineered to accommodate the change. Slab foundations must be cut and ground excavated for the proposed depth.

STEAM SHOWERS

Steam showers consist of three components: the steam generator, a controller, and a steam head (Figure 7-26). The location of the steam head and generator is critical, as these elements must be accessible for servicing. Locate the steam head so that it will provide a steam flow without directly contacting the body.

Evacuating the volume of steam must be considered in the ventilation capacity. Most steam showers vent steam directly out of the shower space.

BATHTUBS

Bathtubs vary tremendously in shape and size. The categories include front-apron tubs, top-set tubs, freestanding tubs, soaker tubs, walk-in tubs, water therapy tubs, and whirlpool/spa tubs.

Size, location, the client's ergonomic profile, and the client's tub preference are your first considerations. Tubs are available in sizes ranging from 60 to 72 inches. The typical tub in a production home is a 60-inch by 30-inch front-apron tub (unless it is a feature tub in the master suite).

Front-Apron Tubs

Front-apron tubs are most often used in secondary bathrooms. Many models come with the option of the front panel and can be installed into a tub deck. For planning purposes, determine the size of the available space and whether this application will include a shower system.

Figure 7-26 Steam showers must be fully enclosed to be properly functional. (Photo courtesy of David Dalton, Inc., Los Angeles, www.daviddaltoninc.com)

Tub-Showers

Any tub-shower should be an undermounted tub. When showering, water will flow into the tub and drain properly. A top-set tub-shower creates water pockets that are difficult to clean and allows water buildup that causes mold and mildew and allows water splash to the floor.

One consideration, when either a front-apron or set-in tub is planned, is the wall treatment surrounding the tub. The thickness of the material you use on the walls and the method and sequence of installation will influence your tub selection.

You must also plan before selecting the type of tub-shower enclosure. Glass doors and panels must be properly secured and watertight. Tempered glass is used, so precise design measurements are essential for a successful installation. Tempered glass is required by code, but it is expensive and cannot be recut or trimmed. Always require the installer to make the final measurements for the glass enclosure and framing.

Freestanding Tubs

Freestanding tubs can stand alone or be set into an island platform, thereby creating an island within the bathroom. When the tub is in a window area, privacy becomes an important element of the design. The size of the tub and location of the drain, faucet, and valves will have to be called out at the rough framing stage. If a new home is being built on a slab, these locations must be determined before the slab is poured. If the installation is in an existing bathroom built on a concrete slab, it will involve cutting the slab and installing a new water supply line and drain to the new location. A raised foundation or upper-floor installation may also require new supply and drain plumbing lines. If a top-set tub is being installed in a deck with one side attached to a wall, faucet and valves can be installed on the wall (Figure 7-27).

Figure 7-27 A free-standing "slipper" tub is set in front of a water feature under the window to create a unique and serene bathing experience. (Photo courtesy of Mary Fisher Designs. com, Northlight Architectural Photography.com)

Several years ago, the Soft Bathtub (E) was introduced. A patented soft interior layer, which is extremely durable, provides comfortable bathing, as it yields to the contour of the body. The tub insulation allows the water to lose only 1°F of heat per hour. Such tubs are best as a top-set installation. Ergonomic in design, they also provide the designer with another option: hydrotherapy and in-line heaters are available.

Walk-in Tubs

Providing safety and easy access, the walk-in tub can be the right solution for accessible bathing; however, there are some extra design considerations. Install a ceiling radiant heat source to keep the body warm during the tub fill and then when the tub drains. A hand shower can be useful for the bather to rinse off after the tub drains. A towel warmer near the door of the tub is a nice feature. A dressing bench is always a good idea in any bath.

Whirlpool/Spa Tubs

Whirlpool/spa tubs present various water experiences. Water is pumped through jets to offer an invigorating massage with adjustable intensity. The air bath pushes air through small holes in the tub, creating a true "bubble" bath. Spa tubs are available that offer a combination of air and water massage. Some such tubs, but not all, allow you to use oils and soaps. Check with your plumbing supplier or manufacturer's representative for clarification.

Cast-Iron Tubs

When a cast-iron bathtub is selected, four considerations must be thought about:

1. The weight of the tub
2. Means of moving the tub into place
3. Means of moving the tub through doors or up stairs
4. Location of faucet and valves

Faucet and valves are placed in the wall, installed in the deck, or located on the floor when the tub is placed in an island or peninsula design. Cast iron cannot be drilled for faucet and valve holes after manufacturing. Acrylic tubs are lighter in weight, and can thus be handled more easily; also, holes can be drilled in an acrylic tub after manufacturing for mounting faucets and valves.

SINKS

The first decision to be made when selecting a sink is how many sinks will be used in the space; the second consideration is the decorative style of the space. Design options include the single top-set or undermount sink; vessel sinks that mount onto countertops; pedestal sinks that are mounted on the floor; wall-hung applications that are secured to the wall without cabinetry or support from below; and trough sinks, which are a large single compartment integrated into the countertop. Hand-painted, porcelain, glass, metal, stone, ceramic, fireclay, and solid-surface fixtures are also available to enhance the look of the space as desired.

How the vanity is used, and by whom, must be determined prior to selection of fixtures. As with all plumbing fixtures, the ergonomic profile of the user helps resolve access, safety, and function issues.

FAUCETS

Dual-handle, single-lever, and electronic hands-free faucets are only a few of the selections available to designers to accomplish their design solutions for the space. Fitting the faucet to the grasping ability and wrist agility of the client, along with style considerations of the interior, is the first step. Styles range from modern minimalism to ornamental traditional.

When selecting a faucet set, plan for an ample amount of space between the sink and backsplash (Figure 7-28).

- Is there room for the hand to operate and clear the backsplash and clean the faucet?
- Will the faucet be installed directly on the sink, on the wall, or on the countertop?

Cross handles and levers can be easily operated with wet, soapy hands. Levers are the ideal control for those with limited grasp and hand movement. The single-mix faucet is another ergonomic application of product design.

The placement of the faucet is traditionally behind the sink on the countertop, but wall-mounted fixtures are also popular. When limited reach and body movement are involved, the better design places the faucet to the side or at the corner of a sink. When doing so, be sure the placement will not interfere with lateral movement at the sink.

Figure 7-28 Good spacing of faucet with a vessel sink. (Photo courtesy of Mary Fisher Designs.com, Northlight Architectural Photography. com)

More water is wasted waiting for hot water to travel to the bathroom sinks and shower than any other use. Point-of-use and tankless water heaters can effectively alleviate this problem. In existing bathrooms, a small point-of-use water heater in a vanity cabinet can be installed to improve the water delivery for both sinks and showers. These applications are discussed in detail in Chapter 10.

GRAB BARS

Grab bars should be a staple in the design of bath spaces. Young or old, injured or limited in motion, everyone would be safer if grab bars were part of the total bathing and hygiene plan. Many clients resist the installation of these accessories, because they feel it makes the space look "handicapped." Because of that perception, the designer should specify that frame blocking be installed in the walls to support the future addition of grab bars in the toilet space, tub area, and shower. Grab bars should be placed at a height relative to the user. Use your ergonomic profile for this measurement. Always fit installation to the person.

A grab bar installed horizontally, approximately 38 inches off the finished floor in the bathtub space, is a typical guideline. It is better to fit the location to the person and how he or she gets in and out of a tub, uses the shower, and uses the toilet.

Proper installation of a grab bar is to anchor it to the wall studs or blocking in the walls. When blocking is added, a 3/4-inch, 6-inch to 12-inch-high sheet of plywood is nailed to the studs. This provides the stability needed to secure the bar.

A grip clearance of 1 to 1-1/2 inches from the wall should be allowed. This will vary by model and manufacturer.

Decisions as to the shape and size of a grab bar will depend on use. The length of the grab bar should be based on user fit, the user's ability to grasp and reach, and the length needed.

When trying to lift out of a bathtub, a person will likely need to use both hands, reaching forward, to pull up to the standing position. Not everyone can do this.

Applying a perimeter grab bar in the shower can promote safe access and use. It becomes part of the visual statement and is less obtrusive to homeowners.

Make sure the grab bar can be readily gripped with wet or soapy hands. A texture on the bar can enhance gripping ability. Grab bars installed on a 45° angle serve the reaching ability of young and old; however, wet and soapy hands can slip if there is no grip texture on the bar.

When designing the plumbing system for the bath, a close alliance with your plumbing supplier and plumber will be invaluable. Manufacturers provide needed support materials along with representatives knowledgeable in their product line.

Selecting Bathroom Fixtures

Selecting the right fixtures for the client involves the initial planning information sheets with the ergonomic profile and basic design layout of the space. Confusion can result with all the available options. The following points will help you focus on use, shape, style, and need.

Sinks

- Determine the number of sinks to be used.
- Decide on the type of sink installation: top-set (self-rimming), vessel, countertop or undermount, pedestal, or wall-mounted.
- Observe the number of holes in the sink and their spread (4 inches or 8 inches on center).

- Settle on the spread of the faucet holes: center-single, 4-inch center-spread, 8-inch-wide spread, wall-mount faucet, electronic faucet. Resolve the depth of cabinetry and countertops needed to install the sink and faucet.
- If a vessel sink is planned, establish the proper height for the top of the sink (refer back to Figure 7-28). This will determine the cabinet or shelf support height required for proper installation.

Sink Faucets

Your faucet selection must be compatible with your sink selection. Vessel sinks will require faucets mounted from the wall or taller, hi-arc faucets installed on the counter (deck), designed specifically for the sink. Occasionally, your client may want to use a deck-mount faucet with a vessel sink (refer back to Figure 7-28).

Decide on the faucet style:

- Consider the ergonomic features of the faucet.
- A single faucet has one handle, and it accommodates grasp and hand dexterity limitations.
- Electronic faucets are always a good solution for clients with limited hand use.
- Make sure plumbing connections are accessible and can be easily connected by the plumber.
- Determine whether the faucet is to be installed on the sink or on the countertop (deck).
- When a deck-mount (countertop) faucet is selected, investigate the need for extenders for installation into a thicker countertop material.
- Verify if the rough top can be cut under the faucets to accommodate a thicker countertop in a deck-mount application.
- Plan counter and cabinet depths large enough for hands to operate the faucet controls and clean behind them.
- Clarify backsplash design detail to be sure sufficient space is allowed for faucet operation.
- If a medicine cabinet is directly above the faucet, select faucet heights that allow opening of the cabinet doors.

Bathtub and Whirlpool-Spa Tub Faucets

- Determine whether the tub fill and valves are to be installed on the tub (bath-mount), in the deck (deck-mount), in the wall, or in the ceiling above.
- Decide on a tub-only or tub-shower installation.
- Select tub and shower faucet combination with a single-mix or dual-handle valve.
- Locate the filler spout so that it does not interfere with entering or exiting the tub or bathing.
- Be sure the spout extends far enough over the tub edge for proper water flow.
- Locate the valves within convenient reach for turning on the water flow and testing the temperature of the water at the filler spout. This applies to both single-mix and dual-mix handles.

Toilets

- Determine the size, shape, and features of the toilet to provide design solutions.
- Fit the toilet to the ergonomic profile of the client.
- Make sure plumbing and electrical supply are available for a toilet-bidet.
- Select fixtures that have earned the EPA's WaterSense® label, whenever possible.
- Select dual-flush toilets.
- If a wall-mount toilet is used, have rough-in valves available at the rough plumbing stage.

Environmental Factors

Environmental factors influencing the design and use of the bathroom should be considered as part of initial space planning. The fixtures, lighting systems, ventilation, and adequate water supply are all involved in creating a comfortable, energy-efficient, and sustainable space.

Indoor Air Quality

Several different properties can be found when analyzing the air quality of a bathroom. Moisture, pollutants from sprays and grooming products, odors generated within the space, off-gases from newly installed materials, and stagnant air all contribute to poor air quality. If not properly handled, these factors can lead to the growth of mildew and bacteria, as well as provide the conditions conducive to the growth of mold. The structural damage to an improperly vented space can be enormous. Problems of mold growth can often be traced to improperly vented wet areas of the house.

Many products and materials used in today's construction give off gases while they cure. You can avoid some of this by selecting products and finishes that are natural materials or low in volatile organic compound (VOC) emissions. Materials and finishes emitting gases include some paints, wood products such as medium density fiberboard (MDF) and particleboard, some foam insulation, plastic products, and various mastics and adhesives used in manufacturing and construction. Sealers such as varnish and glazing finishes will also contribute gaseous odors and fumes.

It is critical that an adequately sized ventilation system be planned for the bathroom. More than one vent may be required to exhaust moisture and odors effectively. Refer to Chapter 10 for additional information.

It is important to plan a ventilation system that is quiet and effective so the homeowner will use it. Some codes require the vent to come on as you enter the room. In this case, a switch will control both the primary light source and vent. The Heating and Ventilation Institute (HVI) suggests that a bathroom vent run for 20 minutes after the bath is used to adequately exhaust moist air. A timer is an effective control that will conserve energy; some codes require bathroom ventilation to be on a timer. Operating windows can allow fresh air to contribute to the ventilation system. IRC code R303.3 states that a bathroom is to be provided with aggregate glazing area in windows of not less than 3 square feet, half of which can be opened. Exception: When artificial light and ventilation are provided, the vent must be rated at 50 cfm for intermittent ventilation and 20 cfm for continuous flow. When a single vent is used in the bathroom, it should be located to exhaust moisture and odors from the toilet and shower location. All ventilation must exhaust to the outside (Figure 7-29).

Figure 7-29 Bathroom
ventilation should be as
efficient as possible.

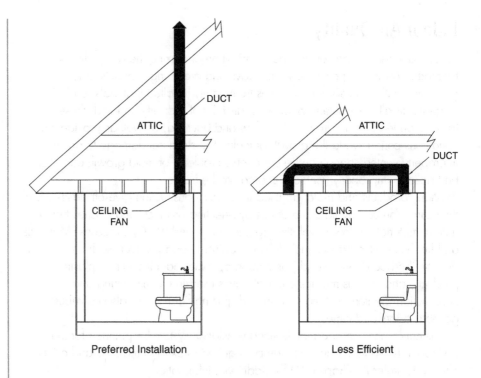

Preferred Installation   Less Efficient

Water Quality and Conservation

Water sourced from municipal agencies is held to EPA standards for primary and secondary drinking water regulations. When a well is the water source for the project, codes and regulations mandate water quality and use for wells. Be sure to check the applicable state and local codes.

What water-quality issues might affect the bathroom?

The term *hard water* refers to water containing high levels of calcium and magnesium. These elements adhere to cal-rod heating units in electric water heaters, gather around the shower heads and faucets of bath fixtures, and leave a ring around many surfaces and fixtures. Filters and water softener systems that reduce the calcium and magnesium content of water can extend the life of these fixtures.

Water consumption is a primary concern when designing the bathroom. Water-efficient fixtures now available can effectively save a substantial amount of water per year. Flow restrictor devices should be used when possible.

Sustainable Materials

Bathrooms are great spaces in which to use recycled materials. Recycled stone, ceramic and glass tile, cabinetry, and lighting fixtures can easily be used.

Bamboo is an extremely popular renewable resource that stands up well to wet areas and is used in a variety of surfaces, including cabinetry, counters, and tile. Recycled paper mixed with bamboo is another countertop material of environmental significance. Refer to Chapter 12 for more information on sustainability.

Energy Efficiency

Energy use and water consumption are closely connected in bath design. The location of the water heater serving the bathroom and the distance to the point of use affect the amount of energy used by the water heater and the amount of water wasted while the user waits for the hot water flow. Insulating the hot water tank and hot water pipe runs will help some. Installing a small point-of-use or booster water heater or pump in the bathroom can be a solution to long distances from the main water heater and eliminate long, costly delays waiting for hot water.

LIGHTING

Bathrooms require some specific applications of light. Entering and exiting the space safely is of prime importance. Specific activities within the space require specific lighting solutions.

- **Grooming:** Requires illumination of the face and head. Wall-mounted light fixtures should be installed so a light source is at eye level. The design of the fixture should be selected prior to rough electrical so the correct finished height off the floor can be specified.
- **Hygiene:** A watertight fixture in an enclosed shower and a separate light fixture in the toilet room are mandatory.

- **Accent lighting:** Accent lighting creates a feeling of serenity and is important to the atmosphere in a spa bath.
- **Dimmer controls and sensors:** All lighting systems should be on dimmer controls. In some code jurisdictions, motion sensors may also be required.

Heating and Air Conditioning

Heating and cooling of the bathroom may be done through the central heating and air-conditioning system, baseboard heaters, heated floors, bathroom radiant heat sources, or any combination of these methods. A radiant heat source may be more comfortable when one steps out of the shower or tub, because it warms the body without evaporating the moisture from the skin (evaporation creates a cooling effect). If a walk-in tub is designed in the bath, a radiant heat source should be planned so that warm rays of heat reach the person who is waiting for the tub to fill or empty. A heated towel warmer nearby is always a good idea.

When a heated floor is selected, proper insulation in the floor will add to the efficiency of the system. Some building codes do not allow electrical lighting fixtures or heat lamps to be installed directly over a tub. Always check local and state codes prior to locating ceiling fixtures.

Sound Control

Sound is emitted by people, mechanical systems, fixtures, moving air, and water. As sound travels within a space, the shape of that space and the finish materials used will either absorb or reflect the sound waves. Controlling the distribution of sound in a bathroom is very important, especially as it relates to adjacent rooms.

Sound control is achieved through construction methods, selection of low-sound-level fixtures, and good equipment and space planning. Locating bath fixtures away from a common wall to a bedroom or living space, whenever possible, is the first step in lowering sound levels. Insulating walls, floors, and ceilings, and wrapping pipes with sound insulation reduce the transmission of sound. Noise-stop board or sound-board and sound-absorbing drywall are effective materials to use on a common wall, along with insulation. Water appliances, such as toilets, shower heads, tubs, and sink faucets, along with water supply lines and drains, all emit varying levels of sound. Insulating hot and cold pipes whenever possible helps to diminish the sound of moving water. Plastic drain pipe emits more sound than cast iron. New, environmentally engineered foam insulation can be blown into wall cavities to create a very efficient sound barrier.

Finding fixtures and products with low sone and decibel ratings should be a priority. (Refer to Chapter 10.)

Because surfaces in bathrooms are typically hard, sound bounces off them readily. Sound-absorbing fabrics, such as towels, fabric window treatments, and area rugs can be used to help absorb sound if they do not interfere with safe movement within the space.

Vinyl tiles, sheet goods, vinyl wood floors, and commercial-grade carpet squares can contribute sound-absorbing qualities to the space. Designing a large bathroom with various floor-covering materials can add color and interest to the space and also lower the sound level.

Sound generated by grooming appliances, such as shavers, hair dryers, and water appliances, especially when added to the sound of bottles, brushes, and curling irons on hard counter materials, can be amazingly annoying. Refer to Chapter 10 for more in-depth information on sound issues.

CASE STUDY ONE
The Loft Bathroom

GOALS:

1. Create a bath that is serene and space-efficient.

2. Select colors, finishes, and materials that work with the loft as a whole.

SOLUTIONS:

1. Multiuse fixtures provide bathing options in a compact space. The wooden soaker tub-shower functions efficiently and sets a serene Asian tone.

2. Clean lines and striking contrasts set the tone for this contemporary space. The sink height must be planned prior to selection of the base cabinetry. Specific storage for bath items is designed into cabinetry (Figure 7-30).

Figure 7-30 The influence of Japanese architecture can readily be seen in the use of platforms. (Photo courtesy of Barbara Houston, Vancouver, B.C.; Ivan Hunter)

CASE STUDY TWO
Water-Feature Bath

GOALS:

1. Keep existing location of sinks.
2. Remove wall between toilet and shower to open up the space.
3. Improve lighting and ventilation.

SOLUTIONS:

1. The vanity was redesigned to include a dressing table and higher countertops. The sinks were undermounted and wide-spread faucet sets selected. Storage at the dressing table includes pull-out cabinets that house makeup and grooming appliances (Figure 7-31).

2. Light fixtures are set to wash the face with light. Dimmer controls and recessed cans are part of the bathroom's lighting system.

3. By removing the wall between the toilet-shower space and vanity, the slipper tub could be located below the high window. Glass panels of the windows are "rain" glass. To create a serene atmosphere in the bath, a water feature was installed from the bottom of the window to the floor (Figure 7-32).

Figure 7-31 (Photo courtesy of Mary Fisher Designs.com, Northlight Architectural Photography.com)

Figure 7-32 (Photo courtesy of Mary Fisher Designs.com, Northlight Architectural Photography.com)

CASE STUDY THREE
Powder Room

GOALS:

1. Create a space that can act as both a guest bath and a powder room.
2. Add some drama to the space.

SOLUTIONS:

1. To carry the weight of the stone and cabinetry, cabinets were mounted on the wall with a French cleat secured to the wall studs. A *French cleat* is a horizontal support, typically made of metal (steel in this case) or wood, which secures the cabinet and stone to the wall.
2. To add drama to the space, onyx was selected for the counter and lit from below with fluorescent light.
3. The client asked for a vessel sink and the waterfall faucet, so creative design solutions had to be found. A custom-built box support with a removable panel for access to plumbing was installed to hold the waterfall faucet set (Figure 7-33).

Figure 7-33 (Photo courtesy of Mary Fisher Designs.com, Northlight Architectural Photography.com)

CASE STUDY FOUR
Design Observations

1. Use color and texture to create interest in small spaces. Moroccan wall and counter tiles complement the limestone floor tile and shower surround. A black rub was used to finish the vanity cabinet mirror and medicine cabinet (Figure 7-34).

2. A soft monochromatic scheme creates a relaxing backdrop for this master bath. Large 18-inch-square limestone floor tile is set on the diagonal with matching grout and bordered with tile cut in half to form a rectangular border.

Honed marble counters are finished with an eased edge, and a limestone backsplash forms the wainscot running throughout the space. The sink cabinet protrudes slightly to lend a more furniture-like appearance to the cabinet as a whole. The countertops are 36 inches high to accommodate a more erect stance. The freestanding tub placed in the window alcove has a floor-mounted faucet set. Recessed lighting and wall sconces make up the light system (Figure 7-35).

Figure 7-34 (Photo courtesy of Mary Fisher Designs.com, Northlight Architectural Photography.com)

Figure 7-35 (Photo courtesy of Mary Fisher Designs.com, Northlight Architectural Photography.com)

3. By separating the vanities in a master suite bath, two different heights could be accommodated (Figure 7-36).

4. Careful consideration of space, light, use, and storage should characterize every bathroom plan, no matter what size the space is (Figure 7-37).

Figure 7-36 (Photo courtesy of Mary Fisher Designs.com, Northlight Architectural Photography.com)

Figure 7-37 Simple lines and understated color give this bathroom a Zen feel. The shower (reflected in the mirror) completes this small bath that doubles as a powder room. (Photo courtesy of David Dalton, Inc., Los Angeles, CA 90019; www.daviddaltoninc.com)

Plumbing

8

Just as the heart and circulatory system deliver fluid and nourishment throughout your body, the residential plumbing system must provide water to various points of use throughout a home.

Understanding how water is supplied and distributed in the home is necessary when designing kitchens and bathrooms that are cost-effective and efficiently planned. A balance must be met between design criteria and economic considerations.

A residential plumbing system is made up of three basic systems:

1. Supply system
2. Drain and waste system
3. Vent system

The *supply system* brings pressurized water from a utility main or private well to the house and distributes the water to appliances and fixtures on demand. When an appliance such as a dishwasher is turned on, a valve opens and water flows to the unit. A *valve* is a device that regulates the flow of a fluid or gas in one direction by opening or closing various passageways. Faucet handles and lever controls, shower and tub controls, gas-line controls, ball-rocker valves in the laundry, and pressure-relief valves on water heaters are all examples of valves used in a residence.

A faucet valve is opened when the handle is turned, allowing water to flow through the faucet. Water pressure "pushes" the water through supply lines, allowing it to flow freely, and the valve permits regulation of the water volume delivered. If the main supply line is regulated correctly, the water will continue to flow at the same rate when other fixtures are turned on. Water pressure to the house must be established prior to the design of kitchens and baths using multiple plumbing fixtures and appliances. For example, planning a master bath shower with multiple fixture outlets will require a supply line compatible with the need. Typically, a 3/4-inch supply line will be needed just for the shower system if it has many water outlets. If the water pressure is less than ideal, a noticeable drop in water flow will occur. Plumbing codes require a pressure-balance valve, which regulates a balance of hot and cold water pressure for showers to help alleviate the problem of potential scalding.

The plumber must check the water pressure available to the house to ensure the correct balance between supply and demand. When adding more fixtures to

an existing home, you may find that the supply line to the house is undersized for the proposed plumbing design. This may require the plumber to install a new, higher-capacity supply line.

It is recommended that you review the new design with the plumber before submitting plans to the client. A thorough review of plumbing applications ensures that codes will be met and a properly sized delivery system will be put in place.

The *drain and waste system* transports *gray water* (used water from washer, dishwasher, sinks, and bathing) and waste from the house to the sewer or septic tank. Most fixtures drain by gravity, with the exception of the toilet, which uses a combination of gravity and falling water. Some low-flow toilets use an injection of air in addition to water and gravity. Occasionally, in a basement level, waste and gray water must be pumped to the sewer line; this is usually accomplished with an electrical sump pump.

Backflow is a concern in fixture design. This term refers to the flow of water in a pipe or line in the opposite direction from its normal direction of flow. In kitchens and baths, this concern centers primarily on contaminated water flowing back into potable water (water fit for human consumption).

An air gap is required at the dishwasher as a safety valve against backflow. This device is used to prevent backflow or siphoning back into the dishwasher when a negative pressure or vacuum occurs. This unit installs on the sink or countertop so water can be diverted into the sink should the need arise. Some dishwashers have air-gap features built into the appliance.

The designer must be aware of the locations of plumbing drain cleanouts (access ports to drain lines). Although most cleanouts are located on outside walls and accessed from the exterior, this is not always the case. Access to plumbing and cleanouts must be maintained so debris that may cause a stoppage in the water drain lines can be cleaned out. The design of cabinetry and placement of fixtures may be affected.

The *vent system* exhausts noxious sewer gases from the house. When a drainpipe is used, sewer gases rise up the vent pipe and out of the house (Figure 8-1).

An island vent allows sinks to be placed in kitchen islands (Figure 8-2). The plumbing and vents are generally placed in a pony wall at the back of island cabinets. The vent loops as high as the cabinet or pony wall will allow and then down under the floor to tie into the main vent system.

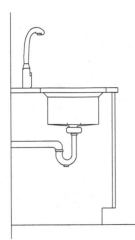

Figure 8-1 A "P" or "S" trap, located below the drain, has just enough water remaining in it to block sewer gases from flowing back through the drain into the house.

Kitchen and Bath Design

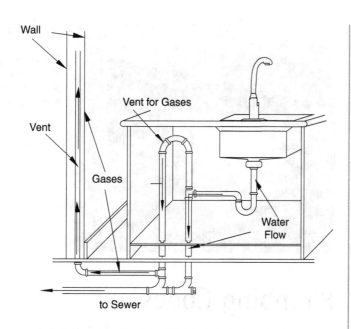

Wall

Vent for Gases

Vent

Gases

Water
Flow

to Sewer

Figure 8-2   Island vent.

The vent system also maintains air pressure in the drain system, helping waste to flow down to the sewer.

Sinks located at a window raise some special concerns related to the sewer vent. The distance from the countertop to the sill of the window can present some challenges. Occasionally an island vent configuration will be used when the window is installed at countertop level and cannot accommodate the angle required for the vent, that is, when the angle is too low to allow proper ventilation (Figure 8-3).

The plumbing system is a simple application of supply and demand. The utility main or private well supplies the water to the house upon demand, and the house drain-waste and vent systems extract noxious fumes and wastes from the house on demand.

Design considerations for plumbing locations in kitchens and bathrooms must reflect the overall design criteria of the client and the water appliances and fixtures specified. Refer to Chapter 5 and Chapter 7 to learn the selection options, size variations, methods of installation, and design criteria for each.

Figure 8-3 Sinks under windows can present a venting challenge. (Photo courtesy of Judy Svendsen, ASID, Raven Interiors/Mary Fisher Designs.com; Don Milici Photography)

Plumbing Codes

Codes covering residential plumbing vary from region to region. The number of fixtures to be installed; the water pressure delivered by the utility or well, which is typically 46 to 60 pounds per square inch (psi); and elevation of the fixture from the water source all contribute to the size of the main supply line from the street or well to the house, as well as the supply lines to individual fixtures or appliances. Supply lines from the water meter and public service are typically 3/4 inch to 1 inch in diameter. Supply lines for risers typically are 3/8 inch, or 1/2 inch to 3/4 inch. These are inside diameters of steel pipe and outside diameters of copper pipe.

Many manufacturers specify the size of a supply line for proper installation of a fixture. If a fixture or valve is located on a third story of a residence or in a high-rise dwelling, a larger supply line may be needed to compensate for this elevation. The plumber is responsible for calculating pipe size in compliance with applicable codes. This is why the designer must communicate with the plumber early in the design process. The designer and plumber must collaborate on the number and type of fixtures planned so that local codes are met and water pressure is appropriate.

Electrical and Lighting Basics

9

The electrical system of a house acts similarly to the nervous system of the body. Every room must have electrical power for lighting, heating, cooling, maintaining air quality, and providing energy for the various electronic components and appliances used. Dispersal of electrical energy throughout the structure is similar to the way in which the brain sends impulses to various parts of the body so that they will function properly.

How Electrical Power Is Delivered to the House

Private or public utility companies generate power and distribute it to the local utility company, which, through a series of transformers, delivers electrical power to the home. Power enters the home through an electrical panel, which transfers the power into various ampere-sized circuit breakers (or fuses in old homes, which by code must be updated to circuit breakers). From the circuit breakers, power is transported through a wiring network to individual outlets and controls throughout the house (Figures 9-1 and 9-2). Within the line voltage of a home, low-voltage applications can be installed, although they will require properly sized transformers.

Lighting fixtures, appliances, and control systems are wired either by *line voltage*, 110/120 volt or 220/240 volt current flowing from electrical wires connected to the circuit breakers; or *low voltage*, current flowing through a wire connection from a transformer that transforms the current to 12 or 24 volts. As noted, when planning a low-voltage system, the transformer must be sized to fit the application. Most installations require more than one transformer, depending on the capacity needed.

Low-voltage systems are a safe, energy-efficient way of lighting both interior spaces and exterior areas (to highlight plants and trees and for security). When dimmer controls are installed, light levels can be finely controlled, enhancing energy efficiency.

When you are gathering project information on site, note the location of the main electrical panel and its rated amperage capacity (amps). The electrician and contractor will use this information to determine whether a larger main

Figure 9-1 Delivery of electrical power to a residence.

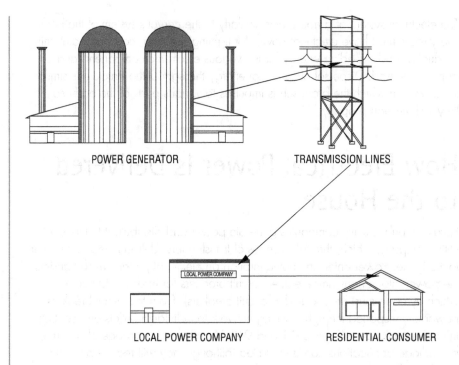

POWER GENERATOR   TRANSMISSION LINES

LOCAL POWER COMPANY   RESIDENTIAL CONSUMER

electrical panel will be needed to power the new design. Note existing appliances and their fuel/energy sources, along with their current location in the space. Lighting, vents, return air grills, and heat registers should be indicated on the plan as well. Review this information with the contractor and electrician to ensure complete compliance with all regulations.

Electrical Terms and Definitions

Voltage (volt): A measurement of the energy flowing in a wire under the influence of a force delivered to the house by the utility.

Wattage (watt): A measurement of the rate at which energy is being delivered or used.

Kilowatt (kw): One kilowatt equals one thousand watts.

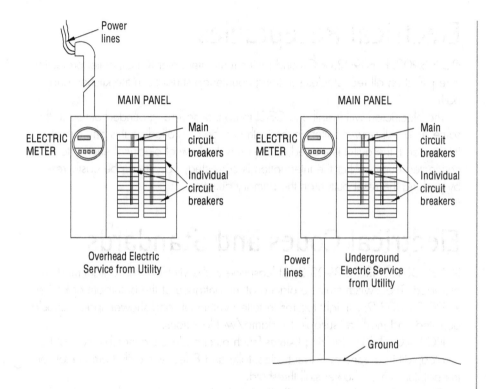

Figure 9-2 Two typical methods by which power enters a residence.

Kilowatt-hours (kwh): The energy transported by a flow of one kilowatt running for one hour.

Ampere (amps): The measurement of electric current strength.

Dedicated circuit: An electrical supply line solely for one appliance; it goes from the main electric panel directly to the appliance.

Circuit breaker: A device that will instantly interrupt the flow of current when the current exceeds the circuit capacity.

The main breaker switch on the main circuit panel is a fire safety device that can be turned off to cut power to all outlets and appliances in the entire house. Individual circuits will be tripped if overloaded by a power surge or short within that particular main circuit. This safety device can easily be reset by switching the circuit toggle switch back to the on position.

Electrical Receptacles

IRC E 3902.1, E3902.6: Ground fault circuit interrupter (GFCI) outlet protection is required on all receptacles servicing countertop surfaces in the kitchen and bath.

The electrician will install one GFCI to control several grounded outlets in the same area. All power outlets in the bath can be controlled on this one circuit interrupter. If the outlet is tripped, it interrupts the flow of electrical energy to all connected outlets. After the interruption is corrected, power can be easily reset by pushing the reset button on the primary outlet.

Electrical Codes and Standards

IRC E 4001.6, IRC E 3903.2: At least one wall-switch-controlled light must be provided. That switch must be placed at the entrance of the bathroom or kitchen.

IRC E 4003.9: All light fixtures installed within tub and shower spaces should be rated and marked "suitable for damp/wet locations."

IRC E 4003.11: Hanging fixtures [such as chandeliers over tubs] cannot be located within a zone of 3 feet horizontally and 8 feet vertically from the top of the bathtub rim or shower stall threshold.

IRC E 3901.6: At least one GFCI-protected receptacle must be installed within 36 inches of the outside edge of the sink.

IRC 3902.1: All receptacles must be protected by ground fault circuit interrupters (GFCIs).

IRC E 4001.7: Switches shall not be installed within wet locations in tub or shower spaces or within reach while standing in the tub or shower unless installed as part of the listed tub or shower assembly.

It is critical that the designer refer to local code constraints for the number of convenience outlets and the distance required between them. Most codes require 4-feet-on-center installation.

Outlets placed in backsplash locations can be installed either vertically or horizontally. Plug strips or four-plex outlets are often used in mix or baking centers where many small appliances are used. Plug towers are now available that

Figure 9-3 Countertop plug tower. (Photo courtesy of Mary Fisher Designs.com, Northlight Architectural Photography.com)

are code certified to be installed into countertops (Figure 9-3). Check with your local inspector to verify that use is approved in your location.

Careful attention must be paid to the activity at each work station throughout the kitchen so electrical requirements can be met. Most small appliances or fixtures are rated at 1650 watts or less and operate on a 15- or 20-amp circuit. Any appliance rated over 1650 watts must be controlled by a 20-amp (or higher ampere) circuit. Manufacturers' specification sheets contain a wealth of information for the designer and electrician. The appliance wattage, amperage, and location of wiring are specified in these materials (Figure 9-4). When preparing the project specification book, highlight this information so that it will be useful and accessible to all contractors working on the project.

Figure 9-4 Sample appliance specifications. (Courtesy of Sub-Zero/Wolf Photograph)

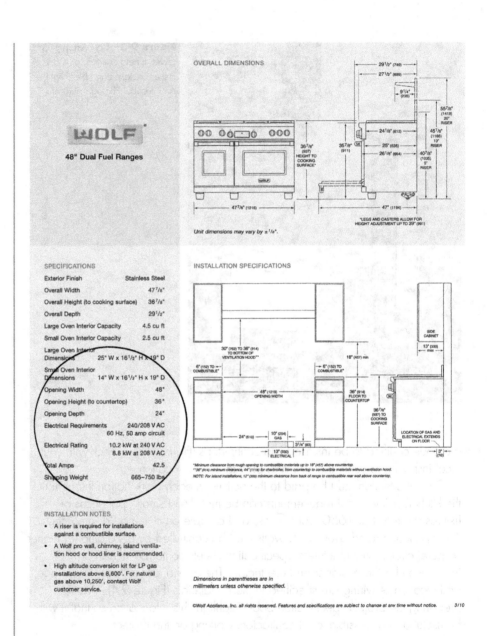

OVERALL DIMENSIONS

Unit dimensions may vary by ± ⅛".

WOLF

48" Dual Fuel Ranges

SPECIFICATIONS

Exterior Finish	Stainless Steel
Overall Width	47⅞"
Overall Height (to cooking surface)	36⅞"
Overall Depth	29½"
Large Oven Interior Capacity	4.5 cu ft
Small Oven Interior Capacity	2.5 cu ft
Large Oven Interior Dimensions	25" W x 16½" H x 19" D
Small Oven Interior Dimensions	14" W x 16½" H x 19" D
Opening Width	48"
Opening Height (to countertop)	36"
Opening Depth	24"
Electrical Requirements	240/208 V AC 60 Hz, 50 amp circuit
Electrical Rating	10.2 kW at 240 V AC 8.8 kW at 208 V AC
Total Amps	42.5
Shipping Weight	665–750 lbs

INSTALLATION NOTES

- A riser is required for installations against a combustible surface.
- A Wolf pro wall, chimney, island ventilation hood or hood liner is recommended.
- High altitude conversion kit for LP gas installations above 8,600'. For natural gas above 10,250', contact Wolf customer service.

INSTALLATION SPECIFICATIONS

*Minimum clearance from rough opening to combustible materials up to 18" (457) above countertop.
**36" (914) minimum clearance, 44" (1118) for charbroiler, from countertop to combustible materials without ventilation hood.
NOTE: For island installations, 12" (305) minimum clearance from back of range to combustible rear wall above countertop.

Dimensions in parentheses are in millimeters unless otherwise specified.

In addition to traditional wiring in the kitchen and bath, low-voltage applications, WiFi systems, and cable bundles for television, security, and audio/visual systems are frequently utilized. Wireless remote controls and air switches are options that may be used for specific installations.

Electronic toilet-bidets and bidet seats that come separate from the toilet require electrical power for operation. A GFCI should be located on the plug side of the toilet to facilitate concise installation. The seat has a cord and plug that may hang down and be unsightly. Remote controls for operation of the bidet seat should also be planned.

Lighting Systems

General or ambient light, task light, accent light, and decorative light all play important parts in the effective and efficient design of the lighting systems for kitchens and baths.

IRC E 4001.6: At least one wall-switch-controlled light must be provided in the kitchen and bath. Switch must be placed at the entrance.

Health and safety issues regarding the kitchen and bath are prominent in the design of an efficient lighting plan. The goal of design is to specify various light sources and applications to make a space safe for occupants and create a comfortable atmosphere. Creating lighting "scenes" within a kitchen and bath should be the goal of the kitchen and bath designer. Flexible light levels for each application in the space will provide control for various tasks. Working with a lighting consultant on large projects can be very beneficial.

Planning an effective lighting system for a kitchen or bath is an exercise in problem solving and layering. It is critical to:

- Identify tasks to be performed.
- Plan safe conditions.
- Plan for occupants' ergonomic traits.
- Create visual interest with decorative applications.

All effective lighting systems consist of different layers of light. Each layer should be controlled separately.

Two additional factors can modify these layers and must be considered:

1. An understanding of the relationship of natural light to artificial lighting
2. Effective dimmer controls on each system

Three basic layers make up a well-planned lighting system.

LAYER 1

General or ambient lighting is initially switched on when someone enters the room. This is accomplished with structural and surface-mounted fixtures for safe entry into the room and is switched at one or more locations within the space (Figure 9-5).

Figure 9-5 (Photo courtesy of Sub-Zero/Wolf Photograph)

Architectural or *indirect* lighting systems are those built into the structural elements of the room, such as coves and hidden light boxes, which function as the general light system. All light systems must work together, sometimes at different levels, to be effective. A good lighting design allows for the mix of natural and artificial light during the day and flexibility in light levels at night.

Structural fixtures consist of built-in recessed and indirect light sources.

Surface-mounted fixtures are installed with a j-box in the ceiling or wall (Figure 9-6).

Recessed downlights are currently the most often used source of general lighting in residential spaces because of their architectural appeal and even light distribution. Although one downlight may be all that is needed in a shower stall, pathways require multiple downlights to evenly light the floors without shadows. Kitchens and baths require twice the level of light of a bedroom or living room.

Figure 9-6   Chandeliers, ceiling lights, sconces, and track lighting systems are examples of surface-mounted fixtures. (Photo courtesy of Mary Fisher Designs.com, Northlight Architectural Photography.com)

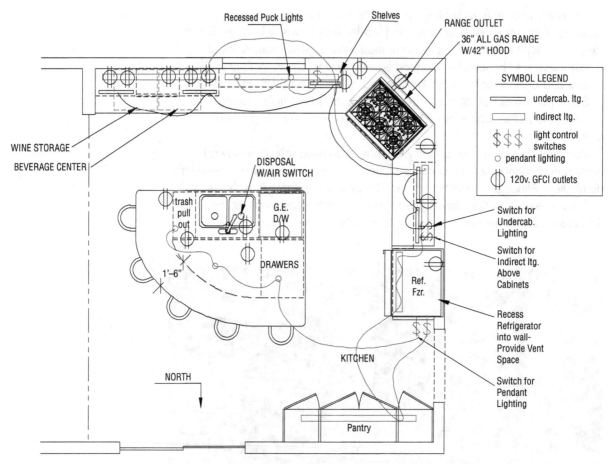

Figure 9-7 Electrical layout for a kitchen.

Up to 50 foot-candles per square foot is typically calculated for kitchens and bathrooms (Figure 9-7). (See the definition of *foot-candle* in the "Lighting Terms" section.)

A number of factors affect the placement of downlights. The length, width, and height of the space to be illuminated determine the quantity and wattage of the downlights used. To obtain uniform lighting in a room using flood lamps, a rule of thumb is that each downlight may cover an area up to four times its mounting height.

For example: In a 10-foot ceiling, a single downlight should illuminate 40 square feet of space on the floor (5 feet by 8 feet). Calculating the dimensions of the room will allow you to determine the number of lights needed and to create a lighting plan consisting of symmetrical rows and columns of downlights that will provide the proper uniformity. It is acceptable to let your planned light patterns overlap to eliminate unlit areas.

LAYER 2

Task lighting delivers high levels of light in specific areas where work is done. It is accomplished with structural and surface-mounted fixtures. Downlights should be oriented directly over the work area in front of the person. When downlights are installed above or behind the person, undesirable shadows are cast on the person and over the work space (Figure 9-8).

Certain ergonomic considerations must be planned into the design. Older eyes need a stronger level of light than younger eyes. The goal is to eliminate

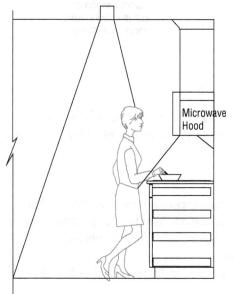

Figure 9-8 Overhead lighting can cast a shadow; undercabinet light will illuminate the task area.

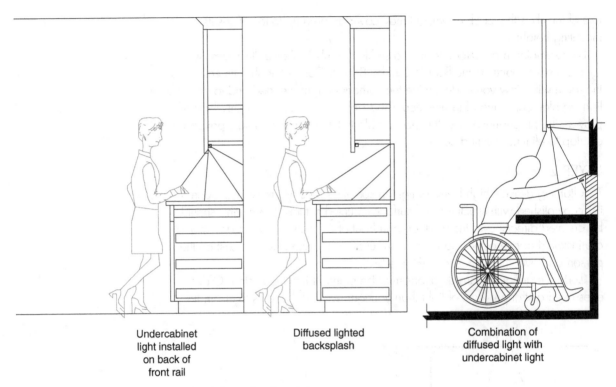

| Undercabinet light installed on back of front rail | Diffused lighted backsplash | Combination of diffused light with undercabinet light |

Figure 9-9 Undercabinet lighting options.

glare and reflections on glossy or metallic surfaces and to place fixtures so they eliminate shadows. Plan for the proper placement of undercabinet lighting so that it is even and nonglaring (Figure 9-9).

LAYER 3

Accent and decorative lighting brings focus to specific items and areas in the room. It can highlight textures within the space and add the visual interest that pulls a room together (Figure 9-10). *Task lighting* provides the light levels necessary for work stations in the space.

As a general rule, downlights should be placed 18 to 36 inches from the wall and spaced equally along the wall.

Figure 9-10 Wall-washing fixtures add visual interest as they illuminate a textured wall. (Photo courtesy of David Dalton, Inc., Los Angeles, CA 90019; www. daviddaltoninc.com)

Modification of perceived light and energy use can be realized by careful planning.

MODIFIER 1

Natural light is one of the best ways to conserve energy. By incorporating larger windows, skylights, clerestory windows, and cupolas into the design, you ensure that the kitchen or bathroom will be efficiently lighted during daylight hours. When natural light sources are considered early in the space planning process, artificial light can be planned to supplement lower light levels on overcast or stormy days without additional fixtures. Geographic orientation and exposure (north, south, east, or west) must be considered. Seasonal variations in the geographic direction of light will influence the quality and amount of received light, as well as affect the perception of the color of light. Southern and western exposures tend to cast warmer light, while eastern and northern exposures tend to shed cooler light.

By designing layers of light on separate dimmer controls, efficient levels of light can be utilized. For example, on a cloudy day, undercabinet lighting may be the only artificial light necessary to make the work space functional. When the various layers of light are on dimmer controls, the correct amount of light can be adjusted for maximum efficiency.

Lighting engineers state that the intensity of light near a window can range from 100 to 5,000 foot-candles, depending on the orientation of the window, time of year, and latitude. These three factors also affect color designed in the space, which is why you must examine colors and finishes in the room that you are designing at different times of the day/night.

On a sunny day, unobstructed sunlight has an intensity of approximately 10,000 foot-candles. On an overcast day, that same point of measurement may indicate an intensity of only around 1,000 foot-candles.

The direction of natural light entering the room at various times of the day and during different seasons of the year will affect glare and light reflection off surfaces and metals. For this reason, you must plan window and glass door treatments that control the light streaming in. Effective lighting systems are designed primarily to light a space at night.

MODIFIER 2

Dimmer controls installed for each layer of light provide an energy-efficient way to set the stage of a space. Adjustability of light levels creates various "scenes" within the space, allowing for intense levels at work spaces and lower intensity, where and when ambient light is preferred.

Lighting Terms and Definitions

To learn what fixture (*luminaire*) to specify for each application and what light levels and quality of light fixtures deliver, we need to know the terminology of the industry.

Lumen: A unit of measurement of the amount of light produced by a lamp. Lumen is the metric equivalent of foot-candle and should be the means of measuring needed light levels. As a reference, a 100-watt incandescent lamp emits about 1,600 lumens.

Luminaire: A source of light; a fixture.

Ballast: A piece of equipment required to control the starting and operating voltages of fluorescent, neon, and high-intensity-discharge (HID) lights. The modern type of lighting ballast is electronic with solid-state circuitry instead of electromagnetic; an electronic ballast greatly reduces or eliminates any flicker in the lamps.

Foot-candle: The measurement of the brightness of light given off by one candle 12 inches to one square foot of surface or object; a unit of measurement used to calculate lighting levels for work spaces. One foot-candle equals one lumen per square foot of surface.

For most kitchens and bathrooms, 35–50 foot-candles of illumination is sufficient. For detailed work, 200 foot-candles of illumination or more provides more accuracy and less eyestrain.

Lamp: Replacement term for *light bulb*.

Kelvin: Scale of perceived color produced by a light source. 2,700–3,000K are warm tones; 3,600–6,500K and higher are cooler tones. A color temperature of 2,700–3,000K is generally recommended for most indoor general and task-lighting applications.

Beam spread: The spread of the beam of light as it broadcasts to the surface or object.

Correlated color temperature (CCT): The color of the light source. By convention, yellow-red colors are considered warm and blue-green colors are considered cool. Color temperature is measured in Kelvins (K). High Kelvin temperatures (3,600–5,500K) are considered cool and lower color temperatures (2,700–3,000K) are considered warm.

Color Rendition (Rated) Index (CRI): How colors appear when illuminated by a light source is referred to as *color rendition*. It is considered a more important lighting quality than color temperature. Most objects are not a single color, but a combination of many colors. Light sources that are deficient in certain colors may change the apparent color of an object. The CRI is a 1–100 scale that measures the ability of a light source to render colors the same way sunlight does. The top value of the CRI scale (100) is based on illumination by a 100-watt incandescent lamp. A light source with a CRI of 80 or higher is considered acceptable for most indoor residential applications (Figure 9-11).

Figure 9-11 Light sources affect how colors appear in a space. (Photo courtesy of David Dalton, Inc., Los Angeles, CA 90019; www.daviddaltoninc.com)

Controls/Switches

You will have to carefully select and then locate the controls for each light system on your electrical plan. Sufficient wall space must be allowed, particularly for switches controlling the general light of the room. Local and state codes will influence the light source that must be switched when you first enter the room. If you are designing a remodeled space, you will want to incorporate existing switches whenever possible. New construction gives you a blank canvas on which to work.

Switches controlling the light as you enter a room are often three-way or four-way switches. This switch allows you to control lights from different locations. If a tall cabinet is located next to an entry door, a minimum of 8 inches of wall space from the opening of the door to the side of the cabinet must be planned to enable the j-box of the light switch to be installed. It may be necessary to locate the switch on the side of the cabinet next to the door.

DIMMER CONTROLS

Dimmer controls provide variable levels of light for incandescent and fluorescent lamps. When you dim lamps, it reduces their wattage and output, which helps save energy.

Off-the-shelf dimmers for incandescent fixtures are inexpensive and provide some energy savings when lights are used at a reduced level. Dimmers also increase the life of incandescent lamps significantly. Dimming reduces their lumen output more than their wattage.

Dimming fluorescent lamps requires special dimming ballasts and lamp holders, but does not reduce their efficiency. Fluorescent dimmers are dedicated fixtures and lamps that provide even greater energy savings than a regular fluorescent lamp (Figure 9-12).

MOTION SENSORS

Motion sensors detect activity within a certain area. They provide convenience by turning lights on automatically when someone enters a room. They reduce lighting energy use by turning lights off soon after the last occupant has left the room.

Sensors should be located where they will detect activity in all parts of the room. There are two types of motion sensors: ultrasonic and infrared. Ultrasonic sensors detect sound, whereas infrared sensors detect heat and motion. Pet traffic patterns should be considered where motion sensors are employed.

WIRELESS CONTROLS

Wireless system controls operate by radio frequency. Entire-room and whole-house lighting scenes can be created and recalled with the touch of a control pad. With open-plan kitchens and spa-type baths, the wireless, remote control systems are very desirable.

Figure 9-12 All lighting systems should be on dimmer controls. (Photo courtesy of NY LOFT, Phoenix, AZ)

LOW-VOLTAGE CONTROLS

Low-voltage systems operate on 12 or 24 volts of power. All low-voltage lighting fixtures require a transformer to reduce line voltage (120 v) to 12 or 24 volts so it can be safely run through a fixture.

LINE-VOLTAGE SYSTEMS

Line-voltage systems operate on 120 volts of power. Lighting fixtures in these systems are wired directly to the line voltage of the house.

TRANSFORMERS

Low-voltage transformers consist of electronic and magnetic versions, typically ranging from 60 watts to 1,000 watts. Transformers must be specified based on the total wattage used by the low-voltage lamps. For example, if an undercabinet lighting application requires 150 watts of power, a transformer rated at 150 watts should be selected. A large-capacity-rated transformer can handle several lighting systems, eliminating the need for several smaller ones.

The new UL 2108 standard devoted specifically to low-voltage lighting systems requires that the transformers used in low-voltage systems be sensitive enough to detect a short circuit several lamps away from the origin and prevent potential harm from heat or fire damage.

Light Sources

Lighting design is both an art and a science. Making informed decisions as they relate to the function and appearance of the space is the designer's responsibility. When you are mixing light sources, give careful consideration to color rating and the Kelvin temperature (color of light from each source). Incandescent, fluorescent, and LED light sources should be close in Kelvin temperature when they are being mixed within the same space.

The source you select will be influenced by several factors, including the purpose of the light, the items to be lit, the decorative style of the space being lit, and the state and local codes governing your project. Location of transformers is an important consideration during the design phase.

INCANDESCENT

The oldest and most common lighting product is the incandescent lamp. It accounts for about 85 percent of indoor home lighting. Incandescent lamps emit

Figure 9-13 Several light sources are available to the designer to establish a lighting system that provides ambient, task, and decorative light. (Photo courtesy of David Dalton, Inc., Los Angeles, CA 90019; www. daviddaltoninc.com)

light when electricity flows through and heats a metal tungsten filament. Incandescent lamps are popular because of their low cost, warm light, and excellent color rendition. They light up instantly and can be used with a dimmer switch. When compared to other lighting sources, they have a short life, generate more heat, and produce less light per watt of energy.

HALOGEN

Halogen light bulbs are hot to the touch and should be positioned so that inadvertent touching does not occur. There is an increase in ambient temperature when halogen lights are used as recessed or undercabinet applications. Interior cabinet space can feel warm when the undercabinet or cabinet interior lights are on. The light output is excellent and can be controlled by a dimmer.

XENON

Xenon light bulbs contain xenon gas that has been introduced into the glass envelope. Because of their small size, xenon bulbs resemble halogen bulbs but are much cooler to the touch than halogen. The light output is excellent and can be controlled by a dimmer.

Xenon is available in line-voltage and low-voltage systems. You must match your dimmer control with the type of system you specify.

FLUORESCENT

Fluorescent lamps produce light when an electric current passes through mercury and inert gases contained within a tube or coil. They require a ballast to regulate the current and provide the high-voltage pulse needed for startup. The use of electronic ballasts to replace standard and electromagnetic ballasts has increased the energy efficiency and eliminated the flicker and noise of this type of lighting. Fluorescent lamps use 25 to 30 percent less energy than incandescent lamps to provide the same amount of illumination. Fluorescent lamps also last about 10 times longer than incandescent lamps. These benefits, along with improvements in the color rendition and temperature of fluorescent lamps, have expanded the applications for this type of lighting. Fluorescent lamps are most efficient when they stay on for longer periods of time. Turning them on and off makes them less efficient and shortens their life span.

COMPACT FLUORESCENT LAMPS

Compact fluorescent lamps (CFLs) combine the energy efficiency of fluorescent lamps with the convenience and popularity of incandescent lamps. CFLs can replace incandescent lamps. Although CFLs can cost several times as much as incandescent lamps, they last 6 to 15 times longer. This longer life, combined with significantly lower energy use, more than offsets the higher initial price of CFLs. These lamps work much like a standard fluorescent and contain a ballast and gas-filled tube. They are designed to screw into a lighting fixture just like standard incandescent lamps. CFLs are especially beneficial in areas where lights are left on for long periods of time. For the best results, you should select high-quality fixtures from reliable manufacturers. Poor quality leads to poor performance.

Turning fluorescent lamps on and off frequently lessens their life. They must start up each time they are turned on.

SOLID-STATE LIGHTING

According to the U.S. Department of Energy, the next frontier of lighting technology is solid-state lighting (SSL), utilizing light-emitting diodes (LEDs) or organic light-emitting diodes (OLEDs).

Light-Emitting Diodes

LEDs have been used to light the controls of appliances for years. Today, task and accent lighting in kitchens and bathrooms are some of the sensible choices for LED products. The development and refinement of LED fixtures has been astounding. Designers prefer this light source for its color temperature, long life, and energy efficiency. The small size, lack of infrared heat, and longevity of these fixtures make them a good source for these applications. The cost of these products continues to come down and the great benefit of energy savings makes LEDs a positive choice in the long run. In addition to planning space for the transformer, it is necessary to include the controller as well. The size of these parts varies with the model selected and manufacturer.

As with CFLs, for the best results, select high-quality fixtures from reliable manufacturers. Poor quality leads to poor performance.

LAMP CHARACTERISTIC

LIGHTING TYPE	EFFICACY: LUMENS/WATTS	LIFETIME (HOURS)	KELVIN COLOR TEMPERATURE	CRI
INCANDESCENT				
Standard bulb	10–12	750–2,500	2,700–2,800	98–100; excellent
Halogen	12–22	2,000–4,000	2,900–3,200	98–100; excellent
Xenon	12–22	2,100–4,000	3,500–4,300	98–100; excellent
Reflector lamp	12–19	2,000–3,000	2,800	98–100; excellent
FLUORESCENT				
Straight tube	30–110	7,000–24,000	2,700–6,500	Fair to good
Compact fluorescent (CFL)	50–70	10,000	2,700–6,500	Fair to good
SOLID-STATE				
LED white	10–12	50,000	2,500–3,500	85–100; good

How to Calculate Light Levels

Calculation of light levels for general and task lighting should be done with lumen or foot-candle measurements. Do not use watts when calculating the light output of your design. Watts represents how much power is being used, not how much light is being generated. For example, according to the U.S. Department of Energy, it takes 100 watts for an incandescent bulb to generate about 1,600 lumens, but it only takes between 23 and 30 watts for a compact fluorescent bulb to generate the same amount of light.

Although 7.5 lumens per square foot might be sufficient for a hallway, you would want 35 lumens per square foot for a kitchen. Proper light levels for each application in the space are crucial. Working with a lighting consultant on large projects can be very beneficial.

Mechanical Applications

10

The correct size and location of mechanical systems will make any kitchen or bathroom comfortable and safe.

Ventilation

Homes today are being built with more attention to air leakage, and to insulation that counterbalances leakage and increases the comfort for occupants. The effort to decrease energy consumption correlates with the need to manage indoor air quality (IAQ) effectively through careful selection of finish materials and the proper use of mechanical ventilation.

Advanced products make it possible to control air quality in every area of the home. Whether the need is to exhaust moisture from bathrooms or cooking odors from kitchens, or to improve overall air quality throughout the entire dwelling, quiet, energy-efficient solutions are readily available. Appropriately designed, installed, and maintained ventilation systems yield positive benefits of better health and better-built houses.

Cooking results in moist air laden with oils from food, odors, and the byproducts of the combustion of gas burners.

During a bath or shower, the humidity level in a bathroom can be as high as in a tropical rain forest. This environment is uncomfortable, hot, and damaging, and is also a perfect breeding ground for mold, mildew, and microorganisms that can affect occupants' health.

Kitchen Ventilation

Overhead and downdraft ventilation systems are typically used in kitchens. Because heated air naturally rises, overhead ventilation is the preferred system for exhausting cooking byproducts. Most professional-style range tops *must* be vented by an overhead system, as mandated by the manufacturers' installation guidelines (Figure 10-1).

In designs calling for open space above the cooking surface, downdraft vents present an alternative for cooktops (Figure 10-2).

Effective downdraft ventilation runs front to back, parallel to the cooking surface. Many manufacturers offer a downdraft system located at the back of the

Figure 10-1 Custom hood liner vents professional style range. (Photo courtesy of Mary Fisher Designs.com, Northlight Architectural Photography.com)

Figure 10-2 A unique overhead vent. (Photo courtesy of BSH Home Appliances Corporation, Gaggenau brand)

cooktop, which allows more base cabinet space below for storage. When in the raised position, the vent must be tall enough to capture and exhaust the steam and byproducts of cooking (Figure 10-3).

IRC guidelines establish minimum requirements for ventilation.

Figure 10-3 A counter-mounted downdraft system. (Photo courtesy of BSH Home Appliances Corporation, Gaggenau brand)

IRC-M1503.1 - Range hoods are to vent to the outside through a single duct. The duct must have a smooth interior, be airtight, and have a backdraft damper. These ducts MUST NOT terminate in an attic, crawl space or other areas in the house. Ductless hoods from manufacturers are the exception.

IRC-M1503.2 - The duct must be made of a single-wall galvanized steel, stainless steel, or copper. **Exception:** Ducts for downdraft exhaust systems are permitted to be constructed of 40 PVC pipe and fittings provided the installation complies with the following:

1. The duct is installed under a concrete slab poured on grade.
2. The trench in which the duct is installed is completely backfilled with sand or gravel.
3. The PVC duct extends no more than one inch above the indoor concrete floor surface.
4. The PVC duct extends no more than one inch above grade outside of the building.
5. The PVC ducts are not solvent cemented.

. IRC M 1507.3 - The required exhaust rate for a ducted hood is a minimum 100 cfm and must be ducted to the outside.

Source: International Residential Code 2009

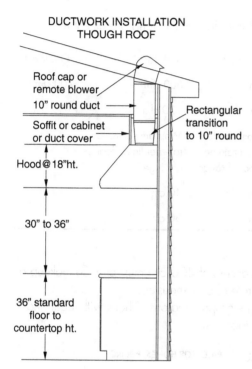

DUCTWORK INSTALLATION
THOUGH ROOF

Roof cap or
remote blower
10" round duct
Soffit or cabinet
or duct cover
Rectangular
transition
to 10" round
Hood @ 18"ht.
30" to 36"
36" standard
floor to
countertop ht.

Figure 10-4 Typical overhead kitchen hood arrangement.

The most efficient method of ducting a hood is to go straight up through the roof (Figure 10-4). However, if ductwork must be directed around a structural member in the attic, a 45° transition duct should be used. When 90° bends in the duct occur, deduct 25 feet from the lineal duct-run calculation.

Most kitchen hoods installed against the wall will be sized between 350 cfm and 600 cfm. This is based on the type of cooking appliance being vented and its width. Island hoods are typically sized at 900 cfm to 1,500 cfm based on equipment type and size being vented. These calculations are based on industry recommendations of 100 cfm per lineal foot width of the cooking surface for wall installations and 150 cfm per lineal foot of cooking surface for island or peninsula installations. An added factor influencing the size of the overhead ventilation system is its exposure to traffic flow and outside air exposure. The more air that circulates where island or peninsula cooking is done, the more powerful the blower must be and the greater the capture space of the canopy must be.

The Home Ventilating Institute guidelines for kitchen vents are as follows.

WIDTH OF HOOD AGAINST WALL	2-1/2 ft (30")	3 FT. (36")	4 FT. (48")
HVI RECOMMENDED RATE	250 cfm	300 cfm	400 cfm
MINIMUM	100 cfm	120 cfm	160 cfm
LOCATION OF RANGE	HVI recommended ventilation rate per linear foot of range	Minimum ventilation rate per linear foot of range	
AGAINST WALL	100 cfm	40 cfm	
IN AN ISLAND	150 cfm	50 cfm	

MAKEUP AIR

IRC M1503.4: Hoods exhausting in excess of 400 cfm must provide makeup air at a rate approximately equal to the rate of air exhausted.

Makeup air requirements vary in geographic regions. Check with local and state codes applicable to the project location.

MINIMUM MECHANICAL EXHAUST	RATES FOR HOMES, PER IRC
Vented space	Ventilation Rates
Kitchens	100 cfm (intermittent use)
	25 cfm (continuous use)
Bathrooms	50 cfm (intermittent use)
	20 cfm (continuous use)
Toilet Rooms	Same as bathrooms

Bathrooms

The correct air movement capacity is an important consideration in any bath. Air movement is typically measured in cubic feet per minute (cfm). Ventilation rates based upon eight air changes per hour are generally suggested.

For most bathrooms, this is one cfm per square foot of bathroom area. For example, a 7-foot by 10-foot bathroom would require a 70 cfm fan. A 50 cfm rating is the recommended minimum for bathrooms 50 square feet (sq ft) and smaller. Larger bathrooms require additional ventilation capacity. The following chart can be used as a guide for proper bathroom ventilation.

BATHROOM SIZE	MINIMUM VENTILATION (CFM) REQUIRED
Less than 50 sq ft	50 cfm
50–100 sq ft	1 cfm per sq ft of floor space
More than 100 sq ft	Add the cfm requirement for each fixture:
	Toilet: 50 cfm
	Shower: 50 cfm
	Bathtub: 50 cfm
	Jetted tub: 50 cfm

Note: These rates represent a minimum requirement. High ventilation rates are also acceptable and will have a minimum energy impact. *Source:* Home Ventilating Institute

IRC R 303.3, IRC M 1506.3: Minimum ventilation for the bathroom is to be a window of at least 3 square feet of which 50 percent is operable, or a mechanical ventilation system of at least 50 cubic feet per minute ducted to the outside.

Other considerations for ventilation:

- An enclosed toilet should have its own exhaust fan.
- Fans approved for installation in wet areas should be located over (near) the shower or tub whenever possible.
- Bathroom doors should have at least 3/4-inch clearance to the floor to allow for proper entry of makeup air.
- Bathrooms with ceilings higher than 8 feet may require additional ventilation.

Heating

Heating and air conditioning of kitchens and bathrooms may be done by a central heat-pump source or from individual sources in the space. You must include the location of heat/AC registers, as well as air returns, in a kitchen or bath design plan.

Radiant heated floors are an often-used feature in bathroom design. Two types of systems are used: electric or hydronic (circulated hot water). Certain considerations arise when you are planning this system:

- What type of finished floor material is planned? (Not all materials are compatible with radiant floor heat.)
- How will the transition from the heated floor space to the adjacent floor space be made? (Installation of a radiant heat system will add height to the floor.)

Radiant heat lamps are recessed into the ceiling and may be part of the ventilation system. Locating a radiant heat lamp near where one exits the shower or tub provides warmth to the body while drying off. Circulating heated air may still be part of the total heating system.

Convection ceiling heaters provide warm air from above. Because the air is moving, it will cause a slight cooling effect on a wet body.

Radiant wall heaters are typically installed in the lower area of the wall. They are not the best solution to heating the space.

Baseboard heaters can provide general heating of the space.

Toe-kick heaters are a popular heat source and are often used when the heat/AC register is in the ceiling to keep feet and legs warm at the vanity. This application can also be located in kitchen toe kicks.

IRC R 303.8: All bathrooms should have an appropriate heat source to maintain a minimum room temperature of 68°F.

Water Heating

Heating water accounts for approximately 15 percent of a home's energy use. High-efficiency water heaters use 10–50 percent less energy than standard models. Actual energy savings from high-efficiency water heaters depend on family size, heater location, and the size and placement of water pipes.

- **Storage (tank) water heaters** keep water hot and ready for use at all times in insulated storage tanks with capacities ranging from 20 to 80 gallons. Many fuel options are available, including electricity, natural gas, oil, and propane. One drawback of these units is that energy is used to keep the water hot at all times; this use is known as "standby losses."

- **Demand (tankless) water heaters** circulate water through a large coil that is heated only on demand using gas or electricity; there is no storage tank continuously maintaining hot water. A possible concern with this technology is the limitation on the number of fixtures that can simultaneously use hot water. However, there is an endless supply of hot water and standby losses are eliminated.

- **Heat-pump water heaters** transfer energy from the surrounding air to water in the storage tank. These water heaters are much more efficient than electric resistance water heaters and most effective in warm climates with long cooling seasons.

- **Solar water heating** can be cost-effective even though the initial purchase price of solar water heaters is high compared to standard models. This is because the sun's energy is harnessed to reduce operating costs up to 90 percent. Solar water-heating systems require a conventional water heater as a backup hot-water source to ensure that hot water is available when solar energy is not adequate. (*Source:* U.S. Environmental Protection Agency)

Sound

Noise level is a consideration when selecting kitchen or bathroom ventilation and appliances.

Sound Control

Sound emissions are measured in sones and decibels.

Sone: A unit of loudness; perceived sound.

Figure 10-5 Many models of high-efficiency water heaters have the EnergyStar® Seal. These should be considered whenever possible. (Courtesy of Judy Svendsen, Raven Interiors, Mary Fisher Designs.com, Photo courtesy of Don Milici Photography)

Decibel (dB): Measurement of the power or intensity of sound. The decibel level ranges from the weakest (0 dB) to the loudest sound possible (194 dB). Most of the sounds we perceive fall in the quiet to loud range.

Decibel Levels

ENVIRONMENTAL NOISE	DECIBEL LEVEL
Weakest sound heard	0 dB
Whisper in quiet library	30 dB
Normal conversation	60–70 dB
Telephone dial tone	80 dB
City traffic (from inside car)	85 dB
Train whistle @ 500 feet/Truck traffic	90 dB
Subway train @ 200 feet	96 dB
Level at which sustained exposure causes hearing loss	90–95 dB
Snowmobile or motorcycle	100 dB
Power mower @ 3 feet	107 dB
Power saw @ 3 feet	110 dB
Loud rock concert	115 dB
Pain begins	125 dB

Source: Galen Carol Audio, San Antonio, Texas

Sounds move within the home either directly or indirectly. Within the home, the layout of rooms and shape of the spaces will act either as a conduit to echo sound throughout or as an absorbent of sound as it moves within the house. Shiny, smooth, hard surfaces reflect sound waves, whereas matte, uneven, porous, softer surfaces absorb sound waves.

With the popularity of the open-space concept in residential design, knowing how to manipulate and minimize sound travel is important. It is extremely important in kitchen and bath design. To isolate sound emissions and treat them effectively, we must be able to identify their source.

Sound Emission Sources

Sound Sources Common to Kitchens and Baths

SOURCE	SOLUTION
Activities in daily living	Sound-absorbing finishes
Ventilation systems	Variable-speed motors, in-line blowers, rubber mounts on remote blowers
Undersized ducts	Size ducts per manufacturer's specification; most noise may be caused by air pressure and movement in undersized ducts
Water flow in drains	Insulate pipes with foam
Water flow in pipes	Insulate pipes with sound-absorbing sleeves
Hard surfaces	Combine with sound-absorbing material
Plumbing fixtures	Install correctly
Equipment vibrations	Use rubber feet or mats when appropriate (but do not impede required air circulation)

Kitchens

Major appliances	Purchase insulated models
Small appliances	Use on a sound-absorbing material
Cooking utensils and cookware	Do not nest when storing
Food preparation techniques	No suggestions; it's inherently noisy
Cabinetry	Self-closing hinges and slides
Partitioned storage	Door and drawer bumpers
Drawer organizers	Drawers with varied inserts (wire grids, wood); storage systems

Bathrooms

Grooming and bathing activities	Personal discipline
Grooming appliances	Store and use in separate space
Personal hygiene	Separate sound-insulated toilet room

Sound insulation techniques and materials common to kitchens and baths:

Sound or noise-stop board

Sound-absorbing surfaces

Foam warps

Quiet-Rock drywall

Insulation

Rougher wood textures

New "eco-conscious" sprayed foam insulation

Cork

Sound-absorbing floor covering

Fabric window treatments

Wrap water and drain pipes

Various shapes within rectangular or square shape space

Sound-absorbing material on walls and floors where applicable

Bathrooms

Bathroom fan sound levels are measured in *sones*: 4.0 sones is the sound
of standard television operation; 3.0 sones is typical office noise; 1.0 sone
is the sound of a refrigerator; and 0.5 sones is the sound of rustling
leaves. For quiet bathroom ventilation, the fan should be rated at 1.0 sones
or less.

Because bathrooms typically have a majority of hard surfaces, which reflect
sound, minimizing that transmission of sound must always be planned.

Construction methods and materials:

Wall, ceiling, and floor insulation

Noise-stop or sound boards on common walls along with insulation

Sound-absorbing underlayment in floors of bathrooms over living spaces

Insulate water pipes and drain pipes

Enclose toilet in a separate room

Plan a ventilation system with the lowest sound level possible (1.0 sones or less)

Insulate ducts with wrap (can help lessen the noise of moving air)

Properly sized ducts

Properly sized valves and faucets

A variety of finish materials, with a balance of soft and hard

Ample space for towels

A radiant heated floor

Because sound travels through air leaks, such as cracks around outlets and switch boxes, foaming around them or using a sound-wrap material will help lessen the transmission of sound.

Surfaces

11

Color, texture, mass, and form all play important parts in the selection of finish materials for the kitchen and bath interior. Skillfully selected materials and finishes contribute to the practical and visual elements of the design.

Natural Stone

Stone tiles, tumbled tiles, of varied shapes and sizes, permit flexibility in design and pattern. Typically, natural stone slabs are fabricated and tailored to meet design requirements.

Because stone is a natural substance, color varies. Stone slabs should be viewed and approved by the client prior to purchase and installation.

Stone is harvested from the earth, so color and pattern will vary as the cutting goes farther back into the mountain. For this reason, slabs and tile coming from the same quarry at different times or in different shipments can vary greatly in color and pattern, even though they are called by the same name. Most slabs ship from the quarry "book-matched." This is particularly important when covering large surfaces such as islands with stone (Figure 11-1).

How the stone was cut in the quarry also affects the look of the stone. A particular stone cut cross-grain looks completely different from the same stone cut going with the grain. The look of the stone changes as the pattern and concentration of color vary.

Overall slab sizes vary according to the composition of the stone. This will determine the number of slabs needed for a project. For that reason, the fabricators should inspect the stone prior to purchase. As they check it for quality, they can recognize any limitations that may influence fabrication. Slabs typically are 3/4 inch (2 cm) or 1-1/4 inches (3 cm) thick. Edge details thicker than 2 or 3 cm are buildups of material and will be discussed later.

Because of the composition of particulates in the stone, some slabs may have a net backing. This helps stabilize the stone slab and should be a cue to the designer to make sure the slab will not be prone to cracking. Do this by working closely with the stone fabricator, and make sure that the desired cutouts and edge details in the stone are possible. For example, sink cutouts typically require 2-1/2 to 3 inches of space from the front edge of the sink to the outside edge of the counter.

Figure 11-1 Book-matched slabs make it easier for fabricators to hide seams. (Courtesy of Cactus Stone, Cactusstone.com)

"MAXIMUS"

CACTUS
STONE

Types of Stone

Granite is a visibly granular, igneous rock ranging in color from nearly white to absolute black and every color in between. The stone consists primarily of quartz, mica, and feldspar, a group of minerals that have similar characteristics. It is the hardest architectural stone, ideally suited for countertops and high-traffic areas. It is imported from quarries located around the world, either polished or honed, in slabs or tiles. The stone fabricator will seal the stone after installation, although the polishing at the quarry begins the process.

Marble is a metamorphic rock possessing a distinctive crystalline texture. Composed principally of carbonate minerals, calcite and dolomite, marble is more porous than granite. It displays distinctive veining and has a wide range of colors. When using marble as a counter surface, it is important to make the client aware of its susceptibility to acid etching and the need to seal the stone frequently. In kitchens, etching occurs when wine, citrus, or food acids are allowed to sit on the stone surface for a period of time. When marble is etched or stained, the surface can usually be reconditioned by a specialist and brought back to its original luster.

Limestone is a sedimentary rock composed primarily of calcium carbonate, dolomite, and magnesium. More porous than marble and granite, it is susceptible to acids and will etch. A penetrating sealer should always be used on limestone.

Travertine is a crystalline limestone with a distinctive layered structure. Pores and cavities appear in some of the layers. These pores and cavities can be left open or filled in with a grout compound. Travertine, which is available in warm earth tones, is one of the most popular stones for interior and exterior flooring.

Onyx, a semiprecious stone, is a sedimentary rock with extremely fine crystal formation. It is translucent and can be backlit for dramatic effect. Cost may be a consideration when planning a design with onyx, as it is quite expensive (Figure 11-2).

Quartzite is a member of the sandstone group. It contains a minimum of 95 percent free silica. Quartzite is similar in appearance to slate but is actually harder and denser.

Figure 11-2 Onyx countertop in powder room is lighted from below. (Courtesy of Mary Fisher Designs.com, Northlight Architectural Photography)

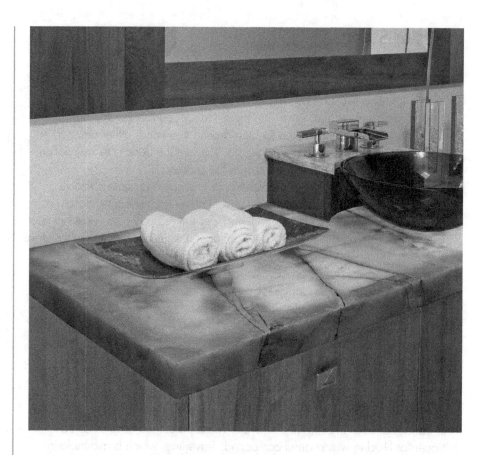

    Sandstone is a very porous sedimentary rock that is considered a soft stone. It is typically used as a floor covering.

    Flagstone is a form of sandstone. It is very porous and is often used as a floor covering, especially in warmer climates where the outdoor living-space floor continues into the adjacent interior space.

    Slate is commonly derived from shale. It is typically composed of mica, chlorite, and quartz. Some slates are harder than others, depending on their geographic origin.

    Shell stone is a sedimentary stone composed of fossils and shells embedded in a mineral body. It is a soft, porous stone that retains less heat than denser stone.

Soapstone is comprised of talc, quartz, and various minerals. Architectural soapstone is relatively soft but is nevertheless often used on counters and sinks. Using mineral oil on soapstone will darken the stone, although it will also achieve a change of color with time.

Edge Details

The selection of the edge detail (Figure 11-3) will influence cabinet reveals, wall returns, and clearances. The extension of the countertop beyond the cabinet face and door must also be determined.

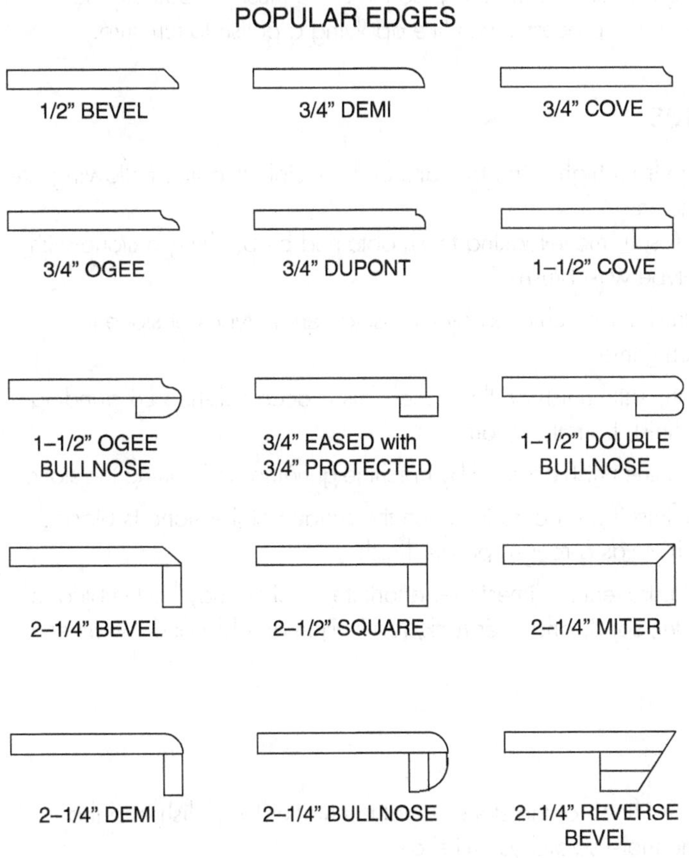

POPULAR EDGES

1/2" BEVEL	3/4" DEMI	3/4" COVE
3/4" OGEE	3/4" DUPONT	1–1/2" COVE
1–1/2" OGEE BULLNOSE	3/4" EASED with 3/4" PROTECTED	1–1/2" DOUBLE BULLNOSE
2–1/4" BEVEL	2–1/2" SQUARE	2–1/4" MITER
2–1/4" DEMI	2–1/4" BULLNOSE	2–1/4" REVERSE BEVEL

Figure 11-3
Popular edge styles.

Sealing Stone

One consideration the designer should pass on to the client is the need to maintain natural surfaces correctly. Penetrating sealers that are allowed to fully penetrate the stone are best. This process takes several applications to fully penetrate the stone. After installation, color enhancers are often added to sealers to bring out the natural color of the stone, especially when the finish of the stone is honed (less than polished).

When a stone surface, such as a countertop, is first installed and sealed, moisture will bead up on the surface. During routine cooking and cleaning of the counter, the sealer gradually wears away, so the stone must periodically be resealed. This is a simple process much like applying a polish to furniture.

Stone Finishes

Stone finishes range from high shine to matte on both slab and tile. Following are some of the most common:

Brushed finish: A soft, matte-looking finish obtained by brushing a stone with a coarse rotary-type wire brush.

Flamed: A textured finish achieved by exposing certain types of stone to intense blowtorch flame.

Honed: A smooth, satin finish on the stone. This is accomplished by grinding off the polished finish from the quarry.

Polished: A high-shine finish attained by machine grinding and buffing the stone.

Sandblasted: A finishing process in which the surface of the stone is blasted with sand, which yields a rough, porous finish.

Tumbled: Marble, travertine, limestone, quartzite, or slate may be tumbled in a solution of water, sand, and river rock, resulting in an old-world, weathered look.

Appearance

A rule of thumb for the finish of the stone is that the higher the polish and the darker the stone, the more scratches will show.

Questions to ask when selecting stone for a project:

How and where will the stone be used?

Will this application be stone slab or tiles?

How will the stone be affected by food and fluids?

What will the edge detail be?

How does the full slab appear? (Never select a stone slab from a small sample!)

How fragile is the selected stone?

Will the seams show because of the pattern?

Can the slabs be book-matched?

What size(s) of tiles are available?

Wall Tile

Because wall tile is installed on a vertical surface, it does not have to be as strong as floor tile. Thinner tile, more delicate finishes, and hand-painted designs can be used successfully.

Layout

Combining various shapes and sizes will provide more visual interest to a space when the decorative scheme calls for it. A variety of shapes are available in tile, resulting in the introduction of line, texture, and color to the room. The pattern created by the field of tile should be viewed in advance of specification.

TIP: Set two mirrors, 90° from each other, perpendicular to the surface. This will show you what the repetition of pattern will be. In addition to pattern, consider how outlets, switches, and plumbing fixtures will affect your design.

Wall tile in the kitchen and bath typically makes up the backsplash material and so should be chosen prior to rough electrical and plumbing. The electrician needs to install j-boxes and switches at the proper depth to accommodate the thickness of the backsplash material and installation. When possible, a sample of the material should be available on the job site.

Installation

Typically, there are two types of installation. The first is mud-set, where a concrete base is made and then tile installed on it; the second is thin-set, where tile is installed directly on a green or concrete board using "thin-set" mortar. A vapor barrier must be provided in both instances.

GROUT

Sanded, nonsanded, or polyblend grout is selected based on the type of tile being installed. The width of the grout joint will dictate the type of grout to be used. Grout joints of 1/4 inch or more use sanded grout, whereas those that are 3/16 inch or less take nonsanded or polyblend grout.

SUSTAINABLE

Reclaiming tile from old structures is one way to reuse materials. These tiles can instantly add the appearance of age to a project when wanted. In some cases, tile manufacturers grind and reuse old and broken tile. These recycled tiles have interesting colors and textures.

ALLOWANCES AT BACKSPLASH

Backsplash heights will vary by the theme of your design. A 4-inch backsplash has been a standard height for years. A full-height backsplash will be the distance from the countertop to the next horizontal surface, usually the overhead cabinetry or hood. The way in which the tile will finish at the side and top is very important. Trim pieces must be compatible with available space.

SEALERS AND MAINTENANCE

Verify the proper maintenance procedure with tile manufacturers and suppliers.

Weight

The additional weight created by the concrete or mortar and tile must be considered at the initial stages of construction.

Tile Categories

A wide range of tile is available to the designer. Each has its own properties and peculiarities.

CERAMIC TILE

Ceramic is the tile most commonly used for vertical and horizontal surfaces. It is made of clay and talc and fired at high temperatures. It comes glazed or unglazed and is appropriate for most uses in kitchens and baths. Be sure that trim pieces are available or plan to use a compatible material as trim when necessary. When designing with an imported tile, allow additional time for shipping from the manufacturer. A working relationship with a qualified and resourceful tile dealer is a necessity.

PORCELAIN TILE

Fired at a very high temperature, porcelain tile is extremely hard and durable. It comes in satin and matte finishes, and many colors and patterns. Some faux stone patterns are extremely realistic. Most patterns have matching trim pieces. When tile is cut to fit during installation, small chips can occur along the cut edge. It may be necessary for the tile installer to do trial cuts with alternate methods to achieve the cleanest edge possible.

GLASS TILE

Glass is naturally impervious to moisture, so it is a great choice for kitchens and baths. This tile is formatted as small mosaic, square, rectangular, and round. Glass tiles are transparent, may be opaque and etched, and come in colors ranging from pastel to bright. Glass tile requires that specific procedures be followed for installation. The installer you use should be experienced in installing glass tile. The adhesive used to install glass tile must be white and will be specified by the manufacturer. **Do not** deviate from the specified procedure!

Glass tile also comes textured, giving you many design options. Nonsanded grouts are typically recommended. Check with the dealer for available trim. If no trim pieces exist, you should meet with the tile installer to develop a recommended design to finish the tile.

The thickness of glass tile ranges from 3/16 inch to 5/8 inch.

METAL TILE

Stainless steel, copper, brass, and zinc are some of the metals available in tile form. Each has its benefits and limitations. All are soft and scratch easily. The grain of the metal will influence the direction you install the tiles. Random or symmetrical patterns can be realized by how you install the tile. Metal tiles are difficult to keep clean but will develop a beautiful patina with aging. The thickness of metal tile varies greatly and thus influences the installation, which must be expertly handled.

MOSAIC TILE

These small tiles come with a net or paper backing for easier installation. Made of ceramic, stone, glass, or porcelain, mosaic tiles are ideal for curved surfaces.

STONE TILE

Natural stone tile can be polished, honed, or tumbled. Marble, granite, limestone, travertine, and slate are the types most commonly used. The thickness of the tile will range from 1/4 inch to 5/8 inch, and weight is again a consideration. Grout joints with polished granite and marble tiles tend to be 1/8 inch wide, although a butt joint (with no grout line) is also popular. Stone material that has been tumbled will require a 1/4-inch sanded-grout joint.

CONCRETE TILE

Color, pattern, and finish are some of the reasons for selecting this material. Concrete tiles come in square and rectangular shapes ranging from 6 inches to 16 inches square. They are very hard but should still have a sealer applied.

LEATHER TILE

Durable leather tiles and tiles made of recycled leather are available for wall and floor surfaces. Proper installation and care are required. These tiles are typically 3/16 inch to 1/4 inch thick and can be used in specific areas of the kitchen and bathroom.

Tile Trims

Trims serve a dual purpose as decorative and finished exposed edges. Trims will define patterns within a space and must be considered in space allowances for their proper finish. Tile trims are available in surface bullnose, quarter rounds, beaks, v-caps, liners, and crowns. It is very important that the designer work closely with the installer and tile dealer to make sure the correct materials are being ordered and used.

Floor Coverings

Ceramic Floor Tile

Tile floors in kitchens and baths must be safe to walk on, easy to clean, and durable, and must fit the decorative scheme. Combining various sizes, borders, and accent tiles can create a surface that complements the space as a whole.

If tile is being installed on a floor that is above a raised foundation or second floor, it will be necessary to allow for the thickness of concrete board or a mud-set base. This additional weight and height will affect the structural sizes of the floor joists, the transition to other spaces, and the swing clearance of doorways.

Hard surfaces adversely affect the legs and back when one stands for long periods of time. Floor surfaces that have some resiliency are a wise and ergonomic choice.

Glazed tile with a glossy finish will be slippery when wet. Most manufacturers offer glazed tile that is slip-resistant. This is extremely important in wet areas such as kitchens and baths. Unglazed tile such as Saltillo or quarry tile can be effective but should be treated with a penetrating sealer to make it easier to clean. Some porcelain tiles come with a texture, making them more slip-resistant.

Stone Tile

Natural stone tile comes in sizes ranging from 1/2-inch mosaic to 24-inch-square tile. Shapes tend to be square or rectangular. Creating borders and patterns can add visual interest to a space. Polished, honed, tumbled, sandblasted, and acid-wash finishes provide the designer with a great palette from which to work. Unpolished stone should be sealed with a penetrating sealer.

Natural Linoleum

Natural linoleum is made of linseed oil, pine resin, wood powder, limestone dust, natural pigments, and jute. It is a resilient floor covering product suited to kitchen or bath floors. It is available in tiles and sheet goods. Designing an inlay pattern with linoleum can create a distinctive look for any kitchen or bath.

Bamboo

As a flooring product, bamboo is durable and easy to care for. It comes in stained colors ranging from light to dark. Bamboo is similar in thickness to other wood floors, ranging from 1/2 inch to 3/4 inch.

Leather Tile (E)

New leather tile is made from recycled leather, natural rubber, and acacia bark. It is practical, easy to clean, and kind to your legs. These tiles develop a patina over time and reflect the uses of the space.

Vinyl Flooring

Available in tile and sheet goods, vinyl floor covering can be a cost-effective floor surface. The subfloor on which it is installed must be smooth and even. Any pattern or texture on the underlayment will show through the vinyl material. This floor has some resiliency and will be comfortable to stand on.

Laminate Tile

Laminate flooring comes in tile and strip form. It is hard and easy to clean. It can have a "hollow" sound to it when walked on, which is sometimes overcome with a sound-absorbing base. It is a synthetic product of a hard base material with various color patterns of thin plastic adhered to the base.

Figure 11-4 Combination wood and slate tile. Photo courtesy of Mary Fisher Designs.com, Northlight Architectural Photography. com

Wood-and-Tile Floors

Combining floor tile with wood can result in a durable, easy-care surface that distinguishes a high-traffic area from the social area of the space. An installer acquainted with the material characteristics and unique installation requirements should be used. It is advisable for the designer to coordinate with the installer regarding particular aspects of the installation. Certain allowances and clearances may be required.

Thickness of material: Typically, stone floor tile varies in thickness from 3/8 inch to 3/4 inch. There are some exceptions. Wood flooring thicknesses range from 1/2 inch to 3/4 inch. Each material used should be the same thickness. A thinner tile can be set with a thicker wood only when the installer builds up the thinset or mastic to the equivalent height of the wood (Figure 11-4). This is very time-consuming and therefore adds cost to the job.

Figure 11-5 Cork Floor.
(Courtesy of Judy Svendsen,
ASID, Raven Interiors; Mary
Fisher Designs.com; photo
courtesy of Mary Fisher
Designs.com, Don Milici
Photography)

Moisture barrier: Transfer of moisture from tile, grout, or thinset to wood is a concern when combining these two materials. The wood must be thoroughly sealed to protect it from the transfer of moisture from mastic and grout.

Joint compounds: Grout joints must account for the natural expansion and contraction of wood.

Sealers: The sealers used on both materials must be compatible.

Cork (E)

Cork floor tiles come in a variety of colors and are easily installed. The resilient nature of cork makes it ideal for standing on for long periods of time. Cork is very durable and has been used in kitchens for many years (Figure 11-5). Made from the bark of trees, this is a renewable resource to consider.

Figure 11-6 Carpet tiles in a kitchen.

Carpet Tiles

Carpet tiles have been available for many years. They create a warm, safe, resilient surface on which to stand. They release soil readily and can be cleaned individually when necessary. They are seldom used in kitchens because most clients want a hard surface, but they make excellent floor coverings (Figure 11 6). In bathrooms, where water is an issue, carpet squares offer an easy-care, safe surface.

Wood Floors

Natural and engineered woods make a durable surface in the kitchen. They can be easily maintained and offer some resilience. If they are installed over a concrete slab, a vapor barrier must be put in place to guard against a transfer of moisture from below. There are a variety of patterns, species, finishes, and thicknesses. The typical thickness of solid wood flooring is 3/4 inch; that of wood veneer 3/8 inch to 1/2 inch; and that of engineered wood 1/4 inch.

Walls

Color, texture, and finish all play an important role in the wall spaces of the kitchen and bath. Many options are available to the designer. Prior to applying any finish, the walls must be cleaned and prepared to resist absorption of water and steam.

Clay plaster applications, available for new and existing walls, give the appearance of Venetian plaster, but with the ease of a new wall installation.

Textured walls, ranging from smooth to orange-peel finishes, are often selected; however, a smoother finish is easier to clean in wet areas, such as kitchens and bathrooms. Satin or semigloss paint offers a coating that helps protect the wall surface from moisture and makes it easier to clean.

Ceilings

Often overlooked as a decorative surface in kitchens and baths, the ceiling can add color and visual interest (Figure 11-7). Moldings, beams, step-soffits, indirect light wells, and metal panels are just a few of the options available.

Counters

Both natural and manmade materials used in kitchens and baths for counter surfacing must be stain-resistant, easy to clean, and durable.

Figure 11-7 Kitchen and bath ceilings should reflect the overall decorative scheme of the design. (Photo courtesy of Sub-Zero/Wolf Photograph)

Stone slabs and tiles are often selected as countertop material. The thickness of the material varies, so select carefully to anticipate the finished thickness and shape of the edge. Stone slab is typically 3/4 inch (2 cm) or 1-1/4 inches (3 cm) thick. This is very important when you are calculating the finished height of the countertop and the thickness of the edge detail of the counter.

Wood countertops can be any desired thickness. A 1-1/2-inch-thick countertop is most common. Edge details can be as high as your design scheme dictates, but you must allow for the drawer or door operation of the cabinetry below. Wood is a great surface for cutting foods and rolling out pastries. A nontoxic mineral oil will seal the wood and minimize knife cut marks. Wood can always be sanded and re-oiled. An island with a wood countertop should have a top-set sink installed rather than an undermount sink. If the sink is undermounted, the cut edge of the wood must be frequently sealed to ward off water damage to the open grain end.

Concrete counters can be installed in two ways: either poured in place in a mold, or formed at the fabricator's shop and installed on site. Concrete is a special mix of water, cement, sand, stone, and pigment and should be sealed unless you wish a distressed look. It has a subtle appearance and can be poured to form a seamless counter.

Solid-surface materials are a formulated mix of mineral compound and polyester and/or acrylic resins. If the design requires a counter, bench, or other surface with contours, the flexibility and formability of solid-surface material can be the solution. Colors and patterns are consistent and can be fabricated so that seams do not show. This material can scratch and crack if exposed to a hot item and may discolor in direct sunlight.

Quartz (E) is a ground stone mixed with resins to make one of the hardest surfaces available. Quartz is nonporous, making it very hygienic, and it does not have to be sealed.

Stainless steel (E) is nonporous, does not chip, and is relatively easy to maintain. It scratches, dents, and will show use. It is hygienic and therefore perfect in food preparation areas. When cleaning stainless steel, you should wipe with the grain of the surface.

Zinc is soft and will scratch and dent. It shows water stains and fingerprints and reacts with food acids. When it is necessary to seam the material, the seam will show. Plan where seams will occur with the fabricator. Maintenance should be prescribed by the fabricator.

Laminate is made of kraft paper, a photographic image on paper, and a melamine plastic coating. It is a cost-effective surface, and most patterns can be formed at the front edge and along the backsplash.

Tile is a very durable surface for countertops. It holds up to heat and water and can be cleaned easily. As a decorative element, tile can add color, pattern, and texture. Grout joints should be made as small as possible to minimize the need for cleaning; although the tile is usually impervious to spills, the grout can stain and discolor.

Lavastone is glazed volcanic rock with a high-fired, enameled finish. A wide palette of bright colors is offered. The nonporous finish makes it a practical choice for the kitchen or bath.

Glass, as a nonporous surface, is hygienic and stain-proof. It will scratch, chip, and break, so give careful consideration to its application. Glass holds up to heat well and is often used as a backsplash at the range area. Varied textures and patterns can be achieved with sandblasting and acid etching. Most glass surfaces in kitchens are raised counters or eating bars. Partition walls with etched or patterned glass are used to screen fixtures in bathrooms.

Paper composite countertops made from petroleum-free resin and 100-percent recycled cardboard are referred to as PaperStone. Scratch-resistant and able to withstand temperatures of up to 350°F, these countertops are very durable and easy to maintain.

Summary

When selecting materials and finishes for the kitchen or bath, style, function, care and maintenance, fabrication, sustainability, and cost all weigh in the decision-making process.

Sustainability

12

Sustainability by definition refers to endurance. When applied to kitchen and bath design, it implies thoughtful consideration of specific materials, energy efficiency, and responsible use of natural resources. Planning the most efficient use of natural resources includes consideration of water use and quality, energy use, air quality, and renewable materials. An integrated approach to residential design begins with the location of the home on the site, and includes landscaping design that enhances positive properties of seasonal changes, a building envelope responsibly built with little impact on the environment, and an interior design that reflects the client's wishes along with wise use of material resources and conservation practices.

Green building is a term that has been around for several years and is interpreted different ways by many diverse groups, including the U.S. Green Building Council (USGBC), Environmental Protection Agency (EPA), Department of Energy (DOE), National Association of Home Builders (NAHB), American Institute of Architects (AIA), and American Society of Interior Designers (ASID). All of these groups agree that buildings that are "green" use resources more efficiently and conserve energy, water, and materials while minimizing the building's negative impact on human health and the environment.

Kitchen and Bath Projects

A new construction project provides the best opportunity to implement "green" building practices. However, in remodeling projects where demolition exposes the existing framework of the structure, the opportunity to elevate the level of energy and water conservation exists.

Sound transmission and thermal heat loss/gain can be addressed with new insulation. Inefficient windows can be replaced, water-conserving fixtures installed, and energy-efficient appliances selected.

Recycling of Materials

Where do old cabinets, appliances, and fixtures go when a kitchen or bath is remodeled? In many areas, recycling businesses take old materials, revamp them, and resell them. In most cases, these companies will come and remove the donated materials. What you can donate will not end up in a landfill.

Older refrigerators and freezers are difficult to dispose of because the coolant chemicals in them are considered hazardous. Certified refrigeration companies can safely remove the coolant and recycle the materials used in manufacturing the appliance.

In 1993, the Association of Home Appliance Manufacturers (AHAM) established the Appliance Recycling Information Center (ARIC), whose mission is to serve as the authoritative source of information on environmentally responsible disposal and recycling of appliances and to undertake research into the recycling of major household appliances. The ARIC is comprised of representatives from the major appliance industry, steel recycling industry, plastics council, and scrap recyclers who met initially to discuss the formation of a resource management alliance. In 2004, 92 percent of all the steel in major appliances was recycled (*Source:* Association of Home Appliance Manufacturers, www.AHAM.org).

The existing materials in kitchens and baths that can be recycled include wood flooring, stone counters, cabinetry, lighting fixtures, and interior doors. Special care must be taken when removing these materials to assure that they can be reused. Occasionally, countertops can be removed and reused in the design of the kitchen and bath.

One way to have continuity throughout the home is to reuse existing interior doors. Not only are you recycling material, but also there is a cost saving once the old door has been refinished to work with the new design. Old interior doors can be installed as pantry doors or pocket doors; if they are wide enough, they can even stay in place.

For years, resourceful interior designers have haunted old buildings that are being torn down, searching for materials and architectural elements to recycle. Craftsmanship from the past that is no longer available is sustained by the reuse of these elements.

Water

Health-conscious people list good water quality as one of the most important attributes of a healthy life. For this reason, the designer should be aware of its effects on kitchen and bath design. A variety of water-treatment processes exist to provide systems that meet specific needs at the point of use.

Municipal and rural water suppliers follow EPA standards for water consumption. However, public water treatment systems may leave mineral deposits behind that influence the performance of water appliances and fixtures.

Residential water-treatment systems can be very confusing to consumers. Basic information on the differences among these treatment methods will equip the designer in guiding the client through the selection process.

Water Filters

Tap water delivered by municipal water companies is as safe as bottled water; however, additives to ensure water quality can often leave a taste or odor that many find unpleasant or undesirable. Water filtration can be the solution to this concern.

No one water filtration system is right for every region. Chemical additives and mineral content vary in rural and urban areas. A filtration system should be selected based on the location of the project and the quality of water supplied.

Manufacturers offer many filtration products to meet specific water-quality needs. Point-of-use installations deliver filtered water specifically where needed.

Basic considerations in selecting a system for water treatment:

- The type and amount of contaminants in your location
- Initial equipment cost
- Maintenance costs
- Operating and storage costs
- Service and warranty
- Ease of use

The first step in selecting a water-treatment system is to have the water tested by a certified water-test technician. This is normally done by the homeowner or contractor.

Four types of water-treatment systems are generally used for residences:

- Carbon or fiber filter
- Reverse-osmosis
- Distillation (limited "spot" use in residences)
- Softeners

CARBON OR FIBER FILTERS

Faucet-mounted, in-line, line bypass, point-of-entry, and pour-through are the most common methods of filtration. In each, water is passed through a filter that traps certain sediments and chemicals.

REVERSE-OSMOSIS

A reverse-osmosis filtration system removes a variety of inorganic chemicals, such as nitrates, calcium, and magnesium, which is usually 95 percent effective. These filters also remove fluoride and are typically used to treat drinking and cooking water.

DISTILLATION

A distillation system produces the purest water but is seldom used in residences. Some minerals in water are desirable for maintaining good body health.

Water Softeners

Hard water is created by dissolved calcium and magnesium. It leads to inefficient laundering, dishwashing, and water heating, because plumbing fixtures build up a mineral deposit that must be cleaned periodically to help extend the life of the fixture.

How Do Water-Treatment Systems Affect a Design?

During the space planning process, the designer must plan storage space for the water-treatment system and access to the equipment for service. The result will be appliances and plumbing fixtures that operate to designed capacity and last longer.

Plumbing

Plumbing fixtures used in home interiors include water heaters, toilets, bidets, urinals, faucets, baths/shower systems, washers, dishwashers, cooking appliances, and drinking-water appliances. Selecting the most water-efficient fixture can be aided by the EPA's WaterSense® seal. This designation is awarded by a program that partners up with manufacturers to identify high-efficient fixtures and to apply EnergyStar® and Energy Guide labeling indicating energy efficiency.

An EPA study on water supply and demand indicated that the residential demand on the water supply constitutes 56.7 percent of the total water demand (Environmental Protection Agency data, 1992).

The breakdown of demand is as follows:

- Toilets, 26.7%
- Washers, 21.7%
- Showers, 16.8%
- Faucets, 15.7%
- Leaks, 13.7%
- Other, 2.3%
- Baths, 1.7%
- Dishwashers, 1.4%

The current standard, set by the Energy Policy Act of 1992 and effective as of 1994, set limits on water consumption of fixtures and faucets sold in the United States. Manufacturers have typically exceeded these standards in the engineering of plumbing fixtures currently available with the WaterSense® seal (*Source:* EPA and the Kohler Company).

- Toilets, 1.6 gpf
    - High-efficiency toilet (HET) 1.28 gpf
    - Dual-flush toilet, 1.6 gpf (solid waste); 0.8 gpf (liquid waste)
    - Pressure-assist toilet, 1.1 gpf
- Urinals, 1.0 gpf
    - High-efficiency urinals, 0.5 gpf or less
- Showerheads, 2.5 gpm @ 80 psi
- Faucets, 2.2 gpm at 60 psi
- Aerators, various flows to 0.5 gpm

Single-flush gravity HETs provide 20 percent water savings with every flush over older models of toilets. Dual-flush toilets allow users to select the flushing volume, saving more than 20 percent per flush.

Water-saving changes include replacing an old toilet or urinal with a water-efficient model, installing low-flow aerators on faucets, repairing leaks quickly, and installing water-efficient products when new appliances are required.

Water Heaters

Long runs of hot-water pipes to points of use throughout the house waste more power and energy because of heat lost while water stagnates in the pipes. A study from the Washington Suburban Sanitary Commission estimated that the conventional shower uses 7–10 gallons of water per minute; with water-saving devices, only 2–4 gallons.

If it takes 1 minute for hot water to flow to an open valve, 7–10 gallons of water can be wasted. If a flow restrictor is used at the valve, only 2–4 gallons may be wasted. However, this does not include the energy lost in heating cold water moving through hot-water pipes. Rectifying this common condition can yield significant dollar savings.

POINT-OF-USE WATER HEATERS

Point-of-use water heaters are designed to fit under a sink and are ideal for water use at remote locations. They are independent of the main source of hot water so they eliminate those long waits for hot water that must travel the entire distance from the hot-water storage to the point of use. Thermostatically controlled point-of-use hot water is instantly available. Another design option is to zone water heaters to areas of consumption.

TANKLESS WATER HEATERS

Energy savings can be realized when tankless water heaters are installed rather than a traditional storage tank unit. Known as an "on-demand" water source, a tankless water heater will heat water only as it is needed. When a hot-water valve is opened, the water heater senses the demand and immediately starts to heat the water. The water flows through a heat exchanger, where it is heated to a preset temperature and then delivered to the opened valve. When the valve is closed, the heater ceases to heat the water. Units are available with electric or gas power (Figure 12-1).

Figure 12-1 Tankless water heater installed in place of the standard tank water heater, allowing additional space for storage and counter. Louvered door provides air circulation. (Photo courtesy of Judy Svensen, Raven Interiors, Mary Fisher Designs.com, Gary Milici Photography)

Pressure-Balanced Thermostatic Valves

Pressure-balanced thermostatic valves control water pressure and temperature at the shower head. This preset temperature helps control heat loss in distribution through water pipes.

Solar Power

Solar water heating, which is discussed in Chapter 10, is just one of the new solar energy technologies on the horizon. Local utility companies and solar societies are good resources for research in this area.

Energy Conservation

Insulation is an essential component of any sustainable design. In the past several decades, the installation of insulation products has become a primary part of the mechanical systems of the structure. Along with the familiar batt insulation, closed-cell spray polyurethane foam supplies amazing thermal insulation properties, in addition to deadening sound transfer from room to room and from outside. Low VOC levels make newer foam technologies attractive for use in remodeling projects and insulating existing homes.

EPA ENERGY STAR PROGRAM

EnergyStar® is a joint program of the U.S. Environmental Protection Agency and the U.S. Department of Energy. It is targeted toward helping consumers save money and protect the environment through use of energy-efficient products and practices.

In 1992, the EPA introduced EnergyStar® as a voluntary labeling program designed to identify and promote energy-efficient products to reduce greenhouse-gas emissions. The EnergyStar® label is now on more than 60 product categories, including major appliances, office equipment, lighting, and home electronics. EPA has also extended the label to cover new homes and commercial and industrial buildings.

Products displaying the EnergyStar® label meet or surpass strict energy-efficiency requirements set by the EPA and DOE. If you want to specify an appliance that does not display the EnergyStar® label, ask the manufacturer about it. As an illustration, a built-in appliance company did not receive EnergyStar® certification on one of its models, because the appliance did not qualify without a door panel when tested; however, it would have qualified if the door panel (which comes from the cabinet company after the appliance is purchased) had been installed. In such circumstances, check the yellow energy-use label from the manufacturer.

Kitchen Appliances

Listed below are annual appliance energy consumption figures related to kitchens and baths.

MAJOR ELECTRICAL APPLIANCES	
Central air conditioning	16.0%
Space heating	10.1%
Refrigerators	13.7%
Freezers	3.5%
Water heaters	9.1%
Dishwashers	3.3%
Range tops	2.8%
Ovens	1.8%
Microwave ovens	1.7%

SMALL APPLIANCES	
Toasters/Ovens	0.2%
Coffee makers	0.5%
Color TVs	2.9%
Cable boxes	0.3%
Desktop computers	1.5%
Laptop computers	0.1%
Printers/Faxes/Copiers	0.2%
Cordless telephones	0.2%
Ceiling fans	0.2%
Lighting (indoor and out)	8.8%
MAJOR GAS APPLIANCES	
Furnace	61.7%
Water heater	21.5%
Range	5.5%

Source: Residential Energy Consumption Survey, American Gas Association, Residential Natural Gas Market Survey, 2007.

Energy consumption guides, such as the Energy Guide (yellow and black label) found on appliances, provide information related to the energy consumption of that appliance. The EnergyStar® label (blue) identifies an energy-efficient appliance that meets EPA guidelines. When an appliance you expect to select does not have these labels, contact the manufacturer's representative and inquire about certification. With all testing facilities, certain parameters exist that affect the certification process. Some major appliances are energy-efficient but do not show the EnergyStar® label.

REFRIGERATORS AND FREEZERS

Refrigerators and freezers continue to evolve into more efficient energy consumers. Insulation technology for new refrigerators and freezers is far superior to the insulation of previous models. More efficient compressors and air-circulation systems enhance the capability of refrigerators and freezers to maintain temperature at proper levels. How the consumer uses the refrigerator and freezer directly relates to energy use of the appliance.

Families with children who frequently open and close the refrigerator door are going to consume more energy than the family that does not.

Wireless monitoring systems by manufacturers help manage the efficiency of the appliance. Selecting a refrigeration appliance that best fits the family's precise needs should be a goal of the designer.

COOKING APPLIANCES (COOKTOPS, RANGES, OVENS)

Gas, electric, and dual fuel (a combination of gas tops and electric ovens) are the energy choices available for kitchen appliances. The most efficient electric cooktop is induction, which uses energy only when the pot or pan touches the cooking surface. (Refer to the discussion of induction cooking in Chapter 5.) Glass-surfaced, halogen cooktops are the next most efficient electric cooktop. Traditional electric coils and hobs heat up and cool down slower than induction and halogen cooktops. Modular cooktops provide a variety of cooking modes, including gas cooktop, induction cooktop, electric cooktop, electric steamer, electric deep-fryer, and gas or electric grills in a smaller size. Steaming, frying, and teppan surfaces can be very efficient, because the appliance itself is the cooking vessel, allowing heat to be transferred directly into the food. Steam cooking often cooks faster and uses less energy.

Electronic ignition has replaced the continuous pilot light of old gas appliances and has made gas a more efficient fuel to consider. If natural gas is not available in the location of the residence, you might want to consider liquid propane (refer to Chapter 5).

When a range or cooktop is installed separate from the ovens, two different-sized ovens should be considered. Efficiency is increased and cost is reduced when a smaller oven for daily and weekly use is combined with a larger oven that is used only when the larger cavity is needed. This reduces use of the large oven capacity for small items (such as two baked potatoes). Newer ovens are fully insulated, making them energy-efficient; when combined with convection air, less cooking time is required for long-term cooking. Note, though, that a convection oven cooking time is seldom faster when operating in the baking mode.

Speed ovens cook extremely fast and can be an energy-efficient choice.

HOODS AND VENTS

Sizing ventilation equipment to properly vent byproducts of cooking enhances indoor air quality. Fabrics, materials, and finishes will last longer, because steam- and oil-laden air is vented to the outside rather than collecting on surfaces within the space.

Of the two existing drafting systems, the most efficient method is overhead ventilation. Downdraft systems are an alternative when overhead ventilation is not possible. Downdrafts that fit between the cooking surfaces are more effective than downdraft systems that run along the back of the cooktop (Figure 12-2).

A ventilation system will operate more efficiently if you turn it on to a low setting before you begin to cook. This allows an air current to develop so that when cooking starts, steam will travel with that circulation of air immediately.

Figure 12-2 (Photo courtesy of BSH Home Appliances Corporation, Gaggenau brand)

Kitchen and Bath Design

DISHWASHERS

Today's dishwashers are engineered to operate more quietly and more efficiently than those of just a few years ago. "Light wash" and energy-saver settings lessen the amount of energy used. Both single dishwasher drawers and full-sized dishwashers offer the option to wash only the top or bottom rack. Dishwashers displaying the EnergyStar® label use 5.8 gallons per cycle or less.

Lighting

The future of clean, energy-efficient light sources is remarkably bright. The technology of LED sources continues to evolve at a rapid pace (see Chapter 9).

Industry experts assure us that the trace amount of mercury found in fluorescent fixtures is miniscule. Nevertheless, a deliberate method of disposal must be followed as mandated by local regulations (see Chapter 9).

Finishes and Materials

Paints with zero VOC emissions are now available. Stains and sealers are now available with little or no VOCs.

Cabinets can be finished with wax finishes and natural pigments. Cork, bamboo, reclaimed wood, natural linoleum, and recycled tile floors are but a few of the flooring materials available. Furthermore, formaldehyde-free and soy-based adhesives are now being used.

Recycled stone and cement countertops can be waxed to seal them.

Natural clay finishes for walls and ceilings make a natural statement on walls and ceilings.

Summary

Sustainability is the determination to select products and materials that conserve and enhance our natural environment whenever possible. Keep materials from the municipal dump by recycling them. Purchase appliances and equipment that are energy-efficient to save both money and resources. Our goal should be to recycle used products to create resources and materials for manufacturing of new products and to perform product installations that enhance the long life of a product.

Appendix

Project Inventory Assessment

Specific, accurate, and detailed information regarding the existing condition of the project and space is necessary for the space planning process to proceed. Allow plenty of time to measure and photograph the space. You will refer to this information often.

Contact Information:

Client Name: _____

Address: _____

       City _____ State _____ Zip _____

Phone: _____ e-mail _____

Project Address: _____

_____

Existing Space:

WINDOWS:

A   Width _____ Height _____ A.F.F. _____ Type _____

B   Width _____ Height _____ A.F.F. _____ Type _____

C   Width _____ Height _____ A.F.F. _____ Type _____

D   Width _____ Height _____ A.F.F. _____ Type _____

E   Width _____ Height _____ A.F.F. _____ Type _____

DOORS:

I   Width _____ Height _____ Swing._____ Type _____

II   Width _____ Height _____ Swing _____ Type _____

III   Width _____ Height _____ Swing _____ Type _____

IV   Width _____ Height _____ Swing _____ Type _____

Existing Appliances:

Range: ☐ Electric (circuit size) ____
             Gas: ☐ Natural Gas ☐ LP Size ____

Range Top: ☐ Electric (circuit size) ____
             Gas: ☐ Natural Gas ☐ LP Size ____

Cook Top: ☐ Electric (circuit size) ____
             Gas: ☐ Natural Gas ☐ LP Size ____

Ovens: ☐ Electric (circuit size) ____
             Gas: ☐ Natural Gas Size ____

Microwave: ☐ Circuit size _____ Physical size _____

Warming Drawer: Size _____

Dishwasher: Size _____

Trash Compactor: Size _____

Refrigerator: ☐ Water/ice in the door
            Size: Width_____ Depth _____ Height _____

Freezer: ☐ With Ice Maker
            Size: Width_____ Depth _____ Height _____

Wine Cooler: Size: Width_____ Depth _____ Height _____

Grill: Size: Width_____ Depth _____ Height _____

Hood: Size: Width_____ Depth _____ Height _____

Misc.   Size: Width_____ Depth _____ Height _____

Plumbing Fixtures:

Sink: Size: Width _____ Length _____ Depth _____ Type _____

Cabinetry:

Is any cabinetry to be reused?
☐ Sizes of cabinets: to remain _____
   (may need to note on separate sheet)
☐ Note the hinge side of the doors _____

Furniture:

Description and size _____

Dimensions _____

_____

Utilities:

Locate and note the size of the following:

☐ Main electrical panel   amperage _____

☐ Gas meter _____

☐ Plumbing locations _____

☐ Water Heater   ☐ Gas   ☐ Electric   ☐ Solar Location _____

☐ Convenience outlets   ☐ GFCI

☐ Switches

      ☐ Single pole _____

      ☐ 3-way _____

      ☐ 4-way _____

☐ Master control lighting system _____

☐ Air conditioning/heat vents (registers) _____

☐ Return air vents _____

Locate these items on your space plan sketch of existing space. If the project is new construction, identify the locations on the plans.

Project Orientation:

Indicate the orientation to the outside   ☐ North   ☐ South   ☐ East   ☐ West

Identify the adjacent rooms

Refer to site-assessment drawing of existing space (art drawing)

Planning Procedure Checklist— Kitchens

Following is a list of steps that will help organize your space planning procedure. As you check them off, you will find that details frequently overlooked are covered in the normal space planning process.

☐ Analyze the space as it relates to the house as a whole.

☐ Create a bubble plan based on how the client uses the space.

☐ Review inventory list and ergonomic information; set priorities.

☐ Lay out space plan and elevation views.

☐ Select appliances and plumbing fixtures.

☐ Create a CoreKitchen™.

☐ Plan storage systems.

☐ Design cabinet types and locations.

☐ Analyze ergonomic information.

☐ Check space clearances.

☐ Adjust the plan to fit finish details.

☐ Create a lighting plan.

☐ Plan sound-control measures.

☐ Verify ventilation location and sizing.

☐ Assemble finish materials.

☐ Create color boards.

☐ Make up specification books.

Planning Procedure Checklist— Baths

Following is a list of steps that will help organize your space planning procedure. As you check them off, you will find that details frequently overlooked are covered in the normal space planning process.

- [ ] Analyze the space as it relates to the house as a whole.
- [ ] Create a bubble plan based on how the client uses the space.
- [ ] Review inventory list and ergonomic information; set priorities.
- [ ] Lay out space plan and elevation views.
- [ ] Select plumbing fixtures.
- [ ] Plan space for accessories (towel bars, toilet paper holder, etc.).
- [ ] Plan storage systems.
- [ ] Design cabinet types and locations.
- [ ] Analyze ergonomic information.
- [ ] Check space clearances.
- [ ] Adjust the plan to fit finish details.
- [ ] Create a lighting plan.
- [ ] Plan sound-control measures.
- [ ] Verify ventilation location and sizing.
- [ ] Locate heating/air conditioning to room.
- [ ] Assemble finish materials.
- [ ] Create color boards.
- [ ] Make up specification books.

Plan Checklist

This list provides you with specific areas to be checked before plans are presented to the client, builder or subcontractors. Attention to detail is most important at this stage. The more complete your plans are, the smoother the bidding process and construction will be.

Appliances

☐ Countertop adjacent to appliance.

☐ Landing space for all appliances.

☐ Island—proper ventilation, energy supply, drains, water supply.

☐ Water and energy supplies properly sized:

    ☐ Water inlet

    ☐ Gas supply line

    ☐ Circuit size

☐ Appliance doors open without interfering with other appliances or cabinetry.

☐ Appliance location does not impede traffic flow.

☐ Surface on which to place items from shelves.

☐ Installed height fits client's ergonomic profile.

Electrical

☐ GFCI outlets.

☐ Switch locations.

☐ 3- and 4-way dimmers.

☐ Note electrical appliance information on specification sheets.

☐ Plug towers—note access after installation.

☐ Air switches.

☐ Verify appliance circuit sizes.

☐ WiFi system.

☐ Phone/charging station.

☐ Cable/satellite.

Lighting

☐ Note type and size of lighting fixtures.

☐ Note if fixture is surface-mounted or recessed.

☐ Detail any special installation.

☐ Indicate the distance from the island countertop or finished floor to the bottom of a chandelier or pendant (e.g., 60" a.f.f. [after finished floor]).

☐ Indicate location of recessed and surface fixtures on lighting plan.

☐ Locate switches, dimmers, and 3- or 4-way controls.

☐ Show location of undercabinet lighting. Installation on back side of front rail of upper cabinet is suggested unless backsplash is mirror.

☐ Extra support for weight of fixture, if needed.

Architectural details

☐ Locate and show space allowances for air circulation and operation of appliances in cabinetry or built-in niches.

☐ Specify special features of any architectural element.

☐ Indicate how countertops, moldings, cabinetry, and appliances fit with the feature.

Plumbing

☐ Note whether sink is undermount, top-set (self-rimming), or front-apron.

☐ Show location of faucet, valves, air switch, air gap, filtered/instant hot water dispenser, and sink accessories.

☐ Locate pot filler on wall or deck, noting the height off the finished floor (a.f.f.) and dimension from adjacent wall or cabinet.

☐ Show where the shutoff valve for any gas supply is located, per plumber. Local codes will dictate access.

Ventilation

☐ Note installed height to the bottom of the hood off finished floor.

☐ Center hood over surface cooking unit/range or cooktop.

☐ Does hood extend 3" on either side of surface cooking?

☐ Note direction of ductwork.

☐ Note size of ductwork. Refer to manufacturer's manual.

☐ Show hood liner as installed in custom hood design (section drawing).

☐ Note location of light and variable speed switch for hood, if a remote control is used.

☐ If an air switch is used, note location in counter.

Space planning

☐ Note clearances in traffic lanes.

☐ Note swing of doors.

☐ Choose location and window type (measure person's ability to reach and operate window).

☐ Define orientation of CoreKitchen™ to natural light and social space.

☐ Doors of appliances and cabinetry should open to 90° without interfering with each other.

☐ Note space clearances when doors are open 90°.

☐ Check sound transmission from kitchen.

☐ Interior air quality: location of vents and return air ducts.

Counters

☐ Determine the type of material to be used and its thickness:

  ☐ Stone

  ☐ Tile

  ☐ Glass

  ☐ Metal

  ☐ Wood

  ☐ Solid Surface

  ☐ Quartz

  ☐ Bamboo

  ☐ Paper

  ☐ Laminate

  ☐ Lavistone

- [ ] Edge details/trims:
  - [ ] Show the edge detail: _____ thickness, _____ shape, _____ protrusion beyond cabinet face
- [ ] Backsplash detail tile design: type, size, direction, and trim pieces.
- [ ] Termination of countertop: Note how the countertop will terminate next to tall cabinets.
- [ ] Show any special detailing of the countertop.
- [ ] Show how counters of different heights terminate on islands and cabinet runs.
- [ ] Show counter edge detail at sink locations (undermount and front-apron sinks).
- [ ] Indicate varied counter heights, material change, thickness, and edge detail. Indicate height off finished floor.

Backsplash
- [ ] Backsplash material thickness provided to electrician so electrical j-boxes and switches can be roughed in at the proper depth.
- [ ] Detail tile design: type, size, direction, and trim.
- [ ] Note grout joint size, material, and color.
- [ ] Show detail drawing of trim and termination points of tile backsplash for either thinset or mud application.
- [ ] Note amount of clearance space behind faucet.
- [ ] Show whether a full backsplash (countertop to bottom of upper cabinet) or less.
- [ ] Show edge detail of backsplash when exposed on wall.
- [ ] Show detail of backsplash from upper cabinet to countertop.
- [ ] Show how backsplash terminates at window or door casing.
- [ ] Thickness of glass or mirror when used as backsplash.

Cabinetry
- [ ] Full-height cabinet depth to accommodate the countertop edge detail.
- [ ] Upper cabinets to have light rail or recessed undercabinet lighting.
- [ ] Base cabinet roll-out shelves and drawers fully extend.

☐ Cabinet doors open without interfering with traffic pattern, appliances, hardware, or other doors.

☐ Pull-out boards are stable.

☐ Interior storage accessories for organization and access.

Hardware

☐ Check hardware protruding on doors and drawers (must pass adjacent hardware in corner areas).

☐ The extension of handles of appliances should not interfere with the operation of adjacent cabinets or appliances.

Floor covering

☐ Note the thickness of the floor covering.

☐ Note the transition of floor covering to adjacent rooms.

☐ Show any pattern or design element of the floor (borders, tile accents, pattern of wood, etc.).

☐ Will doors and casing need to be trimmed?

Windows/doors

☐ Locate and show opening of doors and windows.

☐ Make sure user can reach the window to operate.

☐ Note whether windows and doors are installed in a cased or bullnose opening.

☐ Note the size of casing or bullnose.

Ergonomic Profile

Clearly defining the client's physical characteristics provides valuable information for space planning the kitchen and bath. Explain the purpose of the measurements and questions and how the information will be used to your client. Do not be intrusive. This gives you an opportunity to explain the benefits of universal and ergonomic design, as well as to set yourself apart from other designers.

Ergonomic Profile Measurements

Measuring the physical characteristics of your client is key to locating appliances, planning storage systems, designing cabinets and establishing counter heights.

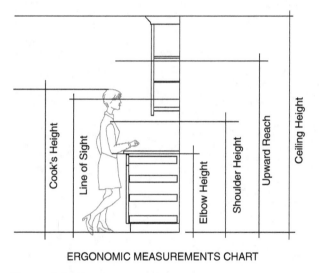

ERGONOMIC MEASUREMENTS CHART

Figure A-1 Ergonomic measurements chart.

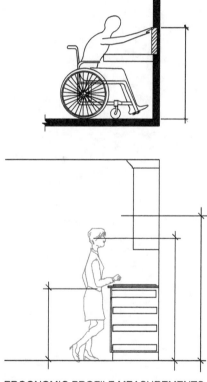

ERGONOMIC PROFILE MEASUREMENTS

Figure A-2 Note the person's ability to reach, bend, turn, and pivot. Indicate the line of sight so you can locate controls where they can be read easily.

Ergonomic Profile Measurements

Glossary

A.A.F.: After-finish-floor: Term for measurement of height of specified item from finished floor.

Access Aisle (E): A person-accessible space between elements such as cabinets, counter edges, appliances, and furniture.

Accessible Route: A continuous unobstructed path connecting all accessible elements and space of the room and residential interior.

Adaptability: The ability of certain building spaces and elements, such as kitchen counters, sinks, and grab bars, to be added or altered to accommodate the needs of individuals with or without disabilities or to accommodate the needs of persons with different types or degrees of disability.

Air Gap: A device used to prevent backflow or siphonage from a dishwasher when a negative pressure or vacuum occurs.

Air Switch (E): A button mounted on the sink or countertop next to the sink that activates the garbage disposer by air pressure. It can be used on spa tubs for air pump control.

Ambient Light: General lighting diffused within an entire room.

Ampere (amp): A unit of measurement assigned to the electrical current passing a given point. Electrical circuits are rated in amperage. Electrical appliances require a certain amperage-sized circuit to operate correctly and safely. The circuit panel will contain circuits of varied sizes.

Antimicrobial Finish: A finish applied to, or ingredient in, the product that inhibits the growth of microorganisms, such as bacteria or fungi.

Apron: Trim attached below a tabletop or window sill.

Argon Gas: A colorless, odorless, inert gaseous element constituting approximately 1 percent of the earth's atmosphere; used in electric lamps, fluorescent tubes, and insulated glass window panes. Because argon is denser than air, it is a good insulator.

Backflow: The flow of water in a pipe or line in the opposite direction from its normal direction of flow. In kitchens and baths, this concern centers on contaminated water flowing back into potable water.

Backsplash: The exposed area between the bottom of the upper wall cabinets and the top of the countertop.

Ballast: A device that controls the current in a fluorescent lamp.

Banquette: A built-in bench along a wall; often used in eating areas.

Barn Door: Door(s) that slide along a wall on exposed track.

Base Cabinet: Lower cabinet, typically 24 inches deep and 34-1/2 inches high.

Beam: A horizontal or nearly horizontal framing member that supports loads imposed perpendicular to the long axis introduced by other framing, such as joists.

Bearing Wall: A wall designed and placed in a position to hold a load above it; usually used around the perimeter of a house and in strategic locations to support floor, ceiling, and roof beams.

Beverage Center: Area containing storage for wine, soda, ice and snacks; features vary by manufacturer/design.

Bidet: A personal hygiene fixture with a hot and cold water supply; used to wash the perineal and genital areas.

Blind-Corner Base Cabinet: A base cabinet usually incorporated into a design to turn a corner with an appliance or other cabinet perpendicular to it.

Blue Board: A type of gypsum wallboard with a blue-colored paper facing; it is chemically treated to provide a bonding surface for plaster or tile adhesive.

Box: Framework of an individual cabinet.

Brushed Finish: A soft, matte-looking finish obtained by brushing a stone with a coarse rotary-type wire brush; a matte-looking finish on stone.

Btu: British thermal unit. Amount of heat required to raise the temperature of one pound of water (at or near 39.2°F) by one degree Fahrenheit. One kilowatt-hour of electricity yields about 3,400 Btu. Used as a unit measurement for natural gas (1,034 Btu = 1 cubic foot of natural gas). One Btu per hour equals 0.293 watt and is represented by the symbol Btu/h.

Built-in Coffee Maker: Built-in appliance that provides options for brewing coffee, espresso, cappuccino, and tea.

Burner: The gas cooking element on a gas range or cooktop.

Butane: A type of natural gas.

Cabinet Run: Continuous span of cabinets along one wall.

Catalytic Cleaning: Process that uses chemicals fused into the interior walls of the oven and the heat of cooking to continuously clean the oven.

Centerline: A line drawn equidistant from the sides of an object, such as a sink or an appliance.

CFM: Cubic feet per minute; a measure of the amount of air a fan can move.

Circuit Breaker: A device that is designed to protect electrical equipment and people from damage or injury caused by overload or short circuit; also, a protective switch that automatically switches off, or *trips*, the power to a circuit in the event of an overload or short in the circuit. It can be reset to resume operation.

Cleanout: A removable fitting that allows access when debris must be cleaned out of a pipe; typically found on outside walls and accessed from the outside.

Clear Floor Space: The minimum unobstructed floor or ground space required to accommodate a single, stationary wheelchair and occupant.

Combi-Steam Oven (E): Appliance that combines steam and convection cooking in a single oven chamber; provides the most flexible use of energy and cooking options. This oven allows cooking with 100 percent steam, 100 percent convection heat, or any combination in between. An energy-efficient alternative that provides healthy cooking methods.

Commercial Refrigerator: Refrigerator designed for use in restaurants and commercial facilities; sometimes installed in high-end residences.

Concealed Hinge: A hinge that is attached to the door and the inside end panel or stile of a cabinet, making it invisible from the exterior of the cabinet.

Concrete Slab: Used for the foundation of a house or building when there is no basement or crawl space.

Conduction: The flow of heat energy through a material. Heat flows from warmer areas to cooler areas of the material.

Conduit: As used in electricity, a metal or plastic tube containing electrical cables.

Convection: The circulation of heated air within the oven cavity for even oven cooking.

Convection Oven: Appliance that circulates heated air within the oven cavity for quick and even oven cooking.

Conventional Oven: The traditional oven-cooking method that uses a heat source at the bottom of the oven; uses the natural process of hot air rising to cook the food.

Cooktop: A surface cooking unit that is built into the countertop; may be fueled by natural gas, liquid propane, or electricity.

Corbel: A decorative support or bracket installed on a horizontal and vertical plane to support the weight of the horizontal plane (e.g., an overhang on an island).

Crawl Space: A small clearance between the underside of a house and the ground, usually high enough to crawl through. Typical minimum space height is 18 inches.

Crown: Molding finishing the top of upper or tall cabinets.

Cupola: A structure located on the top of the roof; may have windows to allow illumination of the space below. When a cupola is part of the natural lighting system of a kitchen or bath, you need to consider how you will light and vent the space.

Diffuser: In heating and cooling systems, a grill or register in a floor or wall that delivers conditioned air to the room. In lighting, a transparent or translucent lens that encloses the lamp.

Dishwasher: Appliances that clean dishes and cookware; available in drawer models and bottom-hinged door models.

Divided Lite: A type of window or door containing several sections of glazing, in which each section (pane) is separated from the other by muntins. If muntins go all the way through the glazing, the assembly is called a *true divided lite*. If the muntins are applied to the face of the glazing, the assembly is called a *simulated divided lite*.

Double-Glazed: Two panes of glass with an air space between the panes that act as a thermal barrier.

Double Ovens: Ovens that are stacked one above the other, encased in a single wrap to form the appliance unit. May be fueled by natural gas, liquid propane (LP), or electricity. Where wall space is limited, this is an efficient way to provide two ovens.

Downdraft Ventilation: A kitchen ventilation system that pulls air (and the byproducts of cooking) down through a vent and exhausts it to the outside; typically, the ventilation system is integrated with the cooktop or installed immediately adjacent to it.

Drawer Bank: A base cabinet containing drawers.

Drywall: A sheet of gypsum-based plaster encased between two layers of facing paper used for interior wall surfaces as a substrate for paint, wallpaper, or tile finishes.

Egress: A continuous and unobstructed way of exit from any point in a building. Also refers to the ability to exit a space in a time of emergency such as a home fire. Windows and doors must meet code requirements regarding the minimum size for egress. A means of egress comprises both vertical and horizontal travel.

Electrical Panel: Enclosed metal box where the electrical breakers are located; usually also the main electrical shutoff for a house.

Elevation: Drawing prepared to scale showing the width and height of one wall of a room. An exterior elevation shows the design, architectural style, and height of the exterior of the proposed building as viewed from any side of the building.

Energy Star®: A program sponsored by the U.S. Environmental Protection Agency and U.S. Department of Energy; intended to identify and promote energy-saving and cost-saving methods, practices, and appliances.

Face Framing: A method of installing joists or rafters, where they attach to the face of the beam rather than running over the top.

Filler Strip: Spacer to allow return at corners and end of a cabinet run.

Fixture: Any permanent part of the structural design, such as tubs, bidets, toilets, and lavatories. In electrical use, any device permanently wired to the home wiring system.

Flamed: A textured finish achieved by exposing certain types of stone to intense flame.

Frieze: Decorative architectural element on vertical surfaces.

Garbage Disposer: A grinder of food waste; sound levels vary by model.

Glazing: Industry term for a pane of glass in a window; the transparent materials in a window or door.

Graywater: Used water from a home's washer, dishwasher, sinks, and bathing.

Halogen: A variation of incandescent lighting in which the filament is encased inside a capsule containing halogen gas, produced by iodine vapor.

Heat Loss/Gain: Heat transfer through glass. Either lost from the inside to the outside or gained from the outside to the interior.

Honed: A smooth, satin finish on stone.

Hood: Appliance installed above cooking appliances below.

Hood Liner: The ventilator and stainless steel box used in custom hoods.

Ice Maker: An undercounter appliance devoted to producing ice only.

Instant Hot Water Dispenser: Appliance that produces hot (200°F) water very quickly. It is often paired with a filtration system, thereby providing hot and filtered water.

Integrated: Appliances designed to receive cabinet panels that create the look of furniture.

J-box: An electrical junction box.

Kilowatt (kw): One thousand watts; a measurement of the rate at which energy is being delivered or used. The unit used for the electrical rating of a particular appliance.

Lift Oven (E): A unique oven that is wall-mounted and features a bottom that descends for access to the oven interior. Should be installed prior to installation of adjacent upper cabinetry. Introduced by Gaggenau in 2007, this oven allows supremely ergonomic design applications.

Line Voltage: Normal current provided to light fixtures and convenience outlets throughout the house.

Low Voltage: Twelve-volt current for lighting systems. Fixtures are connected to wire that has been attached to a transformer; the transformer takes 110-volt current and steps it down to 12 volts.

Microwave Oven: Cooking appliance that uses microwaves. The key element of any microwave is the magnetron tube, which creates radio waves that spread throughout the oven cavity and into the food, activating the water molecules in the food to oscillate at high speed. The oscillation and friction generate heat that cooks the food from the inside out. Microwave ovens come in microwave-only, convection-microwave, and microwave-hood models.

Mise En Place: French term for assembling all ingredients needed to prepare a dish. Typically measured and prepared ready to combine at the point of cooking.

Modular Cooktops: Specific cooking modules that can be installed in the counter at various locations or joined together with connecting strips to make a multifunctional cooktop in a single location. A very flexible appliance. May be fueled by natural gas, liquid propane, or electricity.

Pane: The glass section(s) of a window or door.

Patina: The appearance of a surface or finish of an object, usually achieved over time. Sometimes a chemical or other substance is used to speed up the process.

Polished: A high-shine finish attained by machine grinding and buffing stone.

Post: Vertical architectural support or a vertical structural support larger than a stud.

Potable: Safe for human consumption; usually refers to water.

Pyrolytic Cleaning: Process that uses high heat to clean the oven cavity.

Rail: The horizontal frame member of cabinet construction.

Range: Freestanding unit that contains surface cooking units along with oven(s) below encased in a single appliance. May be fueled by natural gas, liquid propane (LP), electricity, or a combination of fuels (the latter referred to as dual-fuel).

Range Top: Surface cooking units; if not combined with an oven below, the range top must be built into cabinetry or another support base. May be fueled by natural gas, liquid propane, or electricity.

Refrigerator: Appliance that uses a cooling cycle to keep food fresh and extend its useful life.

Refrigerator-Freezer: Combines both cold-storage processes (refrigeration and freezing) in one appliance.

Remote Vent: The part of a ventilation system mounted outside the kitchen space. This application is available in downdraft and overhead ventilation systems.

Riser: In plumbing, a vertical pipe. In construction, the part of a stairstep that is perpendicular to the floor.

Rough Electrical: The distribution of wire throughout the house during the framing stage. If a concrete slab foundation is involved, a conduit (pipe) is laid to run wire through prior to the pouring of the slab.

Rough Plumbing: The installation of distribution pipe, water supply lines, drains, and vents during the framing stage. If a concrete slab foundation is involved, rough plumbing is run prior to the pouring of the slab.

Rough Top: Underlayment on the top of a cabinet box; intended to support and allow attachment of countertop material.

Sandblasted: A rough, porous finish achieved by blasting the surface of stone with sand.

Single-Glazed: Window or opening with only one pane of glass.

Single Oven: Cooking appliance that can be installed side by side with another or in a separate area of the kitchen. Fueled by natural gas, liquid propane, or electricity, ovens are often combined with other appliances such as microwaves and warming drawers.

Soffit: The form created when the ceiling is framed down a predetermined distance and returns to the wall. Soffits provide a raceway for ductwork of hood vents, recessed lighting, heating and air conditioning systems, and other utilities. In kitchens with high ceilings, soffits are used for attaching upper cabinets.

Steam Oven: A crossover appliance from the restaurant industry that uses steam heat to cook and reconstitute foods.

Step Soffit: Multiple-layered soffit; gives ceiling definition and interest and can be utilized for lighting, wiring, and ductwork.

Stile: The vertical frame member of cabinet construction.

Surface Unit: A gas or electric cooking appliance mounted in countertop surface.

Three-Gang Box: A metal or plastic box that houses three plugs or switches.

Trades: Subcontractors specializing in a particular construction skill (e.g., tile installer, stone fabricator, cabinet dealer or shop, etc.).

Triple-Glazed: Three panes of glass with an air space between two of the panes that acts as a thermal barrier.

Tumbled Stone: Marble, travertine, limestone, quartzite, or slate that has been tumbled in a solution of water, sand, and river rock; results in an old-world, weathered look.

TurboChef Oven: Speedcook oven that uses patented Airspeed Technology™ to quickly cook food.

Upper Cabinet: Wall cabinet, typically 12 inches deep.

Valve: A device that regulates the flow of a fluid or gas in one direction by opening or closing various passageways.

Vinyl-Clad: Encased in a vinyl coating or covering. Windows and doors are often clad in vinyl.

Walk-in Cooler: A custom-built walk-in refrigerated space used for bulk storage and as a staging area for foods prepared for entertaining.

Warming Drawer: Appliance that holds food ready for serving, and heats plates and serving pieces. Some can proof dough, and some have a convection mode for distribution of heat.

Watt: A unit of energy assigned to electrical appliances and fixtures to rate their use of energy when operating. For example, a toaster may be rated at 1,500 watts when in use.

WiFi: Layperson's shorthand term for wireless products. In actuality, "WiFi" is a trademark of the Wi-Fi Alliance for products certified to meet IEEE 802.1 (Institute of Electrical and Electronics Engineers) standards. Not every wireless product is Wi-Fi certified.

Window Tinting: A material applied to door and window glass that reduces sun glare and blocks UV rays.

Wine Storage: A cooling appliance that preserves wine at its optimal temperature, whether red, white, or sparkling wine.

Bibliography

Associates III. *Sustainable Residential Interiors*. Hoboken, NJ: John Wiley & Sons, 2009.

Donkin, Scott W. *Sitting on the Job*. Boston: Houghton Mifflin, 1986.

Henry Dreyfus Associates. *The Measure of Man and Woman: Human Factors in Design*. Hoboken, NJ: John Wiley & Sons, 2001.

John W., Hole, Jr. *Essentials of Human Anatomy and Physiology*. Dubuque, IA: William C. Brown Publishers, 1983.

International Residential Code. Country Club Hills, IL: International Code Council, Inc., 2009.

Kroemer, Karl H. E. *Extra-Ordinary Ergonomics*. Boca Raton, FL: Taylor & Frances Group, 2006.

McBride, Kate, ed. *The Professional Chef*. Hoboken, NJ: John Wiley & Sons, 2006.

Mitton, Maureen. *Residential Interior Design: A Guide to Planning Spaces*. Hoboken, NJ: John Wiley & Sons, 2007.

National Kitchen and Bath Association. *Kitchen and Bath Project Management*. Hackettstown, NJ: Author, 2006.

Nissen, L., Faulkner, R., and S. Faulkner. *Inside Today's Home*. Boston, MA: Wadsworth Publishing, 1994.

Panero, Julius, and Martin Zelnik. *Human Dimension and Interior Space: A Source Book of Design Reference Standards*. New York: Whitney Library of Design, 1979.

Saunders, H. Duane. *For Your Back*. Chaska, MN: Saunders Group, 2004.

Steidl, Rose E., and Esther Crew Bratton. *Work in the Home*. New York: John Wiley & Sons, 1968.

Winkel, S. R., Collins, D., Juroszek, S. P., and F.D.K. Ching. *Residential Building Codes Illustrated: A Guide to Understanding the 2009 International Residential Code*. Hoboken, NJ: John Wiley & Sons, 2010.

Index

A page number appearing in italics with an "*F*" after it indicates a figure.

C

Cabinetry, 98–101
  adjustability in, 181
    adjustable shelves, 181
    stationary shelves, 181
  color, texture decorative design, 2
  construction types of, 171
    custom, 171
    framed or face framed, *172F*
    frameless (32 millimeter), 173, *173F*
    modified frameless, 173
    semicustom, 171
    stock/modular, 171, 177;
      specifications of, 177, 178
  custom, 179, *180F*
  design basics of, 51
  dimensions, 174, *174F*
    base cabinetry, 174
    upper cabinetry, 74
  door designs for, 75, *176F*
    flush inset, 175
    full overlay, 175
    half overlay, 175
  hardware selection for, 102
  interior hardware for, 177
  modular or stock, 177
  storage location of, 76 ,*77F*
  terms of, 175
    box, 175
    rail, 175
    stile, 175
    toe kick, 175
    upper cabinet, 175
    base cabinet, 175
    drawer bank, 175
    tall cabinet, 175
    crown molding, 175
    filler strip, 175
    cabinet run, 175
    rough top, 175
California Energy Code,
    Title 24 of, 16
Case Studies, goals and solutions of:
  contemporary design, 116
  design observations, 245
  loft bathroom space, 242
  loft kitchen space, 119
  powder room, 244
  Southern France design, 113
  Sunriver project, 119
  sustainable design, 110
  water feature bathroom, 243
Ceiling heaters, convection type, 280
Circuit breaker, 253
Cleanup center, 80
Codes and standards, building,
    15, 187–205
  Associations/agencies/guidelines/
    common groups, 15
Coffee brewing:
  automatic machine for, 166
  built-in system of, 167, *168F*
  dimensions of, 167
  selection considerations of,
    167
Cooking methods, 138
  conduction, 139
  convection, 140, 151, *151F*
    microwave, 152
    steam, 152
  conventional, 151
  radiation, 140
  sensor laser beam, 140
  range top, 145, *146F*
Compact fluorescent light (CFL),162

Water:
    appliances, 165
    pressure-balanced thermostatic valves
        for, 314
    filters, 309
        carbon or fiber, 310
        distillation, 310
        reverse osmosis, 310
        selection considerations of, 309
    heaters, 312
        heat-pump system, 281
        point-of-use, 312
        solar heating of, 281
        storage tank water, 281
        tankless water, 281, *282F,*
          312, *313F*
    instant hot, 165
    tankless (on demand), 281.
        See also Water heaters
    quality and conservation of, 238
    softeners, 310
    sustainability of, 319
    treatment of, 165. *See also*
        Chapter 12
Wattage (watts), 252
Wheelchair:
    ANSI user guidelines, 107
    turning space, 190, *190F*
Wine storage, 137, *137F*
    selections of, 138
Windows:
    exterior balance of, 29

    outdoor and indoor integration, 29
    plan for kitchen, 61
    selection considerations of, 29
    terms of, 30–32, *32F*
        argon gas, use of, 31
        casing, 31
        divided lites, 31; grilles, 31;
          mullion bars, 31; simulated lites,
            31; spacer bars, 31; true lites,
          31
        egress, 31
        glazing: single, double, triple, 31
        heat loss/gain, 31
        jamb, 31
        low E-II glass, 31
        mulling, 32
        pane, 31
        rough opening, 32
        R-value, 32
        sash, 32
        skylight, 32
        tempered glass, 32
Wood surface finish, 303
Work triangle with CoreKitchen™, 65

X

Xenon lights, 270

Z

Zinc surface finish, 304

Index